The Road to
Full Employment

66

The Road to Full Employment

Edited by

SEAN GLYNN

University of Kent

ALAN BOOTH

University of Sheffield

London
ALLEN & UNWIN
Boston   Sydney

Allen & Unwin (Publishers) Ltd,
40 Museum Street, London WC1A 1LU, UK

Allen & Unwin (Publishers) Ltd,
Park Lane, Hemel Hempstead, Herts HP2 4TE, UK

Allen & Unwin, Inc.,
8 Winchester Place, Winchester, Mass. 01890, USA

Allen & Unwin (Australia) Ltd,
8 Napier Street, North Sydney, NSW 2060, Australia

First published in 1987

British Library Cataloguing in Publication Data

The Road to full employment.
   1. Unemployment – Great Britain –
History – 20th century
I. Glynn, Sean   I. Booth, Alan. *1949–*
331.13′7941   HD5765.A6

ISBN 0-04-330360-9
ISBN 0-04-330361-7 Pbk

Library of Congress Cataloging in Publication Data
The Road to Full Employment.

  Bibliography: p.
  Includes index.
    1. Great Britain—Full Employment Policies—History—
20th Century.   2. Unemployment—Great Britain—History—
20th Century.   3. Unemployment, Structural—Great
Britain—History—20th Century.   I. Glynn, Sean.
II. Booth, Alan, Ph.D.
HD5765.A6R63 1986   339.5′0941   86-14009
ISBN 0-04-330360-9 (alk. paper)
ISBN 0-04-330361-7 (Pbk. : alk. paper)

Set in 10 on 11 point Plantin Light by Oxford Print Associates Ltd, Oxford
and printed in Great Britain by Billing and Sons Ltd, London and Worcester

Contents

PART 2: The Policy Debate

Introduction

SEAN GLYNN and ALAN BOOTH

Unemployment is often said to be the most serious problem facing Britain at the present time and this view has been confirmed by numerous opinion polls. No political party currently offers a short-term solution to the problem and the belief that 'unemployment is here to stay' is becoming broadly established. With current unemployment levels officially recorded at over 13 per cent, and higher on most private estimations, it is inevitable that comparisons should be made with the period between the two world wars, the last occasion on which Britain experienced large-scale unemployment. Unfortunately, the parallels which are drawn are all too frequently devoid of historical context and understanding and misleading statistical comparisons have become common.

The primary aim of this collection of essays is to explore the causes and consequences of the interwar unemployment problem. This area is worthy of study in its own right as a result of both its historical importance and the light which it might shed on contemporary problems. Historical method is an essential part of all social sciences. Social and economic theories, once established in abstract logic, can *only* be tested historically. As a result, the importance of good historical understanding can hardly be overestimated.

These essays were not written in the belief that history repeats itself, but all the authors are aware that there are some fascinating parallels between the present and the interwar years. Comparisons have not been forced, but they will become evident in much of what follows.

In recent years, there has been an explosion of new research and writing on interwar Britain. Extensive use has been made of the state papers which have become available at the Public Record Office, providing new insights into modern British government and administration. Other work has been inspired by new social and economic theories as well as by changing contemporary circumstances. All the essays which follow are by academics who are at the forefront of recent research on various aspects of the economic and social history of interwar Britain.

This collection will make it clear that the Keynesian consensus, which has for so long dominated our perspective on the interwar unemployment problem, has now broken down. The Keynesian approach has certainly not been discarded by historians of the interwar period; it is, indeed, fully represented in this volume. But there are now a number of alternative analyses which also command respect, and they, too, are included. Thus, the views which follow are different and, in some cases, contradictory. At times such as this, when our understanding of the past is undergoing a major reappraisal, historians will tend to disagree not only over analytical perspectives, but also over questions of basic fact. In economic history, such disputes occur frequently over statistical evidence – about which series are the most accurate for specific purposes and especially over the 'correct' choice of base years for measurement. Thus, Chapters 1 and 5 interpret workforce statistics in different ways and Chapters 6 and 7 present orthodox Keynesian views which contrast with interpretations adopted elsewhere. It will be clear that some of the views expressed must be controversial and it is hoped that the collection will give the reader a realistic view of the present range of opinion which runs from new classical to Keynesian and beyond. At the present time, any serious attempt to reconcile contrasting views would be potentially misleading, and synthesis has not been attempted.

The book is divided into two parts. The first analyses the interwar unemployment problem in economic, social and political terms and the second half of the book has a policy focus. In Chapter 1, Glynn presents an overall analysis of the unemployment problem, examining its magnitude and nature. Whiteside considers the social implications of two decades of mass unemployment in Chapter 2 and assesses, in particular, the effects upon living standards, diet and health. The system of unemployment relief is outlined and discussed by Deacon in Chapter 3, and some attention is given to popular protest and reactions to the system. The political background to and effects of unemployment are analysed by Booth in Chapter 4. Capie presents a 'new classical' view of interwar unemployment in Chapter 5 and lays particular emphasis on the years of highest unemployment, 1930–2, when, he argues, there were significant real wage effects on employment. The wage issue is discussed more broadly in Chapter 6 by Garside, who has two main aims. First, he demonstrates that a number of economists in the interwar period gradually came to accept that real wages were 'sticky', and, secondly, that Keynes began to question the basic neo-classical premiss that the real wage and employment were inversely related. The prospects for a Keynesian solution to the interwar unemployment problem by means of an expansion of aggregate demand and a devaluation or depreciation of sterling are considered by Hatton in Chapter 7.

The section on economic policy opens with Peden's discussion of the influences which prevented Keynes from exerting a major influence on interwar economic policy. In Chapter 9, Middleton re-examines Treasury attitudes and presents a new view which is much more sympathetic than previous interpretations. Kirby, in Chapter 10, surveys industrial policy and reveals the factors which prevented the emergence of a coherent, interventionist industrial strategy. The development and influence of progressive attitudes in the Ministry of Labour are examined by Lowe in Chapter 11, and Glynn takes a broad view of interwar economic policies and advances reasons for policy failure. In the final chapter, Booth outlines the major changes which took place during the Second World War and examines the emergence of the government commitment to 'full employment' as presented in the white paper of 1944. In this chapter, and before, it is clearly shown that the road to full employment was long, indirect and not always clearly signposted.

There can be little doubt that the debate about the causes of and cure for unemployment will continue into the future, with few people at present predicting even a medium-term solution to current problems. It is hoped that the essays which follow will inform the obvious comparisons and improve understanding and interpretation not only of the interwar period but also of the future.

Finally, we must explain the system of references. References in the text within square brackets refer to the numbered items of the Bibliography, followed where appropriate, by the page or chapter number in italics, for example [29, *167*] or [142, *ch. 6*].

Part 1

The Nature of the Problem

1

The Scale and Nature of the Problem

SEAN GLYNN

It is usually assumed that interwar Britain experienced exceptionally high unemployment and that the 1930s, in particular, had much heavier unemployment than other periods. The mass unemployment of the 1930s has become a yardstick against which an 'unemployment problem' is often measured. In fact, the issue is not so simple and, from the perspective of Britain in the 1980s, there are very good grounds for revising the view of the period as one of uniquely high unemployment.

Unemployment was a tragedy in interwar Britain because it was prolonged and struck with devastating effects at the heart of the British industrial economy, in regions which had been relatively prosperous, where societies with a pronounced work ethic were geared to regular employment and weekly wage income for adult men. For the first time also, unemployment was officially recorded in a way not open to serious challenge; most of it could not be attributed to idleness or character deficiencies; the official figures revealed sharp increases over the pre-1920 period and truly horrendous levels in some traditional industrial areas. Unemployment was certainly an economic problem, susceptible perhaps to an economic solution, but its major role in modern British history relates primarily to its social, political and psychological effects.

As a result of the interwar experience with unemployment, faith in the market economy was finally shattered and social policies based on notions of 'self-help' were seen to be inadequate. These decisions were taken without any fundamental threat to the political status quo being presented and during a period when the economy progressed on all the usual indicators except unemployment. Living standards and real wages improved, on average, almost continuously and the growth record of the period was good on both historical and international comparisons. Without the unemployment problem the interwar years might now be regarded as a relatively successful period when Britain's relative decline against other industrial nations was reversed and growth in the economy returned to late-nineteenth century levels, or better, after two decades of virtual economic stagnation.

Most of the workforce remained in employment, even in the worst years in the most blighted regions. The fortunate majority viewed unemployment in these years, as always, with a mixture of fear and compassion. At all social levels there was genuine compassion for the unemployed and their dependants and this was a real political force though it was offset to some extent by those who viewed unemployment as good social 'medicine' and by the lobby of middle class taxpayers who resented Exchequer support for the unemployed.

Fear was a more complex reaction: some feared unemployment itself while others feared the unemployed. Unemployment was mainly a moving stream so that, even in the best years, at least four million had direct experience and, counting dependants, as many as twelve million could be directly affected. Fear of unemployment had profound influences on social and political behaviour including industrial relations and work attitudes. Those who were protected from fears about loss of employment often feared the unemployed themselves, though it must be said that during the interwar period there are few examples of unemployed workers perpetrating mass violence. (Indeed, it could be said that they were, on occasion, the victims of police violence, notably in London.) However, the prolongation of severe unemployment was seen as a threat to political consensus and there was a real fear of political extremes which had been manifested overseas and were not entirely absent from the British scene. As Deacon shows in Chapter 3, much of the argument and agitation which did take place related to the system of unemployment relief and unemployment itself may have been seen as inevitable and beyond the control of government. By the 1940s this view had changed.

The Magnitude of Unemployment

There are major problems in defining and measuring unemployment and controversy about measurement is as old as measurement itself.

All practical definitions are socially determined and must be to some extent arbitrary and subjective. All data relating to unemployment has to be used with considerable caution and this is certainly true of the interwar period [95].

The usual measures certainly suggest that the level of unemployment was exceptionally high during the period. The two most important sources of information are the 1931 census and data collected at Labour Exchanges which were established on a national basis from 1909.

National Insurance statistics commence with the registration of defined categories under Part II of the 1911 National Insurance Act which inaugurated the British National Insurance Scheme (hereafter NIS). The NIS statistics provide the basis for the official series for interwar unemployment. They are based on spot daily tallies, taken each month, of the number of people registered as 'unemployed' at Labour Exchanges. This is not the place for a detailed discussion of the statistics and sources, but it should be emphasized that from 1923 to 1939 the NIS covered only 60–5 per cent of the workforce, and also, that registration was not compulsory and that in particular, those not entitled to receive unemployment benefit (most married women, for example) may not have registered. It is quite clear, therefore, that the official or NIS figures seriously understate the number of people unemployed. However, because the 35–40 per cent of the workforce outside NIS was less prone to unemployment, the percentage figures based on NIS returns overstate the national percentage rate of unemployment by some 20–30 per cent. Thus if we compare NIS returns with Feinstein's calculations based on the 1931 census we find that NIS-recorded unemployment was 2.5 million but that total unemployment was estimated to be about 3.2 million [88].

The census statistics are based upon a spot daily tally on 27 April 1931 when heads of households were asked to identify unemployment. Feinstein has compiled unemployment statistics based on revised census data with corrections based on NIS returns and making allowance for the temporarily unemployed. On this basis, using NIS statistics, it is possible to extrapolate from 1931 to get an annual series for the interwar period. Using Chapman and Knight's estimates for man-years of employment, Feinstein estimates percentage rates of unemployment for the *entire* workforce, rather than the 60–65 per cent covered by NIS [54]. The official figures for unemployment of the insured (NIS) workforce are given in Table 1.1, while Feinstein's estimates for the entire workforce are shown in Table 1.2. The former give an annual average of 14.2 per cent unemployment over the period 1921–38 while Feinstein's

Table 1.1 United Kingdom: Percentage of Insured Workers Unemployed 1918–39

Year	%	Year	%	Year	%
1918	0.8	1921	16.9	1931	21.3
1919	n.a.	1922	14.3	1932	22.1
1920	3.9	1923	11.7	1933	19.9
		1924	10.3	1934	16.7
		1925	11.3	1935	15.5
		1926	12.5	1936	13.1
		1927	9.7	1937	10.8
		1928	10.8	1938	12.9
		1929	10.4	1939	10.5
		1930	16.1		

Source: [118, *table 160, p. 306*].

Table 1.2 United Kingdom: Percentage of Total Workforce Unemployed 1921–38

Year	%	Year	%
1921	12.2	1931	16.4
1922	10.8	1932	17.0
1923	8.9	1933	15.4
1924	7.9	1934	12.9
1925	8.6	1935	12.0
1926	9.6	1936	10.2
1927	7.4	1937	8.5
1928	8.2	1938	10.1
1929	8.0		
1930	12.3		

Source: [88, *table 58, p. T128*].

estimates for the same period average 10.9 per cent. Feinstein's revised series is not beyond criticism, but it is far the best indication of overall levels and rates of British unemployment in the interwar period. Clearly, it should be much more widely used by historians and other commentators. *However, it must be strongly emphasized that the Feinstein series is not comparable with official unemployment figures before, during and since the interwar years.* Census and survey data on unemployment usually reveal much higher levels than registration returns. Like the official (NIS) figures, the Feinstein series is unflattering to the interwar period when compared with official series before and since.

Data problems and deficiencies make really accurate comparisons of interwar unemployment levels with other periods virtually impossible, but such attempts are often made and the phrase 'worst since the 1930s' has been frequent in recent years. In the four years since 1982 the official annual average rate of unemployment in Britain has been 11.5 per cent or more and has averaged 12.4 per cent. A multiplier of 8/13 has been suggested in order to adjust interwar NIS figures to approximate comparability with those for the postwar period [194]. On this basis the interwar NIS average of 14.2 per cent becomes 8.7 which makes unemployment levels in the 1980s seem relatively severe. On the same basis of comparison, the worst annual figure of the interwar years, 22.1 per cent in 1932, converts to 13.6. The official figure for 1984/5 is 13.2 per cent. However, on the pre-1982 basis, this is estimated to be 13.7 per cent [276]. On this basis it can be said with reasonable confidence that unemployment in the 1980s has been much worse than during the interwar period and has reached levels comparable with the 1930s peak.

Comparisons with the pre-1914 period are more difficult. While trade union returns are available from the mid-nineteenth century they are based upon a relatively limited and undoubtedly biased sample of mainly skilled workers in highly unionized industries. In the interwar years unskilled workers were twice as likely to be unemployed as skilled. Before 1914 it is clear that even in boom years there was a 'chronic surplus' [193, 82–3] of unskilled labour in the larger urban areas [254, *Part I*] and there was heavy emigration. Also, it is usually assumed that casual labour and underemployment were more common and these were manifestations of a slack labour market with endemic poverty resulting from inadequate earnings. Even the trade union returns indicate that levels of 10 per cent unemployment occurred during cyclical troughs. While pre-1914 comparisons must lack precision because of inadequacies of data, it is possible to suggest that for a large part of the workforce the incidence of unemployment in the interwar years may not have been much worse than that experienced before 1914 at least during cyclical troughs. This may be one factor in explaining public quiescence during the interwar years.

The major differences with pre-1914 lie in the disaggregated pattern, with a reversal in the relative regional impact, and in the persistence of heavy unemployment over the entire trade cycle. Before 1914 the old industrial areas on the coalfields of Britain were relatively prosperous and had a lower incidence of unemployment than London, the Midlands and the South. After 1920 this pattern was reversed and a hard core of persistent, non-cyclical unemployment emerged in the traditional industrial areas. This particular manifestation is the most distinctive feature of the interwar unemployment problem [175].

Disaggregated unemployment statistics (unemployment by duration, region, industry, occupation, age, sex) are invariably drawn from NIS returns [95]. These also have many deficiencies arising not least from variations in workforce proportions insured, administrative influences and under-registration, and should be viewed with major reservations.

It is possible to make a number of cautious generalizations. Long-term unemployment (usually defined as one year or more) was relatively low in the 1920s at 5–10 per cent of total unemployment. It then rose sharply from 1929 and a hard core of about 25 per cent had developed by the early 1930s and tended to persist. This compares with about one-third of the official total in the middle 1980s. Long-term unemployment was self-reinforcing and cumulative and there is much interwar evidence to suggest that, after long periods of unemployment, men became mentally and physically unfit for work and, in effect, were outside the labour market (see Whiteside in Chapter 2).

There were considerable variations in levels of unemployment according to age and sex. Juveniles were, unlike the 1980s situation, less likely to be unemployed than other age-groups. The reasons for this are unclear and complicated. However, the answers which suggest themselves are in terms of lower wages, lower benefits, non-entitlement to benefits and under-registration. Older men in the over-40 age-groups were more prone to unemployment not because they were more likely to be dismissed but because of lower chances of being re-hired if they became unemployed.

Female unemployment is obviously subjected to massive under-recording because of 'discouragement'. Most women were not entitled to unemployment benefits in their own right and saw little point in registration if it was unlikely to lead to employment. During the First World War there had been a sharp rise in female 'participation' in paid employment. The reversion to pre-1914 levels after 1920 cannot be explained simply in social or even 'sexist' terms. Indeed there is a good deal of evidence to suggest that female participation was economically determined. In textile areas, for example, it was traditionally higher than elsewhere. During the interwar years there was considerable regional variation in female participation and, in areas where acceptable employment was available, it increased sharply over prewar levels. In London, for example, office work became increasingly available to women and the demand for labour in general was more buoyant. That situation was reflected in increasing participation rates. This evidence together with experience since 1945 suggests that there may have been widespread female unemployment and underemployment which we cannot measure [26, 615–17].

Unemployment also had an occupational and social dimension, tending to diminish with social ranking, levels of skill and education. Unskilled workers were twice as likely to be unemployed as skilled. As Whiteside suggests in Chapter 2, unemployment acted as a filter for discrimination on social, racial and other grounds. Those groups and individuals which were subject to discrimination of one kind or another were disproportionately represented among the unemployed. This could apply to those with physical and mental differences, racial and ethnic minorities, social deviants and indeed anyone who failed to fit the acceptable stereotype. However, a series of investigations during the 1930s indicated that the Irish, who were perhaps the largest racial minority, were less likely to be unemployed than the population as a whole [100, 50–69].

Poverty, squalor and enforced idleness were certainly not new to interwar Britain. What was new was to find these conditions concentrated in the traditional industrial heartlands on the coalfields. The economic deceleration of the staple industries and the regions where they were concentrated was aggravated by linkages with other industries and through regional multiplier effects. In a relatively good year, such as 1929, NIS unemployment levels could vary regionally from 5.6 per cent in London and the South-East to 19.3 per cent in Wales. In a bad year such as 1932 differences were relatively less with unemployment at 13.5 per cent in London and 36.5 per cent in Wales. On a district basis, of course, much wider differences could be found. The pattern then is one of great regional and local variations in levels of unemployment with a fairly clear division between 'Inner Britain' (London, the South and the Midlands) and 'Outer Britain' (the rest).

The Theory of Unemployment

Understanding the unemployment problem has been complicated by the fact that economists and in particular econometricians with different theoretical approaches seem to find little difficulty in fitting their theories to interwar experience. This may reveal more about the methods of economic and econometric analysis than about the quality of economic theory or the realities of economic history. It should also be said that the quality and quantity of interwar economic data does not often justify sophisticated econometric analysis.

There are basically three theoretical economic approaches: classical, Keynesian and new microeconomic (sometimes called monetarist or neo-classical).

The classical view was probably held in one form or another by most interwar economists and was influential in the Treasury, Westminster and the City of London. Based on Say's Law, or the notion that supply creates its own demand, and the average wage-marginal product identity, the classical view was associated in particular with Pigou [227] (but see Garside in Chapter 6). Essentially the classical view was that full employment was normal and coincided with (Walrasian) equilibrium. The economy would tend towards full employment of labour and the existence of involuntary unemployment was attributable to temporary market imperfections. Invariably, the classical view, at least in its simplest forms, attributed unemployment to 'wage rigidity', that is to real wages being too high (see Garside in Chapter 6). As heavy unemployment persisted throughout the interwar years and the anticipated adjustment failed to materialize, the classical view became increasingly untenable. Classical economists, including Pigou, came to recognize the social and political problems which lay in the way of real or even nominal wage reductions as a cure for unemployment and many favoured public works as a means of relieving distress arising from the problem. By the late 1940s this theoretical view of unemployment appeared to have been completely superseded. However, in recent years it has re-emerged in a more sophisticated and controversial form and a version of this is advanced in Chapter 5 by Capie.

The Keynesian view failed to win broad support or to significantly influence policy until the later 1930s and the reasons for this are discussed in Chapters 8 and 9 by Peden and Middleton. Until quite recently it was conventional wisdom that the interwar experience had completely vindicated the Keynesian view. However, there are considerable problems in defining the latter in precise terms and the academic treatment of Keynes and Keynesianism is now an enormous subject in its own right. Keynes himself changed his views during the interwar years and the *General Theory* of 1936 has been subjected to important modifications, notably by Patinkin [141, 60-3]. Involuntary unemployment arising from deficient demand is the central feature of the Keynesian explanation which certainly appears to encompass historical reality in relation to the 1920s and 1930s in its view that the economy could experience a long period of unemployment without necessarily generating its own adjustment

10

In a situation of 'Keynesian unemployment' producers cannot sell output which it would be profitable to produce at the existing level of wages and prices. There is therefore a quantity constraint imposed by lack of market demand. Lower wages cannot help this situation and producers can only respond by reducing output and employment below the optimum level. Many economists and historians still accept an orthodox Keynesian view and the implications of this approach are examined in Chapters 6 and 7 by Garside and Hatton.

The new microeconomic theory developed by Friedman and others in the past two decades may be seen as a partial reversion to the classical or (Walrasian) equilibrium view with the addition of a number of important refinements. These incorporate certain market imperfections or structural rigidities (including the effects of union power, unemployment benefits and market mismatches) into a new equilibrium concept which is termed the 'natural rate' of unemployment [93, 2]. It is assumed that there is a Phillips-curve-type trade-off between wages (and prices) and unemployment and the 'natural rate' of unemployment is consistent with non-accelerating inflation (or deflation). The 'natural rate' is defined as the non-accelerating - inflation rate of unemployment or NAIRU. The terminology clearly suggests theory developed to explain post-1960 circumstances but the new microeconomic theory has been applied to the interwar period. The persistence of unemployment above the equilibrium or 'natural rate' is explained in terms of 'search theory' which sees individuals indulging in voluntary unemployment while seeking to maximize future wage income by investing in information or job search. Unemployment is seen therefore as a supply-side phenomenon. Because of information deficiencies and other market imperfections, the adjustment of wages and employment to equilibrium may take some time and this may explain situations of abnormal unemployment.

Obstensibly at least, the 'natural rate' hypothesis and 'search theory' seem to have almost as many difficulties in explaining the heavy and persistent unemployment of the interwar years as were experienced by the classical theorists. British wages and prices apparently failed to adjust over two decades and search theory is seen as a rather unsatisfactory explanation of the mass unemployment of the 1930s even by some of its own adherents [185, 273]. However, this has not prevented Benjamin and Kochin presenting a new classical view of British interwar unemployment which sees the bulk of unemployment as essentially voluntary. This issue is discussed below by Garside (Chapter 6) and the possibilities for a supply-side solution are examined by Capie (Chapter 5). The policy implications of different theoretical approaches are examined in the second part of the book.

11

Over the past century many different ways of classifying unemployment have been suggested. Different classifications often reflect analytical views about causes and remedies. The voluntary/involuntary categorization has already been used. At a more fundamental level the four most common types defined are seasonal, frictional, structural and cyclical unemployment. Seasonal unemployment may arise from regular supply and demand mismatches which are usually attributable to climatic variations which occur on a regular calendar basis. Frictional unemployment is defined as that arising from short-term adjustments in the labour market and it is accepted that, since some workers will always be between jobs at any given time, there is an irreducible minimum. Clearly there are close similarities between frictional and search unemployment although all frictional unemployment cannot be defined as voluntary. Structural unemployment arises from mismatches in the labour market, which may be locational, industrial or occupational, and can be seen as a longer-run supply-side problem. However, structural unemployment is instigated by changes in the pattern of demand which result, for example, from changes in technology, location or taste. Cyclical unemployment is essentially a short-run problem resulting from deficient demand and is sometimes called 'Keynesian unemployment' since it was clearly identified by Keynes during the interwar period as indicated above.

Economists' explanations of interwar unemployment run the full gamut from 'Keynesian' involuntary demand deficient on the one hand to 'supply-side' voluntary benefit-induced. The range of these views is explored below.

It has been argued elsewhere that the interwar problem is too complex to yield to a monocausal explanation. Most historians would accept that different causes of unemployment were present but some feel that it should be possible to identify a major cause, according to preference, on the demand or supply side of the economy. Clearly there were cyclical peaks in unemployment and these were especially prominent in 1921 and 1931/2. But there was also a more persistent core of non-cyclical unemployment running through the period from 1920 to the Second World War. Even at the cyclical peaks there was a minimum of 9–10 per cent (NIS) unemployment. It has been suggested that much of this 'irreducible minimum' could be defined as 'structural' unemployment and linked with the declining old staple industries and with the so-called 'structural problem' which a great many writers have identified in modern British economic history [233, 66–75; 3, ch. 5]. In order to understand unemployment it is necessary to examine Britain's industrial pattern and the problems of British industry.

Unemployment and Industry

It is impossible to analyse interwar unemployment without paying close attention to the so-called 'old staples' – the pioneer industries of the Industrial Revolution, concentrated on the coalfields of Britain, and heavily dependent on export markets. The most important old staples were coal, cotton, heavy engineering, shipbuilding, railways and iron and steel. In the later decades of the nineteenth century Britain remained heavily and perhaps dangerously dependent, especially for export earnings, on this small group which was characterized in part by low productivity, low productivity growth and low wages [68]. Between the turn of the century and the end of the First World War there are strong indications of poor overall economic performance and virtually no growth in real income per head and productivity [193]. It has been suggested that the pre-1914 economy was the victim of a low wage/low productivity trap which delayed structural changes [26]. British levels and distribution of consumer income may have failed to provide an adequate basis for new consumer goods industries which eventually provided at least a partial solution to the structural problem. With demand weak and skilled labour plentiful and relatively cheap, production in Edwardian Britain tended to be skill-intensive and low volume in a range of consumer goods with potential for long-run growth [126]. The evidence for supply-side constraints in terms of capital is also very limited and, in view of the very high rate of overseas investment for very modest returns, could only be presented in terms of market imperfection.

This situation may have been intensified by the First World War and related developments. Many of the older industries were stimulated and experienced sharp expansion during the war and postwar boom. Employment in coalmining, for example, reached record levels in 1919–20. At the same time, war circumstances accelerated developments which threatened the future of staple industries. The basic difficulties arose from loss of markets, and especially overseas markets, because of market restrictions (usually tariffs), substitution and reduced competitiveness. Rising unit costs resulting from inflation, rising wages and shorter shifts meant that British products were less competitive abroad [82]. The new reality hit the staples in 1920–1 when there was a dramatic shake-out of labour.

The cause and effect of the decline of the staple industries as employers of labour is rather more complex than is sometimes suggested but the process has a central role in explaining interwar unemployment. Indeed, these industries may have contributed *directly* at least one-third and up to one-half of total unemployment in the best years of the interwar period [68, *169*, 3, *146*]. Indirectly, of course, employment decline in the staples influenced other industries and regions and the national economy. The traditional industrial areas with high concentrations of staples experienced higher average levels of unemployment overall and in all industries [53]. Clearly there were important links between structural and regional problems in the economy.

While it is suggested that the difficulties encountered by the staple industries after 1920 played a central role in the interwar unemployment problem, this cannot be the whole story. Industrial decline is a feature of all modern industrial economies but it only gives rise to a severe problem of unemployment where workers from declining industries fail to be fully absorbed in expanding industries. New and expanding industries certainly existed in interwar Britain and the service sector also expanded and provided increased employment. However, this was clearly insufficient. Employment in manufacturing industry failed to regain the 1920 level (7.14 million) and total employment did not exceed the 1920 level (19.01 million) until 1935 [179, *table 3*, 8]. Supply-side influences and productivity growth exacerbated the problem. Birth rates had been on a downward trend since the late nineteenth century and during the interwar years people of working age formed a higher proportion of total population than before. Emigration was lower than it had been in Edwardian Britain and the net flow became positive during the 1930s. Productivity increases occurred across most industries as management and technology improved even in declining sectors. Indeed, as might be expected, some of the sharpest increases were recorded in industries which were being rationalized and reorganized [81]. In the staple industries employment tended to fall more sharply than output and capital stock. However, these attempts to reduce unit costs were largely unsuccessful in pricing British industry back into overseas markets. In classical theory the problem could be solved by wage reductions, but the real-world problem was more complex. Barriers to trade were flexible and increasingly so during the interwar period. Where import substitution had newly developed it was usually protected as necessary. Where open competition remained possible, Britain had clearly lost its comparative advantage which rested on the cheapness of skilled industrial labour [275].

In general, growth industries were based on the home market and on sales of consumer goods, though some, such as the motor industry, eventually became major exporters. Could employment have expanded more rapidly, especially in the new and expanding manufacturing industries and in the service sector? It has already been suggested that consumer demand was relatively shallow in Britain. The demand for motor vehicles, for example, appears to have been a direct function of income levels and it is scarcely surprising that vehicle rates per capita in Britain were some thirty years behind those of the USA. Of course, the skewed distribution of income in Britain may well have favoured motor production since in this period motor cars were clearly a middle class luxury. The demand for other consumer products may also have lacked social depth despite improvements in real income. The 'new' industries accounted for only 14 per cent of net output of all Census of Production trades in 1924. Although this grew to 21 per cent by 1935 the group was clearly too small to have had a substantial impact on the unemployment problem [42]. The establishment of new firms and branches took place mainly in London and the South-East and the Midlands where consumer income was higher or better maintained [92].

Thus we have some of the elements of a vicious circle. Britain's international comparative advantage had been established during the nineteenth century on the basis of a relatively small group of staple industries [68]. In the 1920s these industries faced a severe market access and cost problem which had been accelerated by the First World War and related developments. Low productivity and wages in these industries had prevented or delayed the emergence of substantial consumer-based industries which provided the main hope for economic restructuring. The problems of the staple industries could only be solved by cost reductions which implied lower wages. The growth industries required growth in consumer demand in order to expand output and employment.

Viewing the problem in these terms it is possible to suggest the concept of a 'dual economy' and this has important implications for the debate on economic policy which is taken up in subsequent chapters [105]. It is simply incorrect to attempt to apply single-market demand and supply analysis to the interwar economy where different equilibrium levels operated between different markets. In the staple industries real wage levels may well have placed a constraint on output and employment, but in the new growth sectors the essential constraint was lack of consumer demand. Both classical and Keynesian unemployment were present.

During the past two decades quantitative historical estimates and analysis have redeemed the interwar period. The image of gloom and decline has, at least in part, been removed and the period is now seen as one where growth returned to levels achieved in the third quarter of the nineteenth century and consumers made substantial real gains. Between the 1890s and the 1920s there was very little growth in the economy and the heavy unemployment of the interwar period was in larger part a legacy of the Edwardian failure and the effects of the First World War. The improved growth rates of the interwar years should not be allowed to conceal the fact that the interwar economy had fallen well below the long-run trend levels which might have been attained if the modest growth of rates of the late nineteenth century had continued.

One thing at least should be clear; we are dealing with a highly complex, multicausal problem with both short- and long-run aspects. The chapters which follow will attempt to illuminate some of the many facets of the unemployment problem in interwar Britain.

2

The Social Consequences of Interwar Unemployment

NOEL WHITESIDE

Social investigation in Edwardian Britain had focused principally on pauperism and poverty. In the interwar period, this orientation changed. Increasingly, attention was given to the rising incidence of unemployment and to the social evils that might be ascribed to it. A variety of academics and journalists set out to experience, observe and record the sufferings of the unemployed. Diet, mental and physical health, social habits, political attitudes, all became grist to the mill of social enquiry. The results were published not merely in social science journals, but also as literary comment, fictional writing and personal memoir. Never before has so much information been available about unemployment in terms of its incidence, distribution and evident social consequences.

Not surprisingly, the news brought from the industrial areas by these self-appointed messengers was not good. It flew in the face of the argument perpetrated in official circles, which stressed how well the British unemployed were treated when compared with their American and European counterparts and asserted that the British people were withstanding the impact of the slump rather well. In the course of the 1930s, political debate raged over the damage unemployment was doing to the social fabric of the nation. In the immediate term at least, official credibility was somewhat dented. In the immediate postwar years, the 1930s established their reputation as an era of social degradation and waste, characterized by political instability abroad and depression at home. Mass unemployment, associated with widespread hardship, was never to be allowed to return.

Recent historical scholarship has disputed the degree of suffering caused by unemployment in the interwar years and the threat the situation posed to social and political stablility at the time [3; 4; 256 295]. Folk memory, some have argued, ignores the benefits o growth and industrial restructuring – of which unemployment wa: an unfortunate but unavoidable part. In spite of mass unemployment national trends in morbidity and mortality continued to improve The British people were better clothed, housed and fed than thei Edwardian forefathers had been. Interwar poverty in absolute term was neither as severe nor as widespread as it had been before the First World War. Contemporary middle class investigators, some o whom made no secret of their left-wing sympathies, were too easil shocked by conditions in industrial areas which had long shown propensity to lag behind prevailing national trends of socia improvement. Against this, other historians have denounced th official statistics for underestimating the damage done by poo housing and bad diet to the health of the unemployed and thei families [188; 282; 283]. They also condemn the school of historica writing which has emphasized national averages, allowing the poo performance of the depressed areas to be masked by escalating rate of social improvement in the Midlands and South-East. In addition one or two studies have noted the correlation between risin unemployment and the incidence of sickness, disability, homelessnes and vagrancy during the 1930s [171; 287]. Some recent publication have tried to evaluate – even to reconcile – these conflicting view [66; 255].

In examining the social consequences of unemployment, therefore we are moving beyond simple questions of human suffering an social conscience. If unemployment damaged physical and menta health, this had important implications for public expenditure ove and above the cost of the dole. Further, unemployment had a impact on social and political behaviour, on the incidence of crim and the proliferation of demonstrations and marches. As we know Britain never experienced the degree of political instability foun elsewhere in Europe. This does not mean that mass unemploymei had no political repercussions. On the contrary, the widesprea popular acclaim which greeted the Beveridge Report in 1942 ougl to be understood as a reaction against the 'do-nothing' politics whic had characterized the previous decade. In short, the significance social conditions fostered by unemployment lies not merely in wh; they were actually like, but also in their impact on political life i subsequent years.

Unemployment and Poverty

Thanks to the endeavours of those many social investigators, the incidence of poverty – and the contribution unemployment made to it – became reasonably explicit. Contemporary research in nutritional science allowed the development of a more sophisticated diagnosis of the relationship between diet and health than the one employed by Booth and Rowntree before the First World War. Converted into cash terms, basic dietary requirements generated a poverty line somewhat higher than the one used in prewar days. When measured against the old yardstick, poverty had clearly declined. However, by contemporary standards alone, the picture found in the depressed areas was less rosy.

Of course the degree of poverty among the unemployed varied by area and by the year in which each survey was made. Surveys of Merseyside, Southampton, Bristol, London and York – undertaken during or after the 1929–33 slump – found between 15 and 31 per cent of working class households had insufficient income for their basic needs, and that in about one third of these cases, destitution was directly due to unemployment [66, 25–6]. The length of time out of work was a particularly significant factor. The proportion of unemployed out of work for 12 months or more increased as the decade wore on. Hence in Sheffield in 1931, 43 per cent of the unemployed were in poverty while in York, 5 years later, this figure stood as 73 per cent. By the late 1930s, almost four out of every five clients of the Unemployment Assistance Board (UAB) – who by definition, had been out of work for at least 6 months – were in poverty [255, 280–1]. According to the Pilgrim Trust, investigating the problem in six towns in the mid–1930s, state allowances represented between 44 and 66 per cent of previous earnings. [66, 27]. In the depressed areas wages were often not high to begin with. Hence, unsurprisingly, the sudden drop in income was most acutely felt by those with large families [188, ch. 5].

The association between unemployment and poverty was, of course, mediated by the changes in relief for long-term cases introduced in the course of the 1930s, as Deacon's Chapter 3 demonstrates. Until 1931, all claimants had received the full amount of benefit available to them, irrespective of other resources, if they satisfied the unemployment insurance scheme's other regulations. The advent of the household means test changed all that. Those who had exhausted their right to unemployment benefit had to submit to what was, in effect, a Poor Law evaluation of their circumstances. Not only was this disgrace bitterly resented – especially by skilled men – but also it allowed the re-entry of regional variations and anomalies in both assessment and scales of relief. Thanks to the 'Standstill' introduced after the creation of the UAB, which allowed the long-term unemployed to claim local public assistance if it gave them more money, these iodiosyncrasies persisted until 1937. Hence claimants in Merthyr Tydfil were more likely to be assessed at the full rate than the unemployed in Scotland or in the North-West [77, 21]. The early annual reports of the UAB chronicle a saga of administrative complexity and unjustifiable discrepancies as similar cases in neighbouring areas were granted different levels of relief. An official survey in 1933 asked 80 country boroughs to assess nine 'specimen' cases. The results were predictably haphazard, ranging from the total sum of £12 11s (£12.55) apportioned by West Ham to £3 12s 6d (£3.63) from Blackpool, the latter typifying the tight-fisted approach characteristic of the Lancashire Poor Law [207, 117] Hence, while the means test generally reduced the incomes of the long-term unemployed, it did greater damage in some areas than in others. Similarly, the introduction of unemployment assistance in 1934 was a positive blessing in those areas where Poor Law parsimony was particularly severe.

In some areas, especially among large families, unemployment relief scales did overlap the bottom rungs of the wage ladder, albeit in only a tiny minority of cases. While some social surveys showed that those dependent on benefits tended to fall below the poverty line, low pay remained a prominent cause of poverty in its own right In cities such as Liverpool, which was renowned for its use of casual and irregular labour, poverty was endemic among large families employed and unemployed alike. A national study, setting official earnings data against Rowntree's 'human needs' minimum for a family of five, revealed that substantial numbers of workers – in textiles, clothing, mining, railway work and construction – earned below subsistence wages. Including dependants and the unemployed an estimated 10 million people in Britain (over 20 per cent of the population) were living in poverty [172]. In some respects these findings have to be taken with a pinch of salt. Not all workers had three children (although some had more) and the author failed to note that, in cotton textiles, two-wage households were relatively commonplace as married women's work was not unusual. However such conclusions reinforced Sir John Boyd Orr's contention in 1936 that 50 per cent of the British population were inadequately fed, a statement subsequently modified by the BMA to a sum total of 8 million people [282, 121].

These findings do not sit easily with official data, showing that real wages rose during the 1930s. However, official wage statistics have distinct shortcomings. Based on industrial agreements, these take no account of the many firms who paid less than the recognized rate, nor of reductions in earnings due to short-time working in times of slack trade. In textiles, mining, and other trades, short-time was the traditional response to depression. Throughout the interwar period, between 25 and 33 per cent of the registered unemployed were short-time or casual workers. As the 'count' was based on returns for a single day, we must assume that only around half of these would be registered as 'unemployed' at any one time. Hence the official figure for workers returned as 'casual', 'short-time' or 'temporarily stopped' can be roughly doubled in order to reach a crude estimate for the total numbers involved in irregular employment of some type. All of this points to the conclusion that poverty due to low take-home pay cannot be divorced from destitution due to unemployment *out court*. Both causes stemmed from different responses to the same problem.

Unemployment, Nutrition and Health

If the social commentators and nutritionists were right, the financial plight of the unemployed should have produced a less adequate diet and, given time, poorer health. Arguments concerning the impact of unemployment on physical and mental well-being were heated – both at the time and since. On the face of things, national data on morbidity and mortality failed to reflect the consequences of poverty associated with unemployment. Further, a series of official surveys conducted in 1932 on the health of the unemployed found little cause for concern. The Ministry of Health argued that the depressed areas had always displayed worse rates of morbidity and mortality: if anything, the gap was closing. Such evidence indicated that unemployment caused little physical suffering among its victims. In the immediate term at least, infant mortality rates failed to reflect the impact of the slump [295; 296]. Viewed from this angle, the impressions recorded by political malcontents like Hutt and Hanning-ton appear unworthy of serious attention [125; 144].

In a reassessment of the 'optimistic' view, Charles Webster has exposed the fallacies in the official statistics and the political factors that influenced their composition [282; 283]. As questions of health and nutrition were linked to income, they were politically sensitive. Rates of public relief could not be raised without damaging work incentives, or providing a case for higher wages, or both. None of these developments, in the Treasury's view, was conducive to industrial recovery. Hence the Ministry of Health, far from responding to evidence of worsening maternal mortality and th slowing of improvement in the incidence of pulmonary tuberculosi in the depressed areas, tried to demonstrate that the criticisms o Boyd Orr and his sympathizers were ill-founded. Official estimate of malnutrition among schoolchildren – as reflected in early signs o rickets and anaemia – were invariably far lower than the estimate made by independent investigators. The basis for official diagnosi and assessment was revised during the 1930s; this indicates tha critics within the system, identified by Webster, clearly had cause fo complaint.

The precise impact of unemployment on health is hard t measure. Mortality statistics are a peculiarly crude indicator; no on would claim that unemployment kills. Official morbidity data relie largely on the reporting of notifiable diseases and hence did no reflect either developments at the subclinical level or illness tha never received medical attention. Although infants under a year old schoolchildren and working people (including the unemployed could claim some form of subsidized medical care, no genera provision existed for the whole population, outside the loca authority services. Some of these services, inherited from the Poo Law, were means tested and catered mostly for the destitute an chronic sick. Women in general and married women in particula were singularly ill-protected. Outside periods of pregnancy an parturition, official interest in their state of health was minima Unofficial investigations revealed, time and again, that it was th wives of the unemployed, not their redundant husbands, who bor the brunt of associated hardships. [66, *31*]. The Pilgrim Tru estimated one in three of the wives they visited was in poor healtl due to 'nerves' or inadequate diet; the needs of husbands an children were dominant at mealtimes.[1] Such evidence helps t explain the high incidence of death – or incapacity – as a result o childbirth in the depressed areas. The maternal mortality rate in pa of the Rhondda fell dramatically when a voluntary agency provide free food for pregnant women in 1934, an experiment whos implications were, characteristically, ignored by the Ministry Health. [207, *115*].

Further evidence that all was not exactly well with the nation health can be found in the official returns of the national heal insurance scheme. Contributory health insurance was undermined much the same way and for much the same reasons as th unemployment scheme. Industrial depression led to falling contrib tions and rising dependency. As with unemployment benefi coverage was extended and redefined to allow the jobless to clai sickness benefit, should the need arise. It did. In the course of th

1920s, numbers of short-term claims rose sharply, especially from women workers. Following the slump, there was a marked increase in the number of long-term disability cases which paralleled the rise in long-term unemployment. Investigation revealed rheumatism, arthritis, circulatory and respiratory complaints and nervous disorders lay at the root of the problem.[2] However, many of the long-term unemployed themselves suffered a degree of physical or mental impairment which rendered them 'unemployable' in contemporary eyes; distinguishing one group from the other was no easy matter. At it stands at present', the *National Insurance Gazette* noted in April 1938, 'the [disability] benefit is practically a pension to many in impaired health . . .' A few years earlier, the Royal Commission on Unemployment Insurance had concluded that the health of a substantial proportion of the unemployed was far from good and had, unsuccessfully, tried to effect their transfer to sickness benefit. The distinction between the two groups was less self-evident than might be supposed [287; 295].

The question remains, of course, how far was unemployment responsible for this state of affairs? The answer lies partly in the way employers tried to rationalize the workforce, partly in the way that stress and falling income actually caused physical and mental deterioration. In the first place, employers facing financial difficulties tended to rid themselves of less productive workers and to eliminate non-productive jobs which had served as 'pension posts' for faithful retainers: night-watchman, porter, sweeper-up and so on. At the same time, depression was worst in those industries most associated with industrial diseases and accidents. Victims whose recovery was less than perfect were the most likely candidates for the dole queue. In terms of physical capacity, as with skill, it is possible to see a 'filtering down' process at work, with the better-qualified and fitter workers tending to take over the jobs of the unskilled and less healthy, who therefore became disproportionately represented among the unemployed [178, 160–9]. In a depressed labour market with few opportunities, a physical impairment might assume the characteristics of a major disability – especially in the eyes of the sufferer whose chances of work were repeatedly ruined because of it. Seen from this perspective, the difference between sickness and health can be understood as relative: chronic sickness was less caused by unemployment than revealed by it, for we know nothing of that army of workers whose health was probably not good but who clung to their jobs rather than risk redundancy by taking time off to recover [287].

We cannot conclude, however, that unemployment itself did not affect the health of its victims. Reduced circumstances and stress were as capable of exacerbating existing maladies as they were of creating new ones. Although hard evidence on this point is not easily produced, contemporary commentators constantly referred to the 'deterioration' of the long-term unemployed, which would render them unfit for future employment, should jobs become available. Men once capable of continuous heavy manual work were losing the capacity and the will for it. Official policy thus tried to prevent – or at least contain – the rising numbers of 'unemployables'. Local authorities and voluntary agencies pooled resources to provide instruction courses, keep-fit classes, voluntary work centres. The unemployed were encouraged to take full advantage of these amenities, but compulsion was only exercised in the case of juvenile claimants to unemployment benefit who had to attend Juvenile Instruction Centres. Juveniles were deemed particularly at risk thanks to the propensity for employers to throw out 'boy' – and less frequently 'girl' – workers once they were old enough to command an adult rate [147]. Policy aimed not only to prevent physical and mental 'deterioration', to reinforce the desire for work, but also to stop the young in the depressed areas 'settling' to a life on the dole.

Evidence indicating that depression and unemployment were inflicting medical damage was provided by investigations into the rising numbers of chronic disabled in the mid-1930s. These revealed that a quarter of claimants for disablement benefits were institutionalized and that about a third were suffering from severe nervous disorders.[3] Psychiatry was gaining respectability in medical circles but changes in diagnostic practices cannot be the sole explanation for the increasing incidence of psychological disability and psychosomatic illness. Nor can the impact of the First World War be held largely responsible; over half of the 'nervous' cases would have been below the age for military service at the time of the Armistice. Research in Europe and the United States proved that unemployment itself damaged mental well-being. Loss of work stimulated a similar pattern of reactions. Initial shock was followed by determined effort to find work; prolonged failure produced disillusion and apathy. In the absence of a regulated time structure, the loss of social contact and the disappearance of nearly all collective activities, individual identity, self-esteem and confidence were undermined. At worst, this led to social maladjustment, neurosis and depression [85; 145].

In Britain, similar evidence supported these conclusions. In Glasgow, a survey of a thousand health insurance claimants revealed that illness in 33 per cent of cases had psycho-neurotic rather than organic causes. Furthermore, only one third had been in work when sickness struck.[4] The impact of unemployment took its toll on men's minds and bodies alike. Skilled men in shipbuilding or engineering probably suffered more than unskilled casual workers, because the were less accustomed to the social disgrace associated with job loss. Rising rates of vagrancy also indicate the difficulties experienced by some of the unemployed in adjusting to their status; far from malingering at public expense, a proportion carried official encouragement to move in search of work a little too far. Once such cases started having regular recourse to the casual words – the 'spike' in common parlance – they were no longer regarded as part of the labour market. Subject to separate relieving agencies, their predicament was largely attributed to their personal, psychological deficiencies, not to the consequences of the slump [171].

The Politics of Public Order and Social Expenditure

Casualism and vagrancy may not have been seen as a consequence of rising unemployment, but crime rates and political disaffection most certainly were. Crime rates in general, juvenile delinquency in particular, rose in the early 1930s. However, there are reasons for believing that unemployment cannot have been the sole cause. In spite of the views voiced by public officials and the press, crime rates continued to rise even when the economy was recovering later in the decade. More significantly, the correlation between unemployment and crime tended to collapse when examined at local level: prosperous Norwich had higher crime rates than depressed Gateshead between 1934 and 1936, for example [66, 41–2]. If the unemployed appeared more prone to crime, it could be because those of more dubious character had greater difficulty in finding work. Employers tend to discriminate against those with a criminal record under any circumstances. In a depression, the chance of a 'new start' must be further reduced. Unemployment did not necessarily force the honest to resort to illegal practices. Rather, it probably exerted the greatest pressure on those already experienced in petty burglary and theft.

The early 1930s witnesed an escalation in the size and incidence of demonstrations and marches against rising unemployment and the introduction of means-tested relief, as Deacon's chapter shows. Deprived of the benefit of hindsight, the government did take this evidence of disaffection seriously enough to tighten up on law and order, to police the marches carefully and – when MPs from the depressed areas joined ranks with the protesters – to modify the impact of the Unemployment Assistance Board. However, historians now argue that, despite official fears, there is little to suggest that the National Unemployed Workers' Movement posed a threat to parliamentary democracy, or even intended to do so. Britain remained politically stable. Extremist organisations – the British Union of Fascists and the Communist Party – certainly expanded at this time, but neither presented a viable threat to the political establishment and neither recruited extensively among the jobless. Reasons why the slump and its consequences were accepted relatively calmly range from the personal to the political. In the first place, those in search of work were unlikely to do anything to prejudice their chances on the labour market and, as psychologists noted, latent depression and apathy provided poor foundations for political radicalism. On the political level, in Britain at least, the slump came not as a break in prosperity but as an accelerated deepening of existing depression in the Northern manufacturing towns. Finally, the British system of unemployment relief – in spite of its inadequacies – proved more reliable than its Continental counterparts [256, *ch. 14*].

The economic consequences of mass unemployment were severe and were not confined solely to the burden imposed by unemployment relief. In spite of every official effort to contain it, public expenditure on the social services rose from £306.634 million in 1920 to £513.783 million in 1935 [113, 6–7]. The direct cost of unemployment in the latter year was less than one fifth of the total [41, *21*]. Although £82 million of the remaining difference can be attributed to the introduction of contributory pensions and public housing schemes this is largely offset by savings in war pensions of £54.4 million over the same period. The cost of poor relief (public assistance) in England and Wales rose from £13.47 million in 1929 to just under £20 million 10 years later, in spite of the transference of the long term unemployed to the UAB in the interim [41, *365*]. These figures illustrate the general growth of social dependence in this period, over and above the rising incidence of unemployment *per se*. The social consequences of unemployment were thus reflected in rising social costs.

Arguably, unemployment helped increase reliance on public funds. Rising numbers of disabled and old age pensioners were 'topping up' on public assistance, perhaps because earlier spells of unemployment had eroded their savings or had rendered children incapable of helping elderly relatives. Other means-tested social services also rose in cost, which helped some poorer families eke out their income. School meals and medical services, subsidized milk and welfare clinics for pregnant women, municipal medical services and so on were all provided, if somewhat unevenly, by local government or by rate-aided voluntary agencies. And well before the advent of the Commissioners for the Special Areas in 1934, local authorities were subscribing to a variety of job creation schemes notably the provision of allotments, but also work designed to improve local amenities – as part of the general effort to alleviate the plight of the unemployed.

Such provision remained, however, very varied and – thanks to the inability of the poorest authorities to raise sufficient funds – tended to be provided in inverse proportion to local need. Hence the depressed areas were often associated with the most rudimentary services administered under the strictest means tests; this affected a whole range of provision, from free school meals to local medical services, slum clearance to public transport [283]. The poorest authorities were caught in a double bind: where dependence on the social services was already strong, any attempt to raise higher rates or further loans to improve matters was liable to alienate potential industrial investment. Although the extension of local authority services was impressive in some areas, provision remained distinctly patchy. Investigations revealed, for instance, a low geographical correlation between the incidence of malnutrition and the provision of free school meals. On the other hand, some Labour-controlled local authorities – like Sheffield in the late 1920s and the London County Council later in the following decade – expanded municipal health and education services in an unprecedented fashion. These initiatives showed how public welfare could be used as a general supplement to working class living standards, without involving the hated means test.

This piecemeal and illogical provision of services provoked criticism from a variety of professional groups – not only nutritionists and doctors, but also those economists who were arguing that the free market was not going to produce an automatic solution to national problems. Although hardly at the forefront of the political agenda, the social consequences of structural economic imbalances did stimulate debate about the merits of greater state intervention. The contribution of political parties and other social and political groups to this process is discussed in Chapter 4. The point here is that the period witnessed a spate of publications concerning the duty of government to ameliorate social and economic ills. In an approach reminiscent of the early Fabians, scientific investigation became the basis for collectivist solutions designed to reduce inefficiency and waste in industry and the social services alike [29; 219; 220].

It is, perhaps, easy to overestimate the influence of these reformers and to exaggerate their unity of purpose [29]. Any proposals for more government action flew in the face of accepted economic wisdom, which dictated prudence, not largesse, in matters of public expenditure. However, although they failed to disturb the political status quo, these new movements did make state intervention more politically respectable than it had been at any time since the Armistice. The new attitude was evident in the work of the Royal Commission on the Distribution of the Industrial Population (Barlow: Cmd. 6153) in the late 1930s. Both evidence and report describe the counterproductive consequences of allowing industry a complete free rein. This had produced problems not only in the depressed areas but also in expanding ones, where overcrowding congestion and poor social amenities combined to hinder efficient industrial expansion. The solution lay in greater central involvement in the locational decisions of private enterprise. Government should encourage industrial diversification and sponsor effective regional planning. This would promote the more even distribution of production, employment and wealth over the nation as a whole, and thus increase industrial efficiency [115].

The Second World War and After

The 'national efficiency' question came into its own at the outbreak of the Second World War. Extensive state controls were no longer a question for political conjecture, but a matter of national expediency. The unemployed were no longer an unfortunate but unavoidable by product of industrial restructuring, but a treasonable waste of manpower resources. They were reabsorbed into the labour market with other 'marginal' categories – the disabled, the sick, the 'retired' the vagrant. In the Second World War, as in the First, the label 'unemployable' proved to be relative; many previously condemned as incompetent or inefficient showed themselves capable of holding down a job of some type. The expanded role of the state provided the framework within which the rationalization of social welfare services could be discussed. The Beveridge Report of 1942, the blueprint for the postwar welfare reforms, followed the Barlow recommendations in advocating the permanent extension of state powers – but for nationalization of welfare rather than the relocation of industry [116]. The significance of the report lay less in its recommendations – it contained few proposals that had not been under consideration in the interwar period – than in its reception. It was the most popular document ever published by HMSO. It proved politically impossible to ignore demands for its implementation. Notably, the promise of universal benefits, available as of right, tapped a major source of public resentment against the indignity and the injustices of the means test. The interwar years had, however, shown that state social insurance was financially unfeasible in the context of mass unemployment. If the future collapse of Beveridge's universal system of benefits was to be avoided, then full employment – or something like it – had to become a central component of public policy.

The war itself must be held responsible for the transformation of the economic and political climate within which social policy was discussed. Mobilization in general and evacuation in particular brought home the plight of families in the depressed areas in a way that the hunger marches, the novels and all the social investigations of the 1930s had never been able to do. Class antagonisms and social divisions were laid aside in the common struggle; even in ruling circles, there was a widespread assumption that the war would lead to a more egalitarian society. Leaving aside its enormous impact on public economics, the conflict thus rekindled not only faith in government as an agent for social improvement, but also a positive determination that the injustices and waste of the prewar decades should not be allowed to return. For the next quarter-century, mass unemployment was widely viewed as intolerable in a civilized society. Its eradication was one of many signs of social progress, much like the elimination of typhoid and cholera in the previous century.

With time, of course, the sense of revulsion has diminished and collective folk memory has played a dwindling role in shaping popular opinion about the 'devil's decade'. The publications of the social investigators have been re-examined and official statistics reassessed, in order to reach a more balanced view of the 1930s and, specifically, to query the degree to which unemployment itself can be held responsible for working class poverty and associated social problems. However, this subdivision of poverty by its principal causes may be statistically attractive, but it is hardly socially realistic. In the first place, it is not possible to distinguish poverty due to unemployment from that ascribed to low pay. This last was often the consequence of short-time working or worsening conditions in casual trades; these were both manifestations of a falling demand for labour in specific industries. Second, as unemployment rose in the early 1930s and fell again with recovery, rearmament and the war, apparently self-evident distinctions between sick, disabled, retired, vagrant and unemployed became blurred. Social surveys, because of their static nature, tended to distort a dynamic process. Less efficient workers – a category incorporating the elderly, the mentally unstable, the unskilled, the physically impaired – were shaken out of the labour market as demand fell, only to be reabsorbed when it picked up again. Rigid systems of classification cannot reflect changes in human judgement. Unemployment as a cause of poverty cannot be assessed in isolation. The links with destitution nominally ascribed to old age, ill health and physical disability are too strong.

29

Furthermore, in many instances, the degree of impairment, howeve initially caused, might easily have been exacerbated by the impact o unemployment itself.

Historians are generally reluctant to apply past conclusions t present day circumstances. Situations invariably change and history has a nasty habit of not repeating itself. However, the experience o the 1930s does show current developments in an interesting light. O course, absolute poverty today is nowhere near as intense or a widespread as it was in the interwar years. Jobs have expanded in white collar and service sectors, the workforce is less dominantly male and there is less premium on simple physical strength tha there was before the war. None the less, rising unemployment today has been associated with social developments which, althoug different in their intensity, are reminiscent of those experienced in the interwar years. Again psychological research has re-explored and reaffirmed the damage inflicted by unemployment on mental well being. Again, escalating rates of disability and vagrancy have ru parallel with rising long-term unemployment. Again political debat rages over whether unemployment should be seen as a primary caus of ill health and of rising rates of juvenile crime. Again, questions o law and order are moving to the forefront of public discussion. Suc common features might, of course, be fortuitous. Alternatively, th labour market is responding to the current recession in much th same way as it did before the war – and with similar socia consequences.

Notes

1 Public Record Office: AST 7/255: Pilgrim Trust Interim Paper no (1936).
2 Public Record Office: PIN 4/58: Central Committee on National Healt Insurance: minutes of 75th meeting, 4 February 1938.
3 Ibid. Also ACT 1/582: papers of the Ministry of Health's Disabilit Committee (1936–37).
4 Articles by Dr J L Halliday in *British Medical Journal* 9 March an 16 March 1935.

3

Systems of Interwar Unemployment Relief

ALAN DEACON

At first sight, the history of unemployment benefits between the wars is puzzling. On the one hand, the benefits are widely regarded as having been generous. Certainly, they rose substantially in real terms, and they were markedly higher than the benefits paid to the sick and to the old. They also rose relative to wages, and it was seen in Chapter 2 that some writers have argued that by the 1930s the level of benefits had become a significant disincentive to work. On the other hand, the benefit system was the focus of considerable unrest and the cause of intense bitterness. Moreover, the memories of the dole queue and of the 'hungry thirties' were to have a crucial influence upon attitudes and policies in later years. How is it, then, that the same benefits could be seen as so generous as to dissuade some from work and yet be so harsh as to generate riots and hunger marches, and to leave such bitter memories?

Part of the answer, of course, is that the unemployed were not a homogeneous group. The treatment of those who were out of work for short periods was often more favourable than that of the long-term unemployed. More fundamental, however, is the distinction between the level of benefits and the rules and regulations which determined who was eligible for those benefits. Much of the unrest and bitterness was caused not by the amounts paid, but by the manner in which it was paid and the way in which benefits were withheld from some of the unemployed. Of particular significance here, of course, was the operation of the household means test in the 1930s.

The benefit system in turn reinforced the prevailing attitudes towards unemployment itself. The benefits were sufficient to underpin the passive resignation of many of the unemployed, while the operation of the means test provoked the anger of those affected and provided a continuing focus for the activities of groups such as the National Unemployed Workers' Movement (NUWM). The latter aspect was remembered most clearly in later years, and it was the administration of benefit which was to constitute the 'bitter legacy' of the 1930s.

This chapter, then, has three purposes. First and foremost, to provide a brief outline of the development of the benefit system, and of the economic and political pressures upon it. Second, to explain the response to those benefits of the unemployed themselves, and, third, to discuss the way in which the operation of the benefit system affected attitudes towards the wider issues of unemployment and of political change.

Unemployment Insurance in the 1920s

Unemployment insurance had been introduced by the Liberal government in 1911. Originally, the scheme had been restricted to some two and a half million workers, virtually all of whom were men [98; 133]. For those who were covered the scheme represented a marked break from the Poor Law tradition of the nineteenth century. Workers who had paid a sufficient number of contributions to establish a right to benefit could draw that benefit without reference to either their personal character or the income of the household in which they lived. True, they had to meet various conditions – such as being available for work – but anyone refused benefit on these grounds had the right to appeal to an independent tribunal. It was this emphasis upon legal entitlement which made insurance attractive to contributors and distinguished it so sharply from the Poor Law [77, 6]. The level of benefit, however, was lower than that paid by the strictest Board of Guardians, and it was officially described as a supplement to the worker's own savings rather than as a subsistence income. More importantly, the benefits were paid for only a short period of time. No one could claim benefits for more than 15 weeks in any one year and, within this overall limit, an individual was entitled to one week on benefit for every 5 weeks' contributions he had previously paid. It was widely believed that this 'one – five' rule provided an effective safeguard against abuse. Llewellyn-Smith Permanent Secretary at the Board of Trade, argued, for example that with the 'double weapon of a maximum limit to benefit and of a minimum contribution, the operation of the scheme itself will automatically exclude the loafer' [73, *11*]. This, of course, rested upon the assumption that the *bona fide* worker would soon find another job, and that only the undeserving would be affected by the limits on benefit. In the early months of the scheme's operation, however, this appeared to be true, and less than 4 per cent of unemployment occurred after benefit had been exhausted [18, *271*].

The initial reaction of the labour movement was mixed. Some argued that benefits should be financed entirely from the taxes paid by the better off, but the majority believed that some contribution from the worker was essential if means tests were to be avoided [264]. The debate, however, was short-lived. An attempt to extend insurance to particular trades during the First World War was fiercely resisted by the trade unions involved, but there was little opposition to the general expansion of the scheme by the Unemployment Insurance Act of 1920 [285; 181].

The 1920 Act has been aptly described by Professor Mowat as an 'accident of timing' [212, *46*]. Around 12 million workers were covered by the scheme, which otherwise differed little, in principle, from that introduced in 1911. Economic circumstances, however, were to change dramatically. Unemployment in the insured trades stood at 3.7 per cent when the Act went into operation in November 1920; by March 1921 it had risen to 11.3 per cent and by June it reached 22.4 per cent. No longer could the postwar Coalition government claim that benefits were a temporary supplement to wages, or that only malingerers would exhaust their entitlement to benefit.

Ministers now had three choices. First they could do nothing and rely on the Poor Law to meet the needs of those who ran out of benefit. It was generally agreed, however, that this would provoke widespread and damaging unrest amongst the unemployed. Serious rioting had already occurred in several parts of the country and the Cabinet received frequent warnings of impending unrest from the Home Office Directorate of Intelligence (74, *11–13*). Particular attention was paid to the activities of the newly-formed NUWM which, although small, seemed to be the kind of body which had been effective in organizing unrest in Europe [124; 134].

Moreover, ministers became increasingly sceptical of the capacity of the Boards of Guardians to cope with the unemployed in such numbers. Some form of government grant would, of course, be cost-effective if it were channelled to the Boards in the areas where unemployment was highest. Such a subsidy, however, would create more problems than it solved.

A number of Boards were already paying relatively generous relief, either because it was their policy to do so or because they had been forced to make concessions by the threat of disorder. The former were especially worrying for the government because the Representation of the People Act of 1918 had extended the franchise to paupers and there appeared to be a growing tendency for guardians and councillors in some areas to actively court the pauper vote [76]. The best-known manifestation of this is, of course, the celebrated refusal of the Borough of Poplar to levy a rate for the London County Council until the costs of poor relief were shared more equally across the city. At one point in 1921 the Poplar councillors were imprisoned for defying an order of the High Court, but they eventually secured the equalization of the cost of outdoor relief within London. This, of course, represented a substantial subsidy to the poorer boroughs and thereby enabled them to pay higher rates of relief if they so wished [243]. The problem of 'Poplarism' was thus to be an important influence upon relief policy throughout the decade.

The second option open to the government in 1921 was to introduce a new benefit, separate from both insurance and the Poor Law. This was believed to be unnecessary, however, as unemployment was itself regarded as temporary. In consequence, there appeared to be no alternative to the third course, which was to make some temporary amendment to the insurance scheme. Accordingly, an Act of March 1921 provided for the payment of additional benefit for a maximum of 30 weeks. There were to be many such temporary amendments.

In all, there were more than twenty Acts relating to unemployment insurance between 1921 and 1931. The net effect of what was a confused and confusing series of *ad hoc* measures was twofold. First, the real value of benefits rose substantially. Those paid to a man with a dependent wife and two children, for example, rose by 240 per cent between November 1920 and August 1931, those paid to a single man by 92 per cent [109]. Second, those benefits were paid almost continuously and with virtually no reference to previous contributions. At any time after 1921 over half of those drawing benefit would not have qualified under the terms of the 1920 Act. Indeed, in 1924 it could have been claimed by anyone who had ever paid 12 contributions, and between February 1925 and August 1931 the minimum number of contributions required was 8 in the previous 2 years or 30 at any time. The latter was the crucial provision, and by the end of the decade a substantial proportion of claimants had not worked for long periods. On 26 May 1930, for example, benefit was being drawn by around 75,000 men who had paid no contributions in the previous 2 years, and a further 62,000 who had paid less than 9. As Bakke noted,

The title to benefit has shifted, then, from the fact that a man has a financial relationship, a premium-bound contract, to the fact that he is a genuine worker genuinely unemployed. If he has sufficient stamps, it is this latter status which they indicate. If he has not sufficient stamps, . . . he can prove this latter status by some other means. [9, 96]

The task of demonstrating the genuineness of one's unemployment, however, was not as straightforward as Bakke might seem to suggest. In fact, it was made steadily more difficult throughout the decade. The important point was that the hurried abandonment of the contributory conditions for benefit removed the safeguards against abuse which had been seen as an essential feature of the original scheme. In theory, it would have been possible for someone to remain on benefit indefinitely, particularly as it was clearly impossible for the employment exchanges to test the genuineness with which claimants sought work by offering them all jobs [73, 22]. There was also the question of cost. It was impossible to raise contributions by anything like enough to finance the additional benefits, and as the Unemployment Insurance Fund sunk deeper into debt so successive governments sought to reduce expenditure as far as it was politically possible to do so. The result of these pressures was the imposition of a means test upon some claimants and, more importantly, the introduction of the genuinely seeking work test.

The essence of the seeking work test was that it required the claimant to furnish proof that he or she was making every effort to find a job. If they failed to do so, they could be disallowed benefit without the exchange or anyone else having to show that work was actually available in the area. Decisions on individual cases were taken by local committees, the members of which were carefully screened by the Ministry of Labour. This meant that it was relatively easy for the Conservative government of Stanley Baldwin to 'tighten up' the administration of the test between 1925 and 1929. During this period some 17 per cent of applicants for the so-called extended benefit were refused, more than a tenth on the grounds that they were not seeking work [73, 55]. The test was thus an effective, if not savage, method of ensuring that work incentives were maintained in a period of mass unemployment and that the cost of benefits was kept to a minimum.

If the reasons for the introduction of the test are fairly clear, those for its successful operation are less so. After all, extended benefit was only being paid in the first place because of the threat of disorder; why, then, did the test not provoke similar unrest? Part of the answer to this question lies in the fact that in its early years the test was believed to apply primarily to married women who had worked during the war but had since left the labour force. More generally, however, the test was divisive in its impact. Unlike a cut in benefits, it did not affect everyone equally, and inevitably some suspicion fell upon those who 'failed' the test and were labelled as malingerers. Thus it was not until the numbers disallowed rose substantially towards the end of the 1920s that mass protest began to emerge. None the less by 1930 opposition to the test was intense and the second Labour government was forced first to relax its administration and then abandon it entirely [73, 71–5]. This in turn led to a sharp rise in the number of people receiving benefit and still further increased the deficit on the Insurance Fund. Indeed, the cost of unemployment relief was at the centre of the political crisis of August 1931 and the resignation of the Labour government [250].

Throughout the remainder of the 1930s Britain was governed by a Conservative-dominated National government. One of the first measures of the new government was to reduce benefits by 10 per cent and to restrict them to those who had paid 30 contributions in the previous 2 years. This marked a clear break from the policies of the 1920s. For 10 years governments had tried to adapt the insurance scheme in such a way as would enable it to cope with the pressures of mass unemployment. In so doing they had sought to reconcile – or at least balance – the twin demands of political expediency and financial stringency. That attempt was now abandoned, and henceforth insurance figured little in political controversy [99; *179–80*]. The important issue now was what happened to those who no longer qualified for insurance benefits.

Unemployment Assistance in the 1930s

The rate of unemployment in the insured trades rose sharply at the beginning of the 1930s: it was 11 per cent at the end of 1929, 17 per cent in the summer of 1930 and over 20 per cent in the spring of 1931. Equally significant, however, was the steady rise in the number of people who had been out of work for over a year; from 53,000 in 1929 to 300,000 in 1932 and on to 500,000 in the summer of 1933. This increase in long-term unemployment threw into sharp focus the problem of those who had been drawing benefits for long periods. It did so, moreover, at a time when the pressures for economies in government spending were becoming still more intense. In August 1931, the May Committee on National Expenditure painted a graphic – and highly exaggerated – picture of a nation dragged down into indebtedness by the burden of excessively generous social services. These services were themselves seen as the

36

product of ill-advised concessions to the political demands of an electorate which did 'not appreciate the true economic position of the country' [111, *13*]. *The Times* similarly declared that Britain had to choose 'between a comfortable way that leads on to bankruptcy and an uncomfortable way that leads back to prosperity' [77, *19*]. Above all, it was the cost of unemployment relief which was identified as the central problem, and it is important to emphasize that much of this analysis was accepted by politicians in all parties. The second Labour government, for example, accepted the imposition of a means test upon those who had drawn benefit for more than 6 months, and it resigned not over this issue but over the question of a cut in the basic rate of benefit [189, *414–21*].

It was noted earlier that one of the first measures of the new National government was to restrict eligibility for insurance benefits to those who had paid 30 contributions in the past 2 years, and this had the immediate effect of disallowing some 800,000 of the 2,800,000 people who were then drawing benefit. These people were now to apply for transitional payments: a new benefit paid at the same rate as insurance but subject to a means test administered by the Public Assistance Committees (PACs) of the local authorities. The PACs had recently replaced the Board of Guardians in the administration of the Poor Law, and they were told to assess claims for transitional payments in the same way as those for poor relief. In practice this meant that they were to apply a household means test [70].

As its name suggests, the essence of a household means test was that a claim was assessed not on the basis of the needs and resources of the individual claimant but upon those of the household in which he or she lived. It meant, for example, that an older man with (say) a daughter in work and living at home could be told to look to her for support. Conversely, a younger man or woman could be refused benefit on the grounds that one of his or her parents was in work and earning enough to maintain the whole household. These were perhaps the most common causes, but the criterion was not family but simply membership of the same household. Distant relatives and even comparative strangers could be called upon to support the claimant – and face detailed inquiries into their own earnings and circumstances.

The rationale of the household means test was quite simple. Transitional payments were not being paid on the basis of entitlement but on the basis of need. It was thus reasonable to ensure that claimants were in fact in need, and this could not be assessed in isolation from the circumstances of the household as a whole. Milner Gray, Parliamentary Secretary to the Minister of Labour, told the

Commons that transitional payments were 'really a form of public assistance. Let us accept that term because it is a fact' [77, *16*].

It was precisely this association with the Poor Law which explains the bitterness and humiliation of the unemployed who were subjected to the means test. As Bakke observed, it meant an immediate change in status from that of a member of an insured trade to something close to a pauper. 'The filling out of forms, the recurrent knocking of the investigator at one's door, the knowledge that all eyes in the street are on the investigator . . . all these are symbols of one's new status' [9, *191*].

Around one-fifth of those who had previously been receiving benefit were refused transitional payments on the grounds of household income, and a further third had their payments reduced. Overall some 450,000 households were affected immediately and many thousands more in subsequent years [77, *17, 25–6*]. Not only did they suffer a drop in household income, but it was frequently alleged that the obligations which the means test imposed on the other members of the household poisoned family relationships and forced, in particular, young people to leave home [280].

It is perhaps surprising then that the introduction of the means test in November 1931 did not produce an immediate outcry. After all those affected would not be suspected of malingering, and the impact upon some communities in the depressed areas was devastating. Against this, however, was the fact that the means test seemed inevitable. The National government had won crushing victories both in the general election of October 1931 and in the local elections held in the following months. In any case, it was widely known that the Labour government had agreed to something similar.

None the less, protest did emerge and develop during 1932. There were riots in London and Liverpool, and in October the NUWM organized a national 'Hunger March Against the Means Test' which culminated in a 30,000 strong rally in Hyde Park [256, *173–9*]. The NUWM also proved to be effective in putting pressure on individual PACs and it soon became clear that the administration of transitional payments would exhibit the same wide variations between different authorities as had existed within the Poor Law. Again central government was furious at the attitude of some PACs, but again it could do little to control the way discretionary decisions were taken at the local level [235]. PACs such as those in Rotherham, Glamorgan or County Durham disregarded virtually all of the income of the other members of the household and effectively negated the means test. Others were much more severe, but by October Henry Betterton, the Minister of Labour, was warning the Cabinet that 'if the present agitation continued' the government might be forced to 'abandon the means test altogether'. The National government was thus forced into what Miller has called a 'tacit compromise', whereby the two most generous PACs were replaced by Commissioners but the others were allowed to 'ease some of the worst aspects of the test if they did it without openly challenging the principles of government policy' [202, *171*]. The relaxation of the administration of transitional payments which now followed undoubtedly helped to avoid further unrest. None the less, the position was scarcely satisfactory from the government's point of view, and ministers were now convinced that the only solution was to take the administration of unemployment relief out of the hands of the local authorities altogether.

Central control of the administration of unemployment relief was the prime objective of the Unemployment Act of 1934. This created the Unemployment Assistance Board (UAB). The constitutional position was that the UAB was responsible for both the rates of unemployment assistance and the regulations determining entitlement. In practice the scale rates were still decided by the government, but the fact that the UAB was responsible for day-to-day administration meant that ministers could not be asked parliamentary questions on individual cases. More importantly, it also meant that the local officers who decided upon individual claims were appointed by and were responsible to the UAB rather than local authority. This, it was hoped, would ensure that the descretion inherent in any such scheme would be exercised in a manner which was acceptable to the central government and did not vary from one part of the country to another [205; 34]. It was expected that the introduction of the new arrangements in January 1935 would lead to a reduction in the levels of assistance paid in the areas where the PACs had been most generous. In other areas, however, there would be improvements, and so the overall effect was expected to be a slight increase in expenditure.

The opposite happened, and the uproar which greeted the new UAB and the panic with which the government responded to that uproar is one of the more remarkable stories in the history of social policy. Briefly, the assessments made by the UAB's officers resulted in far more reductions than had been envisaged. This was partly because the PACs had become more generous in the period before the changes, but was largely the result of official ignorance as to the prevailing level of working class rents [204, *338*]. In any event the government found itself confronted by mass rallies and demonstrations throughout the depressed areas. Over 300,000 people took to the streets in South Wales alone, and their protests were reinforced by those of church leaders, back-bench Conservative MPs and the local authority associations. It quickly became apparent that the new regulations included benefit cuts for nearly half of those being transferred to the UAB, and after hectic – and heated – discussions with the members of the UAB the Cabinet agreed to what became known as the Standstill. Under this every claim was to be assessed twice: first, in accordance with the regulations of the UAB, and then as it would have been assessed by the PAC. The claimant was to receive whichever payment was the higher. Some indication of the degree of panic within Whitehall is provided by the Cabinet's reaction to events in Sheffield. Initially, the Standstill was to take effect on 14 February, leaving claimants on the reduced allowances during the preceding week. Some 10,000 people marched on the Town Hall to demand immediate increases, and after fighting had broken out ministers authorized an immediate restoration of the old benefit levels in Sheffield alone [204, *343*].

The Standstill, of course, made nonsense of the 1934 Act. It preserved the variations between areas and required the UAB to make payments which it publicly complained were 'simply an abuse of public money' [112, *15*]. None the less, it succeeded in its objective of quelling the unrest and so was allowed to remain in force for 18 months. Even then, the new regulations were introduced gradually and in such a way as to minimize benefit reductions. Indeed, by 1936 the tenor of the UAB's administration had changed, and officers were being encouraged to make generous use of their powers to award discretionary additions. As Millet observed, where 'confusion had once reigned, catastrophe pointed the way. Generosity became more important than the Treasury' [205, *206*]. The UAB also eased the administration of the means test by disregarding more of the claimant's savings and by allowing the other members of the household to retain more of their earnings. This was later to bring accusations that it was being too soft on the long-term unemployed, particularly those who were young. In 1938, for example, *The Times* complained that in 'a considerable number' of the 'chronic or constantly unemployed young men' there was a 'slackness of moral fibre and of will as well as of muscle'. It went on to demand that they be compelled to attend a training or industrial centre. The UAB itself estimated that 30 per cent of its applicants under 30 had settled down on assistance, but broadly resisted benefit reductions and emphasized the need for work creation schemes for this group [75, *63*].

There was widespread concern at the apparent demoralization of the unemployed, but otherwise the UAB enjoyed a relatively quiet life in the later 1930s. By 1937 the number receiving assistance was below 600,000 and the UAB's claimants were increasingly concentrated in the depressed areas. Not only did the rate of unemployment vary widely between regions, but so did the proportion of the unemployed who had been out of work for long periods. Unemployment in the South-East stood at 6.2 per cent in 1936 and 6 per cent of the unemployed had not worked for a year; in the North-East the figures were 21.2 per cent and 26 per cent; and in Wales 32.2 per cent and 37 per cent [256, 287]. This degree of concentration reduced the visibility of the unemployment problem and reinforced the remarkable ignorance of many people in the more prosperous areas as to the hardship endured by the unemployed. Neither that ignorance, nor the fatalistic acceptance of unemployment as inevitable, was to survive the Second World War.

Conclusion

Runciman had argued convincingly that the main reason for the lack of serious and sustained disorder in the interwar years was the fact that mass unemployment appeared to many people to be unavoidable. It seemed 'the consequence not of a detectable blunder but rather of an incurable disease. Its victims did not appear to be the victims of remediable injustice so much as an Act of God' [242, 61]. If there was little any government could do to create work, then there was little point in agitation. Instead the majority of the unemployed 'got by' and 'made do' in a manner chronicled by Orwell and others [216]. It was here that the role of benefit was crucial. It did not prevent poverty and hardship, but it did avert starvation and it did enable the unemployed to retain their homes, their furniture and their self-respect. The margin, however, was often desperately thin, and so the level and administration of relief remained a sensitive and volatile issue. Moreover, nobody regarded the seeking work test, the means test nor the reductions originally imposed by the UAB as an act of God – it was these which were the focus of resentment and protest. That protest was angry and sometimes violent, but it was extremely limited in its aims. As Miller has pointed out, all that was demanded in 1935 was a return to the previous level of payments. Once that was conceded, the unrest ended as suddenly as it had begun [204, 347].

The resentment was more enduring, however, and it was to acquire a new significance in the political and economic climate created by the Second World War. The experience of full employment undermined the fashionable – and comfortable – assumption that many of those out of work were unemployable, while the social divisions of the interwar years were eroded by the operation of the evacuation scheme and by the sense of national unity generated by

Britain's isolation in the aftermath of Dunkirk [268; 1]. It was in this context that the White Paper on employment policy was drafted. As Churchill was warned by his adviser Lord Cherwell, 'the British people' had become accustomed to full employment and would not 'tolerate a return to the old figures. They will demand that the Government produce a programme for achieving comparable results in peace' [75, 62]. The force and emotion with which that demand was made owed much to the system of unemployment relief between the wars.

4

Unemployment and Interwar Politics

ALAN BOOTH

The focus of this chapter is the effect of unemployment on the British political system: its impact on parties, votes and access to power. Before the First World War, unemployment had become a major political issue and concern about unemployment had helped to shape part of the Liberal government's welfare reforms [133; 127; 36]. After 1920, conditions seemed ripe for unemployment to become an even more highly charged political issue; the franchise had been extended to cover many more working class voters;[1] unemployment must have affected directly between 5 and 6 million voters each year; and there was intense three-party competition for votes from 1922 until 1931. However, unemployment assumed top priority in the interwar political debate only very rarely. In only one of seven interwar general elections was unemployment policy the main issue and, paradoxically, this was in 1929, when unemployment was at its lowest point between 1921 and 1939. Other issues took higher priority for much of the interwar period, and the unemployed appear to have acquiesced in this order of precedence. Despite mass unemployment interwar Britain was notable for its political stability. However, social stability was very fragile, as other contributions to this volume have argued. There were marches, protests and demonstrations by the unemployed and the the period also witnessed periods of intense class conflict in industry. Yet Britain's social and political structure emerged comparatively unscathed from the interwar years. Paul Addison has rightly entitled his sketch of politics between 1922 and 1939, 'The Supremacy of Safety First' [1, ch. I]

Two Decades of Conservatism

The years 1917–20 were a period of intense social crisis in Britain, with a real danger of revolutionary activity [99, 5–50]. The labour movement had been strengthened and radicalized by the war, full employment, inflation and the socialist revolutions in Europe. Against this radicalized working class stood a capital-owning class containing groups which were determined to resist any progressive demands from labour. Powerful employers' associations insisted upon the reinstatement of managerial prerogatives in industry. City opinion wanted measures to restore London's international position, especially an effective commitment to return to gold at the prewar parity. There were those on both sides of industry who wanted to preserve the wartime pattern of consensual bargaining, but the attempts to create peacetime corporatist structures were doomed, as Kirby points out in Chapter 10. Thus, these questions about the future of economic policy were resolved through confrontation [278, 45]. Almost every demand of organized labour was rejected. The decisive step was the ability of the Cabinet and the coal owners to withstand the demands for the nationalization of the coalmining industry in 1919 and the final blow came in 1921 with another defeat for the miners' union on Black Friday, 16 April 1921. By this time the labour movement had been enormously weakened by the onset of mass unemployment.

The economic crisis of 1920–1 had much greater significance since it (and similar conditions in 1930–2) helped to shape the political agenda for the entire interwar period. The British economic crisis of 1920–1 was largely caused by a major downturn in the international economy, and was accompanied by increasing international competition in product markets and pressure on the exchange rate. The City and British industry began to call in increasingly strident terms for a sound money policy, reductions in taxation and public spending and the imposition of wage cuts to restore industrial competitiveness [23, 213–4]. Public opinion tended to follow as the press began to echo calls for economy. There was a very strong demand for very orthodox policies to which the government was forced to respond; it cut many useful programmes and was even forced to establish the Geddes Committee to 'axe' public spending still further. In many respects, this policy of retrenchment was simply a reflection of the political power of industrial and financial interest groups in 1920–2. The section of society which suffered when retrenchment was imposed upon an already contracting economy was organized labour, but labour was in no position to demand more generous treatment. Not for the last time in the twentieth century, an international economic crisis brought forth very strong demands for orthodox policies. A very similar process took place in 1930–2, and, again, the labour movement had to bear the brunt of adjustment [23].

The arguments in the previous paragraph may help to explain why certain policy options became almost irresistible at certain times, but they do not explain why it should have been the Conservative Party which profited. The Liberals, after all, could claim to be the party of nineteenth-century fiscal and monetary rectitude. Much of the explanation lies in the personalities of Baldwin and Lloyd George.

As we have seen, the postwar coalition under Lloyd George did respond to demands for more orthodox policies in 1921–2. However, even the Geddes Axe was insufficient for the Conservative back-benchers, who were becoming very troubled by some of Lloyd George's less reputable dealings. Led by an 'almost obscure Cabinet minister' [197, *126*], Baldwin, they believed that they would be better able to take advantage of the new mood in public opinion if the Conservatives left the coalition. The Conservative leaders were forced to obey, and the party went to the polls in 1922 promising, *inter alia*, financial economy. Baldwin rose quickly to become Chancellor of the Exchequer and Prime Minister when Bonar Law was forced to resign on health grounds.

More than anyone else, Baldwin ensured that the Conservatives would benefit from the policy priorities established in 1921–2. His genius lay in his sensitivity to public opinion, his ability to mould Conservative policy to the public mood and his evident popularity with the electorate [197; 289]. He was, of course, assisted by the weakness of his opponents. The Liberals were split after 1916 and remained an 'ill organized miscellany of viewpoints' [1, *23*]. Labour emerged as a national party only in 1918 and remained very much an unproven force against which 'red scare' tactics could be deployed. Baldwin was, thus, able to portray the Conservatives as the most credible of the governing parties. His speeches of the 1920s stressed the co-operation and common sense of the English character and presented the Conservative as the party of social cohesion and national unity, in tune with the virtues of the English character [289, *388–90*]. But he could also adapt to the realities of a political system weighed down by mass unemployment. Under Baldwin, the Conservatives always had enough of an employment policy to give hope to the unemployed. He used the tariff very shrewdly, both to cement party unity and to persuade the electorate that the Conservatives had a uniquely powerful remedy against unemployment. He championed rationalization in a similar manner. As we shall see, towards the end of the 1920s he produced a string of limited, common-sense, pragmatic policies to counter unemployment. In short, he made cautious pragmatism and the unwillingness to pursue bold innovations in policy into a national virtue; he accepted the essence of the policy priorities established in 1921–2, but was ready to make marginal adjustments to preserve social peace and stability. Thus, Baldwin created the philosophy and practice of 'safety first' in the 1920s to enable the Conservative Party to exploit the political possibilities which opened up in the aftermath of the postwar social and political crisis. Having established this philosophy so successfully in the 1920s, Baldwin and the Conservatives were the natural beneficiaries when economic crisis in 1931–2 once again brought demands for retrenchment and, in the process, broke the Labour Party.

Baldwin's philosophy was, however, a false safety first. Lloyd George posed no real threat to political stability and integrity. The Liberal share of the vote was a very respectable 29.7 per cent in 1923, but the Conservatives were determined to take the Liberals' middle class votes. The 'red scare' tactics which the Conservatives introduced in the 1924 general election campaign were designed both to unseat the minority Labour government and to establish the Conservatives as the only safe anti-socialist party. The tactics were extraordinarily successful; the Liberal share of the vote fell to 17.8 per cent in 1924. In 1929, when the Liberals set the terms of the election campaign, their share rose to 23.6 per cent, but the party had to field amost 175 additional candidates to achieve this result. The number of votes per opposed candidate actually fell from that achieved in 1924. Even with Lloyd George's massive employment schemes, the Liberals did not threaten safety first. Nor did the Labour Party. Just as Baldwin nibbled away at the Liberal middle class vote, in 1922 MacDonald made the Labour Party's primary objective the erosion of the Liberal working class vote [189, 793–5]. Thus, Labour moved into the centre of the political spectrum and moderated both its programme and its image as the decade progressed. The Labour Party was certainly not a threat to safety. Nevertheless, it was the Conservatives under Baldwin who captured the middle ground of British politics throughout the period 1922–39.

The 1929 General Election

Paradoxically, when 'safety first' was used as a specific election slogan it was a failure for Baldwin. It was coined for the 1929 general election which the Conservatives lost, much to their surprise.

Significantly, unemployment was the main issue in the campaign and, indeed, the problem had received much more attention from politicians and leaders of the major economic interest groups than at any time in the decade.

Labour had been using the unemployment question to make inroads into the Liberal working class vote. Even before the First World War, the Labour Party had fought vigorously for 'work or maintenance', and this demand was renewed at the end of the war [29, 17–21]. When this policy was apparently conceded with the extension of the NIS scheme in 1920, the Independent Labour Party, traditionally the source of new policy ideas for oganized labour, moved towards new and highly innovative proposals in employment policy. Mosley and Strachey's *Revolution by Reason* and the ILP's Living Wage Commission both promised a challenging and fresh approach to the unemployment problem, most notably with Mosley's idea for credit expansion combined with socialist planning [29, 23–5]. These ideas helped Labour gain parliamentary seats from the Liberals, especially in the coalfield areas, Lancashire and Yorkshire, and the predominantly working class districts of London. A similar pattern is evident in local election results, with significant breakthroughs occurring in 1919 and 1926 [67, 168–9]. In the more prosperous manufacturing areas, such as the Midlands, Labour's progress at both parliamentary and municipal levels was obvious but lower.

Before the Liberals could respond to these pressures the party had to be reunited. However, before a full reconciliation could be effected, a much more serious threat to the Liberal electoral position became apparent. In a three-party-system, the Liberals had to persuade the electorate that a firm compromise between capital and labour was possible. Unfortunately, class tensions came to the surface in the mid-1920s to pose enormous problems for the Liberals. We have already noted Conservative use of a 'red scare' in 1925, but what followed was even worse for the Liberal cause. The General Strike and the right-wing Conservative backlash in 1927 threatened to polarize society and create electoral conditions ruinous to the Liberals. Indeed, government strategy during the strike depended upon the exploitation of social divisions by separating trade unionists from non-unionists, but driving wedges between the miners and the wider trade union movement and, finally, by exploiting divisions within the miners' union [28]. The Liberals, without any secure foothold in class politics, stood to suffer enormously if these divisions were not healed.

Accordingly, shortly after the General Strike the party mobilized its impressive array of academic, professional and journalistic talent to find a solution to the 'industrial problem'. Its report, *Britain'* *Industrial Future*, the Liberal Yellow Book, is one of the most famou party political documents of the present century [176]. It propose reform in two areas: industrial relations and employment policy. T counter unemployment, the Liberals proposed a major public work programme financed by a large loan raised in the City by a Nationa Investment Board. Rationalization would also be encouraged Existing party policy on coal, agriculture and trade was als included. On industrial relations, the Yellow Book proposed distinctly utopian scheme in which employee shareholding figure prominently, but from which trade unions were absent. Thes proposals have been reviewed extensively by historians and hav generally been praised for their imaginativeness, even if definit administrative weaknesses have been identified [46; 272; 29].

Much less frequently noted is the appearance of similar proposal at the same time. Leading representatives of both sides of industr came together in January 1928 in the Mond–Turner talks to explor the possibility of co–operation in overcoming the 'industrial problem Like the Liberals, the Mond–Turner talks proposed a new collaborativ machinery to resolve industrial disputes, a more efficient, capita intensive structure for British industry and a programme of publi works combined with an expansionary monetary policy to reduc unemployment [65]. Progressive Conservatives were in a simila position. A group including Harold Macmillan and Robert Boothb published *Industry and the State* which sought to reduce unemploy ment by the expansion of a rationalized and more planning-oriente manufacturing sector and also proposed to protect and encourage th trade unions into more responsible ways [30].

The need to reform industrial relations in the aftermath of 192 needs no comment, but the reasons for the rise of employment polic and the public works drive, a favoured instrument in the radic; writing of the late 1920s, are far from clear. Despite the persistenc of mass unemployment throughout most of the interwar period, onl in the late 1920s (when unemployment rates were comparatively lo and falling) did the issue become top priority for politicians an public opinion. The political history of public works is similar. A the main parties had been committed to or had introduced 'relie works long before the First World War. Only in the 1920s was major public works programme at the forefront of the politic debate. In the 1930s, when unemployment was on average muc higher, the political resonance of both public works and th unemployment issue faded. Thus, we are faced by another parado. unemployment became a political issue in the most prosperous ye; between 1921 and 1939. There are no obvious developments economic theory or in economic policy in other countries to explain this development. It has been suggested that the rise of the unemployment issue can be explained only in terms of a quest to heal the social divisions which had been opened and deftly exploited in the mid-1920s [28]. The rise of employment policy was as much a product of the General Strike as was the proposal to reform industrial relations, the other side of the 'industrial problem' of the 1920s.

The Liberals undoubtedly believed that they had to exploit employment policy if they were to make political progress in the late 1920s. The public works proposals of the Yellow Book were presented in a more detailed, immediate manner in a new pamphlet, *We can Conquer Unemployment: Mr Lloyd George's Pledge*, the Liberal Orange Book [177]. The reaction of the other parties to this manifesto is illuminating. The Conservative government had tried since 1927 to respond to public concern over social divisions and unemployment with a series of steady, if unspectacular, measures such as industrial transference, derating, export credit guarantees, assisted emigration and the outlines of an imperial development programme [289]. Williamson has argued convincingly that the Conservatives had a choice of electoral tactics in the late 1920s and chose, with considerable confidence, 'safety first' to encapsulate the notion of the government's record of steady progress and performance in contrast to what they saw as the empty promises of Lloyd George [289]. The government also adopted the unusual and unethical tactic of using the bureaucracy to criticize the Liberal programme, and issued a white paper which was, in effect, part of the Conservative election manifesto [107]. MacDonald was also confident. He believed that public opinion, having rallied to the government in the General Strike, had become disenchanted with the policy of isolating, dividing and starving the miners [189, *465*]. He judged that the electorate would swing behind a moderately progressive Labour programme, provided that the Conservatives were given no opportunities to unleash another red scare. Thus, Labour's policy document, *Labour and the Nation*, contained a commitment to reduce unemployment but it offered no hostages to fortune and left specific policy proposals ill-defined and vague. MacDonald's assessment was broadly correct. The electorate did favour parties which promised more radical action on unemployment. The Conservatives won just 38 per cent of the votes (in 1924 the figure had been 48 per cent). Labour and the Liberals, with broadly similar programmes, took 60 per cent. Labour was the real beneficiary, sweeping Lancashire, Yorkshire, Cheshire, the West Midlands and parts of London in addition to its strongholds in South Wales and Scotland.

Unemployment was the issue which brought Labour to office, but it was also the problem which broke the government. Shortly after Labour came to power, the international economy began to contract and continued to decline throughout the government's brief period of office. Labour was faced by ever-rising rates of unemployment. The government attempted to tackle the problem by increasing its public works effort, encouraging industrial rationalization, exploring the potential of imperial development and, above all, protecting the dole. A panel of ministers was created to co-ordinate unemployment policy and when, in 1930, this initiative had clearly failed, MacDonald turned to the experts and established the Economic Advisory Council to prepare new ideas. However, after mid-1930 the government began to run into serious criticism from the financial and business communities and its attentions were diverted more towards crisis avoidance than to positive goals [189, chs, 21–6].

Rising unemployment and the subtle changes in policy priorities strained Labour's internal cohesion. The younger radicals, especially Mosley and Johnston, wanted a firmer commitment to the manifesto promises. The left wanted a more vigorous socialist tone to the government's programme. But both these alternatives to crisis avoidance fell foul of the electoral appeal which MacDonald had so brilliantly developed since 1922. Labour had tried to exploit the unemployment issue while, at the same time, demonstrating that it was a national, not a sectional, party which could be trusted to govern the whole nation. This latter aim obliged Labour to accept the policy agenda established in the postwar social conflict. Moreover, as we have seen, Labour's route to electoral success lay in the centripetal direction of squeezing the Liberal working class vote. The party leadership of the 1920s epitomized this limited, moderate approach. MacDonald, who stood for orderly progress, cautious adaptation and the slow process of persuasion and compromise [189, 544] and Snowden, who displayed Gladstonian severity in his attitude to public finance [250, 86], both exemplified the pragmatic respectability which the majority in the party appear to have desired, not least because it brought astonishing electoral success. Under this leadership, the prospect of Labour developing a radical unemployment policy was always remote. The interesting ideas of Mosley and the ILP in the mid-1920s, had been marginalized for fear of provoking another red scare. This impasse might have produced fierce division in the party at a much earlier stage but for MacDonald's immense national stature and the very woolly, romantic version of socialism with which he maintained party unity. British socialism in the 1920s was not economic. In MacDonald's hands, it was an ethical doctrine which was sustained by the Fabian belief in its inevitable domination of the British political system. The left shared important parts of the perspective and was reluctant to rock the boat when Labour seemed to be so successful.

As a result, the Labour Party of the 1920s was faced by a massive contradiction. The circumstances necessary for Labour to gain office did not permit the party to retain office once elected because the Labour leadership was in no position either to develop or carry through a radical policy to tackle unemployment. In the event, the Labour government failed to make any real impression on the rising unemployment figures and in 1931 the Cabinet entered an interminable phase of anguished argument over economic policy. The government was eventually broken by the power of vested interests. On the one hand, the severe depression unleashed, for a second time, strong demands for retrenchment from industry and the City. On the other, the trade unions resisted any cuts in unemployment benefits because wage rates would be threatened. The Cabinet could not reconcile these opposing forces and the government collapsed.

Planning

When MacDonald, Snowden, Thomas and other Labour ministers formed a new Coalition government with the Liberal and Conservative Parties, the bulk of the Labour Party was vulnerable to the very damaging charge, which had been hanging over Labour's head throughout the 1920s, that it could not be trusted in government and had walked away from national problems because of sectional preoccupations. In the subsequent general election, Labour faced an anti-socialist alliance which won a landslide victory. The number of Labour MPs fell from 287 to 52. Labour did, however, manage to retain the allegiance of the vast majority of its working class voters; its share of the vote fell from 37.1 to 30.8 per cent, an almost identical proportion to that which Labour had secured in 1923. At the local level, the setback was even less significant. The momentum which the party had established during the 1920s was resumed in 1932, and Labour continued to erode the Liberal municipal vote, especially in the Midlands [67, *174–87*]. In Parliament, however, recovery was slower and Labour had only 154 MPs even after the revival at the general election of 1935.

Labour had two main problems, neither of which could be remedied at all easily. First, public opinion had shifted firmly behind the National government as a result of the effects of the slump. Secondly, Labour was divided. To the left, the persistence of mass unemployment was a clear sign that capitalism was economically and morally decadent. To the social democrats, unemployment was an issue to exploit to embarrass the government and this could be done if Labour developed policies to cure unemployment within a managed or planned capitalist society. The split within the party was much more open than in the 1920s as both sides tried to learn from the failures of the second Labour government.

The left became much more tightly organized in a new body, the Socialist League, which strove to commit the party to a five-year programme to prepare the transition from a capitalist to an explicitly socialist, planned economy. It included greater emphasis on state ownership and control of the industrial and financial sectors and recognition that emergency powers would probably be needed to effect a socialist transformation [see 230].

The failure of the 1929–31 government to make any impression on unemployment exposed to the social democrats the lack of economic understanding within the party. The leadership, and especially Dalton, began to consult experts in economics and finance and to bring their ideas into Labour's policy-making processes [231, 203–24]. Elizabeth Durbin's major study of the development of Labour's economic thinking in the 1930s draws attention to the importance of two new bodies, the New Fabian Research Bureau, which provided solid blueprints for policies such as nationalization, and the XYZ Club, a group of Labour sympathizers in the City who tried to improve and develop the party's financial policy [83]. There were in both groups a number of young academic economists who introduced into the party's thinking both Keynesian macroeconomics and the microeconomics of planning.

As in the 1920s, the social democratic ideas eventually came to dominate party thinking, but the left did secure much firmer commitments to nationalization and planning than had been possible under MacDonald. The policy programme which emerged from these debates was a challenging blend of more generous social welfare provision, expansionist finance, nationalization of the 'commanding heights' of the economy and socialist planning for the public and private sectors.

Planning became very popular in other parts of the political spectrum in the 1930s. At a time when the National government looked to a revival of private industry through cheap money, protection and a balanced budget as the only permanent solution to Britain's economic problems, more radical, interventionist programmes also found favour outside the labour movement. The slump was a cathartic experience. It demonstrated to many non-socialist progressives both the full chaotic power of unregulated market forces and the inability of the British political system to produce quick, intelligent decisions in economic policy; policy-makers appeared

ways to lag behind events. The solution to which many non-
cialist progressives turned was planning. Planning implied rationality
d control by human agents whereas market forces seemed to bring
archy and unreason. It could be undertaken by industrialists, and
arranged to create a separate decision-making structure in
onomic affairs, a parallel 'economic Parliament'. Finally, the
anned economies of the late 1920s, Soviet Russia and Fascist Italy,
peared to have weathered the storms of the slump much more
ccessfully than the market economies of Europe and America.

There were numerous non-socialist versions of the planned
onomy for Britain in the 1930s. They tended to have common
atures. To regulate each industry, there would usually be a
anning board which would allocate raw material quotas, oversee
pital expenditure, set output quotas and undertake basic research
r the industry as a whole. The plans of each industry would be co-
dinated and reconciled at the national level by a body usually
lled a National Planning Commission, which would comprise not
ly representatives of each industry planning board but also
nisters and experts such as economists, accountants and engineers.
e Commission would also have subcommittees to produce plans
r investment, foreign trade and essential services such as transport,
using and social welfare provision. The plans put forward by
arold Macmillan in *Reconstruction*, Max Nicholson in the *Week-
d Review* and by many other respectable men of affairs were in
is tradition [51; 29, *58–63*]. The influence of the Italian corporate
ate was obvious and, in the early 1930s, the planners appeared
ntent merely to provide 'self-government for industry' to overcome
nat appeared to them to be a simple problem of excess supply.

In many ways it is impossible to assess the economic viability of
ese programmes since the principal objective appears to have been
devise systems in which the ordinary laws of market economics
ased to function. The political impact was slight. The National
vernment was scarcely troubled by the activities of the planners, as
tailed in Kirkby's Chapter 10. MacDonald and Baldwin had a very
lid appeal in the new political climate after 1931. They were
dependently moving in a similar direction to the planners by giving
itish industrialists much greater scope to adopt market share
reements behind tariff walls [72]. Moreover, the full scope of
orldwide depression induced a pessimistic mood in both politicians
d the mass electorate [203]. The slow and partial recovery which
as becoming evident from 1934 appeared to be as much as anyone
ight hope for. In this defensive, troubled climate, the radical
novations of the planners could be seen as a threat rather than a
lp to recovery.

Aware of these problems, the planners began to look at mi
decade to the creation of a powerful centre alliance and to investiga
an accommodation with the Labour Party. They abandoned many
the fascist-inspired elements and moved towards models in whic
redistributive policies were central and which contained stron
labour representation at the policy-making level. The most importa
vehicle for this strategy was the Next Five Years Group (NFY
which published a manifesto of measures to be implemented in hon
and foreign policy in the lifetime of a single Parliament [213].
NFY contained prominent back-bench critics of the Nation
government and campaigned for a domestic policy almost indentic
to that of the Labour Party (minus the nationalization), it has be
tempting to see the mid-1930s as a period of political agreeme
when a new progressive consensus was forged on the role of the sta
in economic affairs [190]. It would be wrong, however, to exaggera
the extent to which the planners and Labour's social democrat
leadership were in agreement over policy. Nationalization remaine
a very divisive issue. The earlier corporatist enthusiasms of mar
prominent Conservative planners created deep suspicions in t
labour movement about the democratic credentials of NFY leader
Moreover, Labour could not enter a 'united front of the centr
without provoking a storm of controversy from the left, which itse
was pressing for a 'united front of the left' and alliances with the II
and Communist Party to campaign for a radical socialist alternati
to government policy. Thus, the most important effect of unemplo
ment on politics in the 1930s was to cripple the opposition
government policy. It is just conceivable that a vigorous campaign
either a strong centre grouping or by a left alliance could have swu
public opinion to favour alternative economic strategies. T
essential ingredient of either coalition had to be the Labour Par
but Labour was forced into introspection by unemploymer
Preoccupied by its internal divisions (which mass unemployme
helped to exacerbate and maintain), Labour could not look outwar
to build a new mass movement. When Labour at last managed
overcome its little local difficulties in the late 1930s, the focus
debate and interest had switched from employment to foreign polic

Conclusion: Political Stability

The dominant theme of this chapter has been the link in interw
Britain between mass unemployment and economic policies of
conservative nature. Three factors have been identified as havi
particular importance in explaining this apparent paradox. First, t

vo severe depressions which dominated the economic history of terwar Britain unleashed demands both from major vested terests and from sections of the mass electorate for economic and nancial policies of an orthodox colour. Secondly, the best hope for ore radical policies in the 1920s was probably the Labour Party, ut to gain power Labour had to come in to the centre to erode the iberal working class vote. This electoral strategy encouraged the arty leadership to regard any radical policy innovations as electoral abilities, or 'flashy futilities', as MacDonald remarked of the ILP .iving Wage' programme. In essence, therefore, Labour also had to :cept the limited economic policy agenda of the 1920s. Finally, in te 1930s, unemployment helped immobilize the Labour Party and iade it difficult for it to lead a vigorous campaign for alternative :onomic policies.

At other times or in other countries, such a policy impasse might ave induced the unemployed and their sympathizers to pursue ktra-parliamentary methods of changing policy. There were protest emonstrations about unemployment in interwar Britain, but the emand for extremist solutions was minimal. Orwell described the embership figures of extremist parties in interwar Britain as athetic' [217, 164]. Membership of the British Union of Fascists as always low and concentrated in specific areas except in 1934 hen the *Daily Mail* gave the party very favourable publicity. Even en, membership rose only to 50,000 [281, 577]. Membership vels were also low in the Communist Party, especially after the :riod of postwar boom and social conflict had passed. The CP's dustrial organization also had minimal impact, in large part :cause it was opposed at every opportunity by the TUC [196, 141]. here were small and isolated communities in South Wales and :otland where a powerful and committed local socialist leadership ·lped to create a militant working class consciousness which turned ;ainst the administration of the dole, the means test and works hemes [186], but they were very much in the minority. As Keith .iddlemas has written: 'The loss of workplace or union as a focus r activity, the onset of apathy, disorientation, undernourishment ·mbined with a low level of political education, geographical agmentation and incompatibility between stratified groups of 1employed workers, all militated against the creation of a mass ovement *from below*' [196, 141]. Deacon's Chapter 3 shows very :arly the important role which the benefits systems played both in aintaining political stability and in provoking resentment and otests which had extremely limited short-term objectives. Those otest marches and demonstrations which were not associated with e administration of the benefits system were largely to bring the plight of the unemployed, who felt politically as well as geographical isolated, to the attention of administrators, politicians and th relatively prosperous communities of London and the Hon Counties. For the employed, especially from the late 1920s onward when the problem took on its pronounced regional–structur character, fatalistic acceptance of unemployment and accommodatic to the realities of life on the dole were only to be expected. For th employed, there were rising living standards and persistent ground for short-run optimism; unemployment was on a downward trend almost every year except the obvious crisis periods of 1920–2 an 1930–2, when external factors could be blamed for the deterioratic in economic conditions. To the vast majority of the population, an certainly to the policymakers themselves, the cautious pragmatism interwar governments was producing results; economic condition were improving.

Thus, we have a series of factors which affected political parti and significant sections of the mass electorate, both employed an unemployed, inducing them to tolerate limited adaptation economic policy and to be suspicious of radical but largely untri initiatives. This does not imply, however, that interwar Britain w happy to endure mass unemployment. As we shall see in the fin chapter, in the very different conditions of the Second World Wa the widespread resentment of interwar unemployment became irresistible force in the planning of postwar policy.

Notes

1 The 1918 Representation of the People Act provided complete manho suffrage for all men over the age of 21 years and also gave the vote women aged 30 or more. Approximately 2 million men and 8 milli women were added to electoral registers. In 1928, a new Franchise A extended the vote to women aged 21 or over.

5

Unemployment and Real Wages

FORREST CAPIE

1 Britain in the years between the world wars there was compara-
vely rapid economic growth. In the 1920s and 1930s total output
rew at a faster rate than it had done for more than thirty years. But
1e period is remembered not for that but rather for large-scale
nemployment. Unemployment was high throughout the period –
ertainly by the standards of 1945–80. Following the 'Keynesian
evolution' and before the growth performance of the interwar years
ad been established and set out, explanations for the 'poor
erformance' of the period, as defined by the knowledge of the
nemployment levels, tended to be couched in terms of deficient
ggregate demand. Doubt was later cast on this view as it became
ndeniable that there had been rapid economic growth. (Indeed
nce growth was above any trend that could have been extrapolated
om the thirty or forty years prior to 1920 there are some grounds
r being sceptical of a deficiency in demand for the long period.)
hat combination of rapid growth and 'high' unemployment became
source of puzzlement for historians. It was regarded as a paradox
ad the explanations began to carry a substantial regional element.
owever, something that has not been evident until very recently
as been a serious reconsideration of the part played by real wages.

The Wage–Employment Relationship

'hy have real wages been ignored? There are many justifications,
ıt the main thrust of the answer that is usually given is that labour
arkets just do not work. Certainly labour markets do not work at

the same speed as, for example, financial markets, but given that the core of economics is demand and supply, then surely that apparatus should be employed as the starting point, and we can see how far it takes us in an analysis.

Before Keynesian analysis was developed, the view that the demand for labour was a decreasing function of the real wage would have occasioned no surprise, since it was simply an application to the labour market of the principle of scarcity which lay at the heart of economics. Since Keynes there have been objections. One is that if product prices are inflexible in the short run then the firm may be forced off its labour demand curve when there are fluctuations in demand. However, once the product price adjusts that problem is over. Another objection is potentially more serious for it is that demand for labour could be an *increasing* function of the real wage. These objections have in fact been dealt with in the literature and a slightly modified labour demand function derived that accounts for both of the objections.

Doubts about the wage–employment relationship have, for many, been reinforced in recent years by the apparent failure of empirical studies to produce results that are not unambiguous. The promise that econometrics seemed to hold for solving such problems has not been fulfilled, and the original enthusiasm has greatly abated. Though it should be said that for the post–1945 period there have in fact been many studies for several countries that have confirmed the close relationship between real wages and employment [see 13; 174].

For the interwar years econometrics never really held much promise anyway because for most exercises there are simply insufficient observations in the data and too few degrees of freedom. It is a short period from 1919 to 1938, with no more than 20 observations, and when changes in these variables are required and lagged variables introduced, then the robustness of the results diminishes and the confidence that can be placed in them dwindles. (In their favour there is a considerable degree of variance in the data.) This of course does not stop people trying and we shall report some of their results later. It must be emphasized that great caution needs to be exercised in reading these econometric results.

This chapter then has a deliberately narrow focus. It looks at only one possible avenue of explanation. It does that in the belief that it provides certain insights to the problem of interwar unemployment. Application of demand and supply analysis is the obvious way to approach the problem. The focus is on supply in this chapter not because of a prior belief that all the explanation lies there, but rather because of the view that any explanation that ignores supply is likely to omit factors of great importance.

58

The emphasis is on the supply side of the question and the view presented is that labour supply is a function of the real wage. The degree of sensitivity may be argued about, but the function is important. We also take it as read (though many do not) that the demand for labour is a decreasing function of the real wage. As we said at the beginning this was the view widely held at the time. In the depth of the depression in 1931 Keynes held these views as a statement to the Macmillan Committee showed.[1] In the *General Theory* he put it like this:

> In emphasising our point of departure from the classical system, we must not overlook an important point of agreement. . . with a given organisation, equipment and technique, real wages and the volume of output (and hence of employment) are uniquely correlated, so that in general, an increase in employment can only occur to the accompaniment of a decline in the rate of real wages. [157, *17*]

If we are agreed that it is essential to think in terms of prices and quantities and accept that the evidence suggests that the demand for labour is a function of its price – the real wage – then when we turn to the supply of labour we would also expect individuals to respond to changes in the real wage. The net outcome will depend upon income and substitution effects. Bear in mind that speed of response may not be fast since there are a lot of other considerations to take account of – in the jargon, the short-run elasticities could be quite low.

Labour Supply and Participation

On the supply of labour consider first the following. In the economy there are a number of people in employment and there are some unemployed. And then there are people outside the labour force. The total of the first and second groups make up the labour force. The unemployment rate is the proportion the unemployed are of that total.

In an economy there will be people leaving one job, or being made redundant and looking for another job. They may move directly from one job to another or they may take time off in between either in order to make a more thorough search of the prospects or simply because they do not find suitable work. At the same time there will be a movement from those who are unemployed into employment. There can also be movements from those in the labour force to outside the labour force and vice versa. For example a 'mature' student, who had taken himself out of the labour force to acquire new skills, could be re-entering. So there will always be a certain

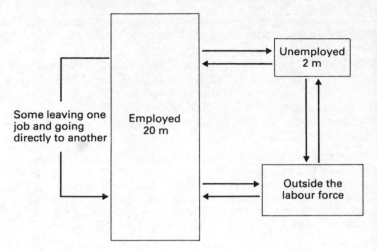

Figure 5.1 Labour supply

amount of movement around these groups. (I myself have been in al
three groups more than once.) All of these movements can be neatl
captured in Figure 5.1 above (which can be related to Table 5.1).

The rate of movement from the employed group to the unemploye
and vice versa are empirical questions and are likely to vary over tim
with different surges of growth in the economy. But assume for th
purpose of illustration that there is a 'job separation' rate (that is
people are leaving employment for whatever reasons) of 1 per cen
and that the unemployed find jobs at the rate of 15 per cent pe
period. Ignore for the moment those outside the labour force. If w
began with a labour force of 22 million with 20 million employed an
2 million unemployed we can see how this would move towards a
'equilibrium'. This is illustrated in Table 5.1. To start with there i
an unemployment rate of 9.1 per cent but there would be
movement, in this example, from that level down to the point wher
20.4 million would be employed and 1.6 million unemployed. At thi
point the rate of losing jobs is cancelled out by the rate of finding an
while the process goes on there is no change in the numbers in th
two groups. The rate of unemployment at this point is 7.3 per cen
and it is this rate that is called the *natural rate*. In other words if ther
were no changes in any other variables and the growth of th
economy were stable this rate would persist [see 11].

Several factors can affect the natural rate of unemployment. Fo
example if the government introduced unemployment benefit it i
likely that some people at the margin would have a greater incentiv

Table 5.1 Dynamics of Employment and the Natural Rate

Period	Employment	Unemployment	Unemployment rate	Number losing jobs at 1%	Number finding jobs 15%	Net change
(1)	(2)	(3)	(4)	(5)	(6)	(7)
1	20	2	9.1	0.2	0.3	0.1
2	20.1	1.9	8.6	0.2	0.3	0.1
3	20.2	1.8	8.2	0.2	0.3	0.1
4	20.3	1.7	7.7	0.2	0.3	0.1
5	20.4	1.6	7.3	0.2	0.2	0.0

Columns (2) and (3) assume a workforce of 22 millions.
Column (4) expresses the *percentage* rate of unemployment.
Columns (5), (6) and (7) express the numbers losing jobs, finding jobs and the net change in *millions*.

to stay in the labour force, to be more willing to have a job separation and to take longer to find a new job. Likely to be more important is a structural change such as a shift away from manufacturing in an economy. The rate of job separation could increase sharply and even though the rate of job finding may increase the natural rate could rise steeply. Other factors such as minimum wage legislation, degree of unionization and so on would also have an effect.

However, the particular focus of this chapter is the role of real wages and we want to examine the effect of this variable. If real wages were 'high' or growing very rapidly we may expect employers at least to slow down their recruitment or, more extremely, lay workers off. On the other side of the equation, more people will offer themselves for work. This would raise the rate of job separation and simultaneously attract people from outside the labour force into the search for these higher wages.

After the sharp recession of 1920/1 the total number in employment stood at about 16.5 million. Apart from levelling off in the year of the General Strike, 1926, that number grew to 18 million in 1929. Employment then fell for two years to just over 17 million (in fact a fall of 800,000) and then grew sharply until the end of the 1930s when it was just short of 20 million. So there was a fairly considerable growth in employment over the period as a whole. The unemployed are, as we have seen, only to a certain extent the other side of the employment experience. The NIS numbers were of the order of 1 million throughout the 1920s but then climbed to 3 million in 1931 at their worst point. (The rise in unemployment between 1929 and 1931 was 1.8 million.) After that the numbers fell to the mid-1930s and remained at a level of 1 million until 1937/8. That figure of 1 million represents an unemployment rate of about 6 per cent when adjusted for comparison with the present day calculation. To put that figure in perspective, that rate is probably quite close to the one that prevailed in the decades before the First World War. But even if it were higher than before 1914 the suggestion would be that this must be close to the natural rate of unemployment for the years before 1939.[2]

The years 1929–32 are particularly critical. Unemployment in that short period grew at a rate that was more than twice as fast as suggested by the numbers of jobs lost. In other words the extra growth in unemployment was as much a consequence of the growth in the labour force (note that this is not a demographic explanation) as the number of jobs lost in the recession. That is, there was movement into the labour force from outside. For this reason the unemployment rate carried on growing during 1932 in spite of the fact that in that year employment grew. In the two-year period within 1930–2 just over 4 per cent of jobs were lost and these were mainly in manufacturing industry.

It is worth reminding ourselves at this stage that but for the behaviour of unemployment in the early 1930s – critically 1930–2 – the period as a whole might not have continued to be viewed in such bleak terms. After all the fall in output in Britain was the mildest of all the industrial countries – a total of 6 per cent of GDP from the peak of 1929 to the trough of 1932. That was very much less than most European countries and a great deal less than the USA where the fall in output was of the order of 33 per cent between 1929 and 1932. Of course there were still some pockets of harsh unemployment in Britain and these account for some of the action taken in the period and also for the gloom that pervades much of our view of that period.

What is of interest is the fact that jobs were lost when the working population was growing and it is these labour market developments that require some explanation. What light can real wages throw on the subject? In discussing real wages attention must be given to both demand and supply. On the demand side the employer is interested in the real cost of labour to himself (what is called own product real wage) and he therefore has a real wage in mind that is the nominal wage he pays deflated by an appropriate price index (in manufacturing it would be that of manufacturing output). For the worker the real wage he has in mind is the nominal wage he receives deflated by the cost of living index. At most times there will be no great difference between the two series, but on some occasions there may be, and it could be that a divergence in the series could have interesting effects on the labour market.

Real Wages and the Interwar Labour Market

Having identified the requirement, it would be satisfying if we could go off and collect the data and carry out the exercise. Unfortunately it is not quite so straightforward. There are many measures of wages. One of the difficulties confronting those who deal with this problem in the labour market is of agreeing on the best series. The own product real wage is the relevant one for the firm and there are various others that might be used as a guide to that for the worker. However, there is no series for manufacturing output prices that runs through the interwar years and it is not easy to find a good proxy for such a series. If wages in manufacturing are deflated by wholesale prices a distortion is introduced since the Board of Trade's wholesale price series was a mixture of input and output prices.

Before returning briefly to this problem let us consider the course of real wages in all industries calculated by deflating total wages by the final output deflator.[3] The course of average annual real wages between the wars rose sharply upwards after 1921 and thereafter, with very occasional and minor exceptions, rose throughout the period. However, as Figure 5.2 brings out, the growth rate is different. After some quiet wild oscillation following the sharp recession of 1921, the growth of real wages showed a steep rise through the years 1928–31 and then a sharp fall in 1932. There was

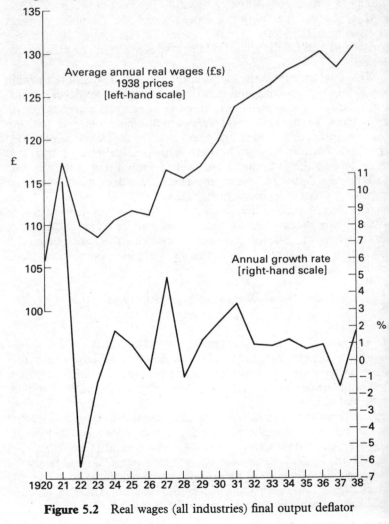

Figure 5.2 Real wages (all industries) final output deflator

then no growth to speak of through to 1936, a fall in 1937, and then a rise at the end of the period.

When real wages are calculated using the retail price deflator the pattern is, as we might expect, similar, but there are some more extreme points. This real wage series (Figure 5.3) rises steeply from 1928/9 and then moderates after 1932. The growth rate shows a dramatic rise over 1929–31 and then collapses until 1937 and it is worth keeping this in view when we think of how workers (whose real wage depends on retail prices) may have been attracted into the

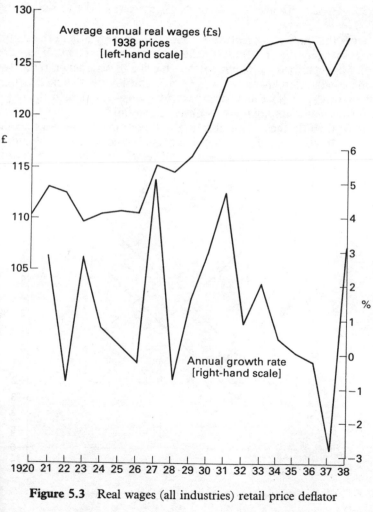

Figure 5.3   Real wages (all industries) retail price deflator

labour force and then discouraged over these years. If we had deflated wages in manufacturing by the wholesale price index we would have seen a rise in real wages of more than 25 per cent between 1929 and 1932, and then a fall of almost 15 per cent by 1937. However as we noted above that would be to exaggerate the movement of real wages for the firm. Probably the best guide available to the own product real wage is annual average wages deflated by the Board of Trade's price index of manufactured articles. Unfortunately this index covers the period only after 1930. But what it shows is a sharp rise in 1931 and then a fall in 1932 and 1933. Then there are two years of slight rises and two substantial falls.

Now the interesting feature is that these movements in the course of real wages were reflected in the path of employment. Whenever real wages surged employment fell back and whenever there was some moderation in real wage growth employment picked up. In other words, at least as a first pass, the close relationship between real wages and employment is observed to hold.

How then do these data fit in to the theoretical framework set out above? In Figure 5.4 real wages are expressed in terms of output prices. If the cost of living were to fall relative to output prices then

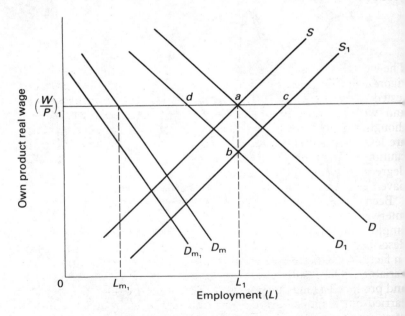

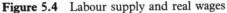

Figure 5.4 Labour supply and real wages

66

he supply of labour increases as workers are attracted by higher real wages and the supply schedule for labour (S) therefore moves out rom S to S_1. This in fact did happen during the early 1930s when he terms of trade moved strongly in Britain's favour. D_m is the lemand schedule for labour in manufacturing and D that for labour n aggregate. A relative fall in the price of manufactures would shift D_m to the left. Thus if a were the initial point with employment at L_1 ind real wages at W/P_1 then L_{m1} would be the number employed in nanufacturing. We could regard a as the position in 1929 and with he schedule moving in the way we have described there should have been a new equilibrium at b with an increased supply of labour and a lecrease in demand. At that point employment in total would have isen and that would have been accompanied by a fall in the real wage. However if W/P did not fall, then with the supply of labour at c ind the demand at d there would be unemployment of dc. This all greatly simplifies the real world and of course that is the point of it in order to capture the essence of what could be happening. We know hat real wages actually rose rather than remaining constant but we an leave that aside in this simplification. Also remember that it is not necessary for real wages to fall to get an expansion in employment because there is generally a secular tendency for productivity to grow.[4]

Conclusions

The views given in the previous paragraphs deserve to be tested more rigorously. The ideal would be a model, fully specified, and then ested econometrically. Some attempts to do this have been made, ind we now turn to the results of these exercises. Remember, hough, that they are all carried out with the same basic series, which ire less than entirely satisfactory and we should also remember the caution at the outset that the period has only 20 observations and few legrees of freedom. It should be noted, however, that similar results have been obtained for the period 1950–83 [191].

Beenstock and Warburton, in the most recent examination of the nterwar years, estimated a demand function for *manufacturing* employment [15]. They use the 'correct' own product real wage as lescribed above and found the effect to be negative and significant. In fact, they experimented with a number of possible versions of the variables. The results of a series of equations were all very similar ind produced a long-run real wage elasticity of around 1.0. They also carried out a similar exercise for *total* employment and the results were confirmed though, of course, the long-run wage elasticity for the aggregate was much lower, of the order of 0.3. In short, and not too surprisingly, they found a downward sloping demand curve for labour both in total and at the disaggregated manufacturing level.

The second part of our interest is in labour supply and the participation ratio. According to the analysis given above, it is a combination of the fall in employment and an increase in labour supply which helps to explain the great growth in unemployment. What, then, is the econometric evidence here? Beenstock and Warburton estimated several 'participation' equations and they show a real wage elasticity of labour supply of around 0.45. Incidentally this is also the kind of result that has been found for recent years. The participation ratio varied directly with real wages. In summary in this study there is quite strong support for the view given above.

Of course, as we might expect, there is as much disagreement over the econometric results as there is over the qualitative account. One reason for undertaking econometric study is to help focus upon exactly where disagreements lie. Many variables can have an impact and much debate centres on what should or should not be included. Because of the lack of observations, only a limited number of variables can be included in any one test. Broadberry [35], for example, estimated a linear labour supply equation in which total population, the real wage (using retail prices) and the proportion of females in the labour force were the explanatory variables. From the results, he concluded that the real wage was not significant in the labour supply equation. One objection to this specification would be that total population was one wrong variable.

Beenstock and Warburton went further and tested the view that real wage behaviour was largely responsible for the growth in unemployment between 1929 and 1932 and its subsequent fall [15]. They did this by dynamically simulating their estimated model. For example, they asked what unemployment would have been if real wages had grown at their trend rate of 1921–8, and what would have happened after 1932 if real wage growth had continued on trend. According to this test, three-quarters of job losses were directly attributed to real wage growth in excess of trend. Moreover, about one-third of growth in the working population can be put down to real wages. Similarly, after 1932 half of the effective job gains came from real wages and the labour supply grew by about half of what it otherwise would have if it had not been for real wage moderation.

In summary, this concentration on the supply side of the labour market question has brought out the possibility that real wage movements go some way to explaining the particularly serious jump in unemployment between 1930 and 1932, years in which the fall in output was comparatively mild by world and historical standards.

Real wage movements also go some way to explaining the path back to equilibrium by the end of the decade.

Notes

1 Macmillan Committee, *Report*, Addendum I [110, *194*].
2 Even if the rate of unemployment were lower before 1914, the interesting question that arises (but is not readily answered) is how was it affected by the flow of migrants abroad?
3 The following few pages are based on the Bank of England Panel Paper by Beenstock, Capie and Griffiths [14].
4 In an attack on these ideas, Dimsdale has made a number of critical points [79]. He has, however, confused the issue of the correct real wage index. The only valid one for manufacturing is that used by Beenstock, Capie and Griffiths [14]. Secondly, he implies that for employment to grow, wages must fall, an argument which ignores the growth of labour productivity. More importantly, he erroneously states that Beenstock, Capie and Griffiths 'do not allow for the effect of the fall in import prices in the depression'. In fact, we stressed that import prices had to be allowed for and, indeed, we disaggregated between primary products and manufactures. He further assumed that raw materials and labour were net complements when the econometric estimates suggest that they were net substitutes. A fuller discussion of these points is given by Beenstock [12].

6

The Real Wage Debate and British Interwar Unemployment

W. R. GARSIDE

The Neo-Classical Theory of Wages and Employment

Many government officials, industrialists and economists between the wars saw a distinct connection between the crisis of unemployment and the prevailing level of wages. There were differing interpretations, however, as to the precise nature of this alleged association and of its consequences for public policy. Nevertheless, the contrast between employment conditions and the behaviour of real wages in the pre-1914 and post-1918 periods, and more particularly the coexistence in Britain in the early 1920s of increased labour costs and falling international competitiveness, convinced contemporary observers that real wages, already 'too high', were a fundamental cause of the prevailing economic malaise.

It was generally conceded that before 1914 British real wages possessed a sufficiently high degree of flexibility to prevent excessive unemployment. Although there was evidence of standard wage rates being maintained while prices fell during the 1880s and early 1890s, in contrast to the experience of the previous thirty years, labour unions during the Edwardian period proved generally unable to prevent wage reductions in times of rising unemployment. Collective bargaining procedures and statutory unemployment insurance had yet to be fully developed; thus the temptation to accept wage reductions rather than endure extreme poverty was strong. At that time, Clay noted,

It was possible to maintain wage rates generally at a level that restricted employment throughout industry; somewhere, usually at many points, wages (in relation to efficiency) could be reduced to the level at which expansion could take place. [60, *154*]

According to the classical equilibrium theory of the labour market, both the demand for and supply of labour were functions of the real wage. The demand price of labour was equal to its marginal product, that is, the extra increment to total production arising from the employment of an extra unit of labour. The supply price of labour was that at which the marginal product of labour equalled the value which the marginal unit of labour assigned to the leisure forgone by working (the marginal disutility of labour). Aggregate labour demand was a negative function and labour supply a positive function of the real wage. It was the real wage, therefore, which served to equate the supply of and demand for labour. Providing that real wages were flexible, market forces would ensure that all those willing to work at a given real wage would in fact be employed; prices would adjust through market competition to reduce any temporary unemployment leaving those not willing to work at the prevailing level of real wages voluntarily unemployed. As Pigou put it:

There will always be at work a strong tendency for wage rates to be so related to demand so that everybody is employed. . . The implication is that such unemployment as exists at any time is due wholly to the fact that changes in demand conditions are continually taking place and that frictional resistances prevent the appropriate wage adjustments from being made instantaneously. [228, *252*]

Classical orthodoxy in other words maintained that the existence of unemployment beyond the frictional level was due primarily to real wages being too high in relation to marginal productivity.

It was not surprising, then, that contemporary observers judged the rapid rise in unemployment after 1920 to be the result of the destruction of the self-regulating character of the labour market, giving rise to a level of real wages incompatible with full employment. The problem was not just that money wages had been boosted during and immediately after the war but that in general they proved resilient in the face of subsequent economic depression, at least after 1922. Until then the imperfections and failings of the labour market system to which informed commentators were later to draw so much attention had not become especially apparent. By 1919 average weekly and hourly money wage rates were more than double their 1914 level. They both continued to rise through to the end of 1920, particularly hourly wage costs following the reduction in normal weekly hours of work across industry during the previous year [82] However the collapse of the postwar boom and the sharp rise in unemployment which accompanied it caused money wage rates to fall relative to prices up to the end of 1922. Sliding-scale agreements operated in many industries permitting wages to follow prices in a downward direction.[1] The index of weekly money wage rates (July 1914 = 100) declined from 276 in December 1920 to 178 in December 1922. Although real wages improved slightly during 1920–1, the pressure on money wages proved greater. Real weekly wage rates (1914 = 100) rose from 104 in December 1920 to 116 a year later but had fallen to 100 by the end of 1922 [82, *442*].

Much of the concern over real wages in the 1920s arose from the fact that the wage flexibility exhibited before 1922 gave way thereafter to a marked degree of money wage rigidity. During 1923–32, in particular, the 'normal' inverse relationship between unemployment and wages broke down. Money wages were proving 'stickier' than money prices. Nominal wages fell at most 2 to 3 per cent per year and actually increased after 1934 in the face of recorded unemployment levels in excess at times of 16 per cent of insured workers. By 1929 money wages were only 1.3 per cent below their 1925 level. The fall in British unit wage costs during the same four year period, moreover, was only one-half of that achieved in the USA and only one-quarter of that in Sweden.[2]

It was natural that the marked degree of money wage stability after 1923 should have occasioned alarm within government and industry given the pressures of high unemployment and weak international competitiveness. If only real wages could be forced down, the argument ran, the prospects of Britain's staple industries could be improved, workers would be encouraged to seek openings in the labour-intensive sectors of the economy, and costs would be reduced by competitive wage bidding, thereby stimulating profits and investment. What worried so many contemporaries was that the labour market had become more rigid than hitherto, seemingly incapable without corrective action of equating supply and demand and therefore destined to exacerbate Britain's relative or even absolute economic decline.

There was no shortage of explanations at the time as to why real wages were 'too high'. Trade unionism had to be partly at fault. The problem as perceived was not the spread of trade unions *per se* (total union membership had doubled between 1914 and 1919 but had fallen by one-third on the eve of the General Strike) but rather the maintenance of their defensive power. Centralized bargaining on a national scale in highly unionized industries together with the enforcement by Trade Boards of industry-wide minimum wages in less organized sectors, it was frequently alleged, had made specific wage/employment trade-offs difficult to achieve, the intertia and clumsiness of collective bargaining acting as a brake on the downward adjustment of wages in times of depression [227]. Moreover, social and political rather than strictly economic criteria had crept into the determination of prevailing wage levels; notions of 'fairness' and of what constituted an appropriate 'living wage' were preventing workers from disturbing existing relativities and of undercutting each other's wage in order to secure employment. Postwar wages policy, Pigou judged in 1927, had been responsible for adding some 5 per cent to the volume of unemployment normally brought about by other factors [227]. Furthermore, commentators anxiously observed, employers after 1926 were proving reluctant to press their advantage against labour resisting systematic wage cuts in order to avoid costly disturbances or at least the disruption of mutually-agreed bargaining procedures [94].

It was self-evident to others that a major cause of labour market rigidity lay in the operation of the unemployment insurance scheme. The extended availability and rising real value of benefit payments down to 1931, critics maintained, had discouraged labour mobility, increased the duration of job search, taxed industry without due regard to profitability, enabled workers to refuse non-customary wage offers without loss of benefit and had encouraged employers to dismiss workers rather than promote efficient production [291; 59; 47]. Trade unionists, to put it another way, now had less incentive to agree to money wage reductions once the responsibility for the employment consequences of their wage bargaining could be shifted on to the state.

Despite the forcefulness with which such arguments were put it proved difficult between the wars and has proved difficult since to establish any significant causal link between unemployment insurance, institutional wage procedures, trade union strength and wage rigidity. The most dramatic fall in nominal money wages occurred during the early 1920s when the union share of the labour force was nearly double that of 1930/1 when wages stayed almost constant at a time of considerably higher unemployment. Economists such as Pigou, Cannan and Clay accepted that the real wage problem was not common to all industries but could not agree whether it was wages in the depressed trades that were too high or whether the prevailing maldistribution of labour was at fault, a problem exacerbated by trade union success in maintaining money wages in the more prosperous industries, thereby reducing the volume of vacancies available to potential labour migrants [52, 55–9].

More recent efforts to resurrect a classical perspective on the interwar period have proved largely unpersuasive. Benjamin and Kochin's strident claim that the array of unemployment benefits available to large sections of the working population between the wars was so 'generous' as to induce a considerable degree of voluntary unemployment has been roundly condemned on economic statistical and administrative grounds [17; 64; 69; 194; 215; 129] There is little substantive evidence to support the view either that money wages held or that competitive clearing of the labour market was hindered because substantial numbers of the unemployed refrained from seeking or accepting available jobs because of the near financial gain from remaining out of work. In a separate reassertion of classical orthodoxy Beenstock, Capie and Griffiths have suggested that the increase in unemployment between 1929 and 1931 can be attributed primarily to the exceptionally rapid rise in manufacturing real wages and that the economic recovery from 1932 owed much to the subsequent moderation of such real wage growth [14]. Dimsdale's careful reworking of the available data, however, demonstrates that both the scale of the rise and fall of manufacturing product real wages and their alleged relationship with employment in depression and recovery have been considerably exaggerated [79].

Given our present state of knowledge, we cannot be certain that high interwar unemployment was caused predominantly by too high a real wage. The question of whether, for example, high labour costs in the 1920s were an independent source of unemployment or simply one unfortunate result of an exchange rate policy which squeezed employers between domestic money wages and world prices is one which cannot yet be answered precisely. What is more probable, as Matthews and others have pointed out, is that before 1930 'rises in the real cost of labour contributed to increasing unemployment' but that 'the effects are difficult to separate from those of other influences tending in the same direction' [193, *316*].

Unemployment and Wages in the 1920s

There was a strong temptation nevertheless for businessmen and politicians, concerned about rising labour costs and mounting unemployment at home and declining international competitiveness abroad, to see in an enforced reduction of real wages a direct and effective remedy for Britain's economic ills. The Chancellor of the Exchequer, for example, appealed as early as September 1921 for unemployment relief expenditure to be the lowest minimum possible to prevent starvation in order that it should not interfere with the more important process of restoring Britain's competitive position in world markets through a systematic reduction in wage costs. In autumn of the same year a committee headed by Hilton Young, Financial Secretary at the Treasury, reported to the Prime Minister that although 'the fundamental causes of unemployment are of a world-wide character' the most immediate influence in Britain was 'the relatively high costs of production caused mainly by the higher rates of wages'.[3] In the preamble to the General Strike, Baldwin's reported assertion that 'all workers in this country have got to take reductions in wages to help put industry on its feet'[4] proved sufficient to galvanize TUC support for the miners' struggle. Early in 1931, with Britain already deeply affected by world slump, employers warned that the only practical solution to the crisis was 'to reduce wages, to let export industries, not sheltered trades, set the wage pattern, [and] to cut unemployment benefit'.[5] Four months earlier Hubert Henderson had warned fellow members of the Committee of Economists that 'in view of the turn which world prices have taken and the extreme slenderness of the chances of substantial recovery. . . we have no alternative now but to face up to the disagreeable reactionary necessity of cutting costs (including wages) in industry. . . That I say is the plain moral of the situation, as plain as a pikestaff.' [140, *70*]

Few denied the attractiveness of short-circuiting deflation on an equitable basis by some sort of national consensus aimed at the simultaneous reduction of money, salary and rentier income. But this was a dim prospect, not least because the TUC adamantly refused to sacrifice wages for jobs arguing that any reduction in working class consumption would merely intensify falling prices and profits at home thus further hindering economic revival. This defence of wages it must be said was less an embryonic expression of Keynesianism than an instinct basic to the whole trade union movement.

To the more perceptive observer, however, it exposed the fallacy of trying to counter unemployment through a direct assault on money wages. At the heart of Keynes's condemnation of the return to gold at the prewar parity in 1925 was his conviction that it would be impossible to secure the required reduction in money wages to offset the effect on an overvalued pound without singling out particularly vulnerable groups of workers (he had the coalminers in mind) who shared a common concern to defend living standards and maintain wage relativities. Keynes did not presume that money wages were fixed or downwardly rigid; what he stressed was that given the institutional and psychological background against which policy had to be framed deliberate wage-cutting as a way of reducing unemployment would prove socially chaotic, politically impracticable and ultimately self-defeating.

By the late 1920s enthusiasm for money wage cuts as a counter to unemployment had certainly waned. 'There was a time', the Conservative administration confessed in 1929,

> when perhaps a reduction in the costs of production was looked upon as largely synonymous with the reduction in wages. In present conditions, it must be sought in the improved organisation and efficiency of all elements of industry . . . in all that is implied in the term 'rationalisation'.[6]

Henry Clay conceded that

> only a concerted and co-ordinated revision of all wage-rates . . . would afford any great stimulus to employment; and for such co-ordinated action there is no machinery . . . Wage revision therefore offers little chance of reducing costs. [60, 156]

Mosley too rejected the idea that if only workers were prepared to accept a lower wage, production would thereby be rendered profitable and full employment restored. In his view wage reductions on any large scale merely destroyed the purchasing power of the community and threatened to intensify the problem of idle capacity [251, 140–1, 199–220]. In his evidence to the Macmillan Committee even Pigou, customarily though unfairly regarded as the arch-spokesman of classical economics, refused to accept that unduly high wages were necessarily the cause of persistent unemployment or that a direct assault on money wages would offer any effective or lasting remedy.

In any event, the enforced suspension of the gold standard in the wake of the 1931 financial crisis transformed official attitudes towards the issue of wages. The floating of the pound provided Britain with a competitive edge in the short term and the hope reigned that when the world economy recovered prices would increase to a sufficient extent to be consistent with profitable trade on the basis of prevailing costs. Britain's trading advantage, however, fast disappeared in the face of the subsequent devaluation of the dollar and the franc. Moreover a wave of economic nationalism abroad strengthened trade restrictions and increased the threat of retaliation against any country seeking unilaterally to improve its cost competitiveness. Prosperity, stability and improved employment were by no means guaranteed even in a country such as Britain whose recovery from economic slump had occurred earlier and was much stronger than in most other industrialized nations.

Keynesian Theory, Unemployment and Wages in the 1930s

It was in these circumstances that Keynes, already convinced of the folly of deflation as a cure for depression and deeply suspicious of the adequacy of the free market system as a guarantor of full employment equilibrium, vigorously attacked any notion of reformulating economic policy along strictly classical lines. The *theoretical* case for attacking real wage costs was as yet intact. In the years before and immediately after the publication of the *General Theory* Keynes himself accepted the orthodox doctrine that with a given capital stock and state of technology the marginal product of labour would tend to fall as employment expanded. Any reduction in unemployment, in other words, would require a cut in the real wage because diminishing returns would effectively raise the supply price of increased output. There was considerable agreement that a reduction in real wages could do much to ease Britain's industrial and trading difficulties: the contentious issue was how best to bring this about.

What Keynes and others came to realize was that the classical doctrine involved such unrealistic assumptions – of a stable, self-regulating labour market with free competition and perfect mobility of labour – as to render it incapable of providing any policy prescriptions valid in the real world. In the mid–1920s both Pigou and Keynes believed that manipulation of wages could in theory increase employment. But because the existing system of wage determination did not in their view possess sufficient flexibility for practical and procedural reasons to secure the required reductions, action to increase employment had to be consistent with prevailing real wage standards. Faced therefore with the reality of institutionalized wage bargaining, with the potentially high cost in economic and social terms of industrial conflict and with a labour movement determined to defend the hierarchy of relative wages, it would be foolish, Keynes maintained, to seek a remedy for economic depression through cuts in money wages. Such reductions, he argued, were an unreliable 'cure' for unemployment incapable in themselves of expanding employment merely because producers' costs has been reduced. Behavioural assumptions which might be valid at the level of the individual firm need not necessarily be so at the aggregate level. A cut in the money wage would increase employment only if prices remained fixed or did not fall by as much as the money wage so that real wages were reduced. But since labour costs governed the supply price of products in the short run, a cut in money wages could conceivably lead to product prices falling in the same proportion as the money wage, leaving the real wage unchanged (unless there was a simultaneous increase in demand). Product prices would chase wages down without any stimulus to expanded output or employment. The resultant redistribution of real income was likely, moreover, to prove unfavourable to spending and employment, drawing income away from those whose marginal propensity to consume was high. Furthermore, Keynes contended, if such wage cuts increased the expectation of future falls in wages and prices the uncertainty and gloom could depress businessmen's incentive to invest. All in all, there had to be a more sensible alternative.

Contrary to what many economists and historians have since chosen to believe, Pigou did not champion the orthodox view. The notion that real wages were 'too high', he informed the Macmillan Committee in 1931, was true only given in the existing demand for labour. As he explained:

> If you have got unemployment, one can say that the cause of the unemployment is either that the real rate of wages is all right but there is not enough demand; or if one takes the demand as given one can say that the real rate of wages is too high. . . So I do not want to say that unduly high wages are the cause.[7]

For prosperity to be restored, he wrote two years later,

> either money costs must fall or money prices must rise. The practical difficulties in the way of the former solution have proved so serious and the friction to be overcome so great that the main body of instructed opinion has turned towards the latter.[8]

'Instructed opinion', in other words, was resolutely seeking some alternative means of stimulating economic activity and employment without recourse to deliberate cost-cutting. Keynes believed that the real wage could only be reduced by an increase in product demand which would raise product prices relative to the money wage. Only then would the real wage fall and employment increase. In his view the government ought to have engaged in deficit-financed public spending to raise the trend level of investment and, at the same time, have increased the money supply in order to keep the rate of interest low, thereby helping to sustain private investment and business confidence. Without such stimuli, confidence would sag and transactors would hold money instead of real assets. The resultant decline in the money value of real assets would discourage investment but encourage transactors to accumulate money balances by spending less than they earned. The demand for real investment would fall, depressing aggregate product demand.

The inference was clear: it was easier to lower real wages by raising prices than by lowering money wages. Workers after all would be more likely to accept an economy-wide price increase (reducing all real wages proportionately) than they would sectional attacks on money incomes which threatened their relative wage positions. By using fiscal and monetary means, it would be the level of employment determined by aggregate demand that would set the real wage; the classical postulate that the real wage determined employment would therefore be turned on its head [265]. Contemporaries feared, however, that in the long run trade unions had the power to neutralize the effects of any expansionary monetary and fiscal policy by linking money wage settlements to the price level, effectively stipulating a real wage. But such fears were largely exaggerated during much of the 1930s. During that time, Casson writes,

> The relatively high level of unemployment, coupled with surprisingly good industrial relations, seem to have prevented the trade unions from forcing the issue in this way. Keynes judged that. . . the British economy could be reflated without inducing a substantial increase in money wages, and he seemed to have been broadly correct. [52, 162–3]

Although the economy displayed an exceptional and relatively short-lived degree of rigidity during 1936–7, this did not deflect Keynes and his followers from their belief in the ultimate value of demand-induced expansion as the more positive and socially equitable way of raising the aggregate level of employment and activity. On the contrary, the persistence of involuntary unemployment mirrored the fact that the labour market did not automatically clear; what was required according to the Keynes of the *General Theory* was a rise in aggregate demand engendered by expansionary fiscal policy sufficient to re-employ workers forced through rising prices to accept a decline in real wages.

Ironically, the offensive launched by informed observers such as Keynes and Pigou denouncing on practical, social and political grounds any immediate recourse to direct cuts in wages as a means of boosting industrial competitiveness and employment, had given way by 1936 to an alternative emphasis upon demand expansion which nevertheless reasserted the belief that a fall in unemployment required a reduction in real wages. The *General Theory* implied as much principally because it remained wedded to the classical view of the diminishing marginal productivity of labour.

But what if in conditions of high unemployment, low output and idle capacity labour's marginal cost did not rise with increased output? The possibility then arose of a positive relation between employment and the real wage. Indeed by the end of the 1930s Keynes himself had come to realize that in an economy operating at less than optimum output with plant and labour only partially employed, the marginal product of labour could rise (and its marginal cost fall) as output expanded and as capacity became more fully utilized [153]. Once the possibility of increasing returns to labour was accepted the classical view that unemployment was high because the real wage was too high made little sense since an expansion of output could permit an increase both in employment *and* the real wage. This at once strengthened the case for a planned expansionist policy since a fall in real wages was no longer regarded as a prior condition for a rise in employment. [265, *23–6*].

Conclusion

These latter considerations help us in hindsight to put the real wage debate into a wider perspective. As prices and profits fell in the 1920s few inside or outside of government could resist the temptation to put a large part of the blame for continued industrial decline, rising unemployment and falling overseas trade upon the failure of money wages to respond sufficiently freely or adequately to market signals. Accepted economic doctrine taught that equality of demand for and supply of labour was ensured by competition in the labour market; persistent unemployment was an indication of the absence of free market forces. From this standpoint it is not surprising that contemporaries were therefore at pains to identify the institutional and attitudinal forces believed to be responsible for such market imperfections. In like manner they sought ways of weakening labour's resistance to the discipline of the market and, when such ways proved either unavailable or unworkable, they were ultimately forced to consider alternative policies aimed at restoring industrial competitiveness by some other more practical or politically feasible route.

This preoccupation with apparent labour market failure in a period of severe economic contraction, however, had a wider significance. It proved to be an important element in the evolution of the radical plea for a more interventionist and managed economy within Britain. Mass unemployment convinced Keynes in particular that whatever pure theory might proclaim, once money wages and prices could not and so obviously did not clear markets, for whatever reason, then some other strategy had to be adopted. If aggregate demand fell but money wages did not, he was to contend, the labour market would not clear. Even if money wages did fall there was a assurance that planned output would settle at a full employment level. The 'problem of wages' in other words helped to focus attention upon the principle of effective demand. In doing so, however, it raised the intriguing question yet to be satisfactorily answered: whether the unemployment associated with a level of interwar real wages above market clearing levels could have been reduced earlier and more substantially by a mildly inflationary policy of fiscal expansion.

Notes

The themes developed in this chapter, together with most of those taken up by other authors within this present volume, are discussed further in W. R. Garside, *The British Unemployment Crisis: A Study in Public Policy, 1919–1939* (forthcoming).

1 The number of workpeople affected by sliding-scale agreements was estimated to have doubled from 1.5 million to 3 million during the period 1919–22. Many of the wage reductions imposed during 1921–2 resulted from the operation of scales attached to the price of the particular industry's product [see 299].

2 Wages did not of course remain uniformly stable in all industries. By the end of 1929 rates were below their 1923 level in textiles, boot and shoe manufacture, coalmining, railways, building and shipping.

3 PRO, Cab 24/128, CP 3363, Proposals of Commander Hilton Young's Committee submitted to the Prime Minister at Gairloch, 2 October, 1921.

4 *Daily Herald*, 31 July 1925. Baldwin later denied the statement.

National Confederation of Employers' Organisations, *The Industrial Situation*, 11 February 1931.

Memoranda on Certain Proposals Relating to Unemployment, Cmd., 3331, May 1929, p. 52.

Committee on Finance and Industry, *Minutes of Evidence*, vol. II, May 1930, p. 48.

The Times, 6 January 1933.

7

The Outlines of a Keynesian Solution

T. J. HATTON

Introduction

In this chapter we address ourselves to the implications of alternative economic policies. Specifically we ask the question: suppose we accept a simple Keynesian theory of the determination of employment, how much difference would such policy choices have made? Developing such alternative scenarios or 'counterfactuals' is now a widely accepted approach to economic history but has its drawbacks in that it depends on identifying and measuring key economic relationships. The more plausible the assumptions, the more believable the argument which follows from them. In this respect two important qualifications must be born in mind throughout. First we are characterizing the economy in a manner which gained widespread acceptance following Keynes's *General Theory* [157]. Not everyone would agree that such an approach with its central focus on aggregate demand is appropriate, even for the time when the *General Theory* was being developed. We pay some attention to possible limitations of the Keynesian approach at the end of this chapter and discussion of the supply-side approach has been given by Capie in Chapter 5. Second, even within the Keynesian tradition there is no unanimity on the magnitude of certain effects which are important for this framework of analysis. For both these reasons, the results of simple Keynesian calculations must be regarded as suggestive rather than definitive.

The counteractuals which are considered need not be policies which were recommended at the time, though these are historically more interesting. It is also worth considering how such proposals might have been modified to achieve a specific goal. Here we consider two proposals associated with the name of Keynes and which have been much debated by economic historians. The first is the return to the gold standard at the prewar parity in 1925 for which he roundly castigated Churchill, the Chancellor of the Exchequer, and his advisers, arguing that a lower rate would have been more appropriate. The second revolves around proposals for a programme of public works expenditure and centres on the specific policies of Lloyd George's Liberal Manifesto of 1929 which were not adopted but were strongly endorsed by Keynes.

The central point in the argument is that the exchange rate and the budget must both be considered when analysing a change in policy. A change in the exchange rate would have implications for the budget via its effect on domestic income and similarly a change in fiscal policy would have implications for the balance of payments and/or the exchange rate. Thus in our counterfactuals we consider how changing one policy might have engendered changes in others and what the outcome of joint changes in policy might have been.

Exchange Rate Policy in the 1920s

Since 1925, many writers have followed Keynes in arguing that Britain's failure to achieve full employment in the second half of the 1920s was, to a large extent, due to the overvalued exchange rate. Keynes himself argued that the return to the gold standard at the prewar parity was a 'policy from which any humane or judicious person should shrink' [137, 218]. In his view Churchill had been misled by his advisers who had underestimated the extent to which domestic prices and costs would have to fall relative to those overseas if relatively high employment was to be restored. Though the issue was contested at the time, subsequent writers have tended to support the view that, as compared with 1913, British prices had risen by more than those ruling overseas [208, 100–6; 237].

Though Keynes suggested that an exchange rate of $4.40 rather than $4.86 would have relieved much of the burden, little effort has been made to assess the consequences of the decision on aggregate employment. This issue is complicated by the fact that the orthodoxy of the day was to limit public expenditure closely to the yield on taxes in order to balance the budget. If the yield on taxes had been higher as a result of the expansionary effects of a lower exchange rate, there might have been more scope for expanding government spending. Given the commitment to the gold standard, orthodoxy in public finance, and the unwillingness to impose a tariff, policy choice was closely circumscribed. In order to protect the balance of payments foreign lending was discouraged and a tight monetary policy imposed. Keynes emphasized that high interest rates were an additional reason for low levels of domestic spending and employment a view which has received some support in recent research [78; 298]

To evaluate the implications of adopting a lower exchange rate, we turn first to the direct effects of the implied change in relative price on the balance of payments. Moggridge made some calculation based on certain assumptions about the price elasticities of demand for imports and exports (−0.5 and −1.5 respectively) to evaluate the improvement in the balance of payments which might have resulted had the exchange rate been 10 per cent lower in 1928. He estimated this at £70 million of which £52 million arose from the improvement in the balance of visible trade [208, 249]. These results are sensitive to the particular assumptions made, especially about the price elasticity of demand for exports.[1] Taking a low value (−1) and a high value (−2) as alternatives but keeping the other assumptions unchanged we obtain estimates of £48 million and £93 million respectively for the improvement in the balance of payments.

By itself this will not tell us the effect on employment because income adjustments have not yet been allowed for. In order to do this, we assume that the improvement in the balance of payments represents a switch to domestic production and estimate the expansion of national income which would occur through the Keynesian expenditure multiplier. The multiplier is discussed further in the next section but, for now, we take the value to be 1. and the resulting rise in income is given in panel (a) of Table 7.1 As result of the rise in expenditure demand for labour would be increased and, using the relationship estimated by Thomas [267, 342], this is calculated at 200,000–400,000. A target unemployment rate of 5 per cent implies a number unemployed of just over a million compared with the actual number in 1928 of 1.54 million. Even on relatively generous assumptions, an exchange rate 10 per cent lower would not have solved the unemployment problem though it would have substantially improved it.

An implication of the rise in income and expenditure would be rise in import demand and hence the improvement in the balance of payments due to expenditure switching would be partially offset and the final change in the balance of payments somewhat smaller. Using Thomas's [267, 342] estimate of the marginal propensity to import gives the estimates of the balance of payments change in Table 7.1 at about two-thirds of the initial effects. These range between £3 million and £68 million and represent a substantial increase in the balance of payments surplus which would have allowed for a less restrictive monetary policy. Lower interest rates might have given

Table 7.1   Effects of a 10% Devaluation (in 1928)

Export price elasticity	Low (−1)	Middle (−1.5)	High (−2)
With no change in government spending			
Initial expenditure switching effect (£m)	48.0	70.0	93.0
Change in GNP (£m)	72.0	105.0	139.5
Change in employment (000s)	199.0	290.3	385.7
Balance of payments improvement (£m)	32.9	48.0	67.7
Improvement in the budget (£m)	28.8	42.0	55.8
With the budget deficit held constant			
Change in government spending (£m)	120.0	175.0	232.5
Change in employment (000s)	331.0	483.9	642.9
Balance of payments improvement (£m)	22.8	11.3	−0.8

se to a greater incentive to invest abroad and together with an
sing of restrictions on lending would have produced an offsetting
ovement on the capital account. More important, lower interest
tes might have increased the incentive for domestic firms to invest
d added a further stimulus to total output and employment. Such
onetary effects are notoriously difficult to estimate but one can be a
ttle more definite about the scope for a more expansionary budget.

Since the increase in income and expenditure would have
creased the yield of taxation and reduced expenditure on subsidies
ich as unemployment benefits, the central government's accounts
ould be expected to move towards surplus. Following Middleton
01, *130*] we assume that for every £1 increase in national income,
e central government budget improves by £0.4. Applying this to
e increase in GNP gives the estimates for the budgetary improve-
ents arising from devaluation in Table 7.1 (a). Given the orthodoxy
 balancing receipts and expenditure we may conjecture that this
ange would have led to higher levels of government spending
hich would have given rise to a further round of expansion in
come and expenditure (and subsequently a further rise in
overnment expenditure as the automatic effect of the stimulus
ntinued). This would have the effect of raising the value of the
ultiplier and in order to incorporate this effect we assume that all
dditional government revenues and savings would have been spent
 that the budget surplus remained at its observed level.

The implications of assuming government expenditure was
panded in this way are given in panel (b) of Table 7.1. Because the
dget is so responsive to changes in activity there could have been a
bstantial increase in government spending without worsening the

budget. As a result the effects of expenditure switching are magnifie
considerably. The range of estimates for the increase in employmer
of 331,000 to 643,000 suggest that had government expenditure bee
expanded in this manner the unemployment problem in the la
1920s might have been substantially reduced. The higher incon
levels also imply increased imports so that the resulting improvemen
in the balance of payments are smaller. Taking the middle estimat
as the 'best guess' we can conclude that the 10 per cent devaluatic
alone would not have been enough to reduce unemployment to
million but expanding public expenditure at the same time to kee
the budget deficit at its historically observed level would ha'
brought the economy close to this goal. It should be stressed that th
would not have required a departure from conventional budgeta
practice and given this orthodoxy such effects would have follow
as a matter of course. One might conjecture that the authoriti
would have preferred to cut taxes rather than increase expenditur
in which case the expansionary effects would have been somewh
smaller. Alternatively they might have chosen to retire the pub
debt more rapidly, in which case the employment effects would ha
been smaller still. But it should be remembered that they would al
have had the opportunity for more expansionary monetary polic
though the greater the budgetary expansion the less scope the
would have been for monetary policy. Nevertheless it could
argued that in various respects these calculations are too optimistic
a point to which we shall return.

Public Works in the Late 1920s
and Early 1930s

In this section we turn to examining the scope for, and efficacy of
programme of expansionary public expenditure as a means
reducing unemployment. A series of calls for expenditure on pub
works were made in the 1920s and 1930s by a variety of differe
groups – most notably from among Labour and Liberal politicians
well as economists and trade unionists [29; 96]. But the set
proposals which attracted most attention was that put forward
Lloyd George in the election campaign of 1929 under the title
Can Conquer Unemployment [177]. This was based on the earli
Liberal Industrial Enquiry [176] and was strongly supported in
further pamphlet by Keynes and Henderson [158, *86–125*]. By tl
time it had become plain that with the restoration of the g
standard and, even with the return to stability in industrial relatior
unemployment remained obdurately high. With the worseni

86

unemployment situation these calls were repeated on the Macmillan Committee in 1931, by Keynes in 1933 and by Lloyd George in 1935 [see 29]. Despite this clamour successive governments in general, and the Treasury in particular, resisted such proposals until forced into expansionary budgets in the late 1930s by the exigencies of the rearmament programme.

Among the alternatives considered in *We Can Conquer Unemployment* was a programme of raising central government expenditure on public works by £250 million per year over two years. Spending was to be focused largely on infrastructure such as housing and roads as well as utilities such as telephones and electricity supply. This was expected to raise annual employment by about 600,000 during the life of the programme. Keynes and Henderson re-examined these proposals taking account of the direct effects of the projects themselves and secondary effects arising from increased demand for intermediate inputs. On these grounds they found that the proposals would have achieved the extra employment claimed. Though the technique of calculating the expenditure multiplier had not yet been fully worked out they referred to the cumulative effects on aggregate demand as potentially powerful. More recently Thomas has estimated an income-expenditure model of the interwar economy to assess the proposal for a spending programme of £100 million a year over 5 years. He finds that the effects on employment would have been relatively modest, rising from 268,000 in the first year to 359,000 in the fifth year, as compared with the half-million suggested by £100 million of spending under the Lloyd George proposals (267, *337*].

Clearly such effects depend on the value of the multiplier, the first exposition of which was made by Kahn [151]. He estimated the secondary effects on demand to be somewhat smaller than the first round effects, making the multiplier around 1.75, and subsequent estimates made in the 1930s put it value somewhere in the range 1.5 to 2.0 [33; 57; 258]. While these often took into account the leakages from the circular flow arising from imports they rarely took into account those arising from increases in tax yields and declining government subsidies. More recently, taking this into account, economic historians have suggested much lower values. Glynn and Howells [103, *41*] estimate a value of 1.26 and Thomas obtained a value of about one in the short run rising to about 1.5 in the long run (12 years). It has, however, been argued elsewhere that both these calculations may be on the low side [130].

In Table 7.2, multiplier values of 1.25, 1.5 and 1.75 are assumed and used as alternatives in calculating the effect of a £100 million spending programme. On the lower estimate it would have generated less than 350,000 additional jobs while the high estimate would be

Table 7.2 Effects of a £100m Public Spending Programme (in 1930

Multiplier value	Low (1.25)	Middle (1.5)	Hig (1.75
a *With a fixed exchange rate*			
Income change (£m)	125.0	150.0	175.
Employment change (000s)	345.6	414.8	483.
Change in the budget (£m)	−50.0	−40.0	−30.
Change in the balance of payments (£m)	−26.3	−31.5	−36.
b *With a floating exchange rate*			
Income change (£m)	167.0	214.0	269.
Employment change (000s)	461.8	591.7	743.
Change in the budget	−33.2	−14.4	+7.
Depreciation (%)	5.1	6.5	8.

more consistent with the projections of Lloyd George. But, as before
one has to consider the implications for the budget and the balance o
payments. Using the same assumptions as earlier it can be seen fron
Table 7.2 (a) that the budget would have deteriorated, though b
substantially less than the original increase in expenditure, rangin
from half, the estimate favoured by Keynes to less than one-third
Perhaps more seriously, a substantial worsening of the balance o
payments is also indicated. Given the precarious state of the balanc
of payments, especially after 1929 one might have expected tha
public confidence in the Bank of England's ability to maintain th
gold standard would have been undermined. It must be conclude
that, at the time these measures were being discussed, even th
relatively modest programme would not have been feasible withou
additional measures such as a tariff to protect the balance o
payments.

In the light of this it is not surprising to find that, as pressure o
the balance of payments increased after 1929, there were renewe
calls for the imposition of a tariff. Having previously opposed tl
return to gold at the old parity, in 1930 Keynes came out strongly
favour of a tariff to provide the freedom for domestic expansic
without the dislocation of the international payments system whic
he judged would follow from devaluation [84, 365]. If we link tl
proposal for a tariff up with that for a public works programme
would have two clear advantages. First, it would have offset the ri
in imports resulting from the expansion in income. Second, the effe
on government revenues would have helped further reduce tl
budget deficit implied by the public works programme. Under tl

assumptions we have already made it is possible to calculate how much the average tariff rate would have to be raised to prevent any rise in the volume of imports. For the low, middle and high estimates of the multiplier respectively it would have needed additional tariffs of 5.9, 7.1 and 8.3 per cent on the value of imports. These magnitudes are roughly in line with the rise in the overall tariff rate when the tariff was imposed late in 1931. The impact on public revenues would have been substantially in excess of that required to balance the budget, though if a greater responsiveness of imports to the tariff were assumed, a lower tariff would have been needed and the relief to the budget would have been correspondingly smaller.[2]

This serves to emphasize again that a combination of policies would have been needed for domestic expansion under fixed exchange rates. But it must also be emphasized that such a policy as that considered above would not have eradicated the unemployment problem. Using the NIS figures, in 1929 there were about 1.5 million unemployed rising to 2.4 million in 1930 and over 3 million the following year. To reduce the unemployment percentage to 5 per cent or so in 1930, these estimates would have to be multiplied by a factor of two or three, that is, to a level not seriously contemplated by contemporaries or by historians.

Once Britain had left the gold standard in September 1931 the pound fell briefly to about $3.40 against the dollar late in the year but then recovered strongly until it rose above par after the dollar devaluation of 1933. From 1932 with the establishment of the Exchange Equalisation Account the Treasury was endowed with reserves in order to manage the sterling exchange rate. Though there was a desire both to steady the exchange rate and to maintain a relatively low value, there was a strong tendency for the exchange rate to rise [14, 55–7]. After the financial crisis had passed, the external constraint on domestic policy was relaxed. Following the debt conversion operation and with the worldwide fall in interest rates the era of cheap money was ushered in. Together with the tariff, this prevented the slump from worsening despite the continuing deflationary forces from overseas.

If we consider the implications of an expansionary programme in the conditions of the early 1930s, they would be somewhat different. In the absence of further increases in the tariff, a domestic expansion would increase imports raising the demand for foreign currency which would tend automatically to lower the sterling exchange rate. If we assume that equilibriating forces in the foreign exchange market would keep international payments in balance then any domestic expansion would automatically bring lower exchange rates. The effect of the depreciation would be to increase exports, adding to the expansionary effects of public spending. If we retain the assumptions made about the effects of depreciation on the balance of payments we can calculate the depreciation necessary to accommodate a given increase in activity keeping the balance of payments constant as a proportion of imports.

As can be seen in panel (b) of Table 7.2, incorporating the effect on exports into the multiplier enhances the effects of a £100 million public spending programme by a third to a half.[3] As a result the final budget deficits are substantially smaller and on the higher estimate there would have been no increase at all. The depreciation required is not great in the light of the observed fluctuations in exchange rates in the early 1930s. Though the employment effects are substantially larger than in the upper part of the table they indicate that such a policy would only have mitigated, not eradicated, the depression.

The Feasibility of a Keynesian Solution

It has sometimes been argued that any attempt to revive the economy either by manipulating the exchange rate or expanding public expenditure would have run into serious economic constraints which would have limited or completely undermined the effects of employment. To a certain extent these arise from taking too narrow a view of the implications of such policies. We will consider several arguments in turn.

In the context of the return to the gold standard it is sometimes argued that other European countries which stabilized their currencies after 1925 would have selected even lower rates in order to maintain their competitive advantage [245, 93]. Similarly, in 1931 a number of Britain's important trading partners (principally those of the Empire) tied their currencies to sterling reducing the competitive advantage of the devaluation. The main problem in the 1920s was a world shortage of dollars, and devaluation against the dollar might have relieved balance of payments strain in a number of countries simultaneously [234, 83]. Such effects may be seen to have operated in the 1930s with the countries of what was to become the sterling area experiencing an early recovery, growth of trade and an easing of domestic policy constraints within the group as a whole. Devaluation is often seen as a beggar thy neighbour policy since each country devaluation has a deflationary effect on its neighbours and sets up a round of competitive devaluations. But we have emphasized that devaluation and domestic expansion were natural complements in interwar Britain and under such a policy combination, the demand or imports would have been higher and would not necessarily impose deflationary pressures on other countries.

Lloyd George and Keynes argued that there was ample scope for useful public works projects and, given the scepticism with which such proposals were met, went to some lengths to claim that these could be implemented quickly and would provide an acceptable social rate of return. In the official reply to Lloyd George's proposals much was made of the argument that such projects would be subject to considerable planning delays and would be administratively difficult to implement in view of the fact that much of the work would have to be undertaken by local authorities. This view has recently been re-emphasized by historians and it has been argued that by comparison public spending for rearmament was much easier to implement than a public works programme would have been [272, 2–6]. Such arguments will depend on the size and nature of the programme, but plans such as those put forward would clearly have involved lags. With the benefit of hindsight one might suggest that projects which came on stream at almost any time from the early 1920s until rearmament would have been a welcome addition to demand. More to the point, accepting that such proposals would have been subject to these limitations does not mean that expansionary budgets in general would not have worked. Though it would have been politically less acceptable, a tax cut would have had a more immediate impact though its ultimate effects would have been smaller, and in retrospect one might think of a combination tax and expenditure policy as appropriate.

It is sometimes argued that budget deficits of the magnitude required for an effective expansionary programme would have produced various side-effects which would make efforts to expand employment ultimately self-defeating. As was emphasized earlier, the eventual size of the deficits required would have been only a fraction of the original increase in spending, especially if the exchange rate were free to adjust. But it should be recognized that there would typically be lags in response of domestic activity to the initial spending and to changes in the exchange rate as well as in the accrual of additional taxes. The most persistent argument has been that a policy of deficit financing would have 'crowded out' private spending in various ways, some of which formed part of the famous 'Treasury View' [210, *ch. 8*]. The psychological effects often referred to apply principally to loss of confidence in financial markets about the ability to maintain a fixed exchange rate which is consistent with our earlier argument about the effects of public works on the balance of payments. These arguments are principally about timing and suggest the appropriateness of gradual as opposed to sudden expansion. In the longer term it has been suggested that loan financing would raise domestic interest rates and discourage invest ment, though this effect might be mitigated by an inflow of capital from abroad. If, as seems likely, additional deficits had been largely financed by the issue of Treasury bills, the rise in interest rates would probably have been mitigated partly by an expansion of domesti credit [132, *443–4*]. Such crowding out as would occur depends also on the interest elasticity of investment about which there is little firm evidence for the interwar period.

One challenge to expansionary policies is that they would have failed to mop up employment where it was most needed and would have given rise to bottlenecks and inflation [26; 105]. Unemployment was highest among workers with specific skills who were displaced by the collapse of the great export industries and located predominately in the so-called 'outer' regions of the North and West where there was least need for the social capital envisaged in public work programmes. For the 1920s there is evidence that this was severely exacerbated by the return to gold and this suggests adopting a lower exchange rate would have eased the regional problem [149] Similarly we have argued that a public works programme would have needed to be accompanied by a lower exchange rate which would have the by-product of expanding export demand. But it seems unlikely that lower exchange rates alone would have solved the regional problem. In addition it should be recognized that at least some of the induced effects of expansionary budget measures, even concentrated on public works in the South, would have spilled over into the outer regions. There is little evidence even in the South-East that bottlenecks in labour supply were an imminent constraint, and unemployment among unskilled workers and those in the building trades remained relatively high. It has also been observed that inter regional migration tended to increase with the level of activity and seems likely that a higher level of aggregate demand would of itself have tended to ease the regional problem [131].

Both among contemporaries and subsequent writers there is strong preoccupation with the inflationary consequences of expan sionary programmes. It should be recognized at the outset, as it was by some contemporaries, that inflation was, in part, the *means* recovery, though we have not been able to consider its impact in the context of the simple calculations made earlier. Raising prices relative to costs would have been a major factor inducing firms expand their output but with such a large margin of unemployed resources it is not clear that this increase would have needed to be large. A lower exchange rate in the 1920s can be considered largely a device for achieving this aim and some allowance was made for these effects. Perhaps the more serious contention is that, either in the late 1920s or the early 1930s, a devaluation would have raised costs by nearly as much as output prices, thereby neutralizing much of the stimulating effect on production. In so far as inputs came from abroad this would be true but, for the economy as a whole, the most important cost is labour. If wage settlements depended on the price of foodstuffs determined in world markets then the benefits of devaluation would be severely attenuated. If on the other hand nominal wages were genuinely 'sticky' or depended on domestic norms such as unemployment benefits the offsetting effects would be much less. As yet the evidence does not enable us to reach a clear conclusion on this issue.

Conclusion

Taking a latter-day Keynesian view of the interwar economy we have argued that had more expansionary policies been followed, the employment effects could have been substantial. But domestic employment and the balance of payments must be considered together in the context of the policy regime in each period. A lower exchange rate in the late 1920s would have allowed scope for more expansionary domestic policy even within the tenets of the ruling orthodoxy. Similarly, in the early 1930s the corollary of a public spending programme would have been a lower exchange rate. In both cases the effects of the alternative policy choice on employment would have been enhanced, which suggests that their potential expansionary effects have often been underestimated.

Notes

I am grateful to Roy Bailey, George Peden and the editors for their comments on an earlier draft of this chapter. Any errors remaining are solely my responsibility.

A number of estimates of the export price elasticity have been made and some, such as that recently estimated by Thomas, fall well below 1. But this was based on an inappropriate relative price measure and the range used here is based on my own results [130, *appendix 2*]. Moggridge applied the elasticities to visible trade but assumed that an exchange rate change would be partly offset by price adjustments. In the case of a 10 per cent devaluation sterling import prices would rise by 9 per cent while, because of higher costs and wider profit margins, export prices in foreign currency would fall by only 6 per cent. Wright [298, *304–5*] has suggested incorporating supply elasticities directly but his alternative calculations yield similar results to those of Moggridge. We follow the latter's method and use his adjustments for change in invisibles throughout.

2 Taking Thomas's import function, the elasticity of imports with respect to income is close to 1 and the relative price elasticity -0.5. In this case, to offset the effect of a rise in domestic expenditure the percentage tariff would have to be twice that of the rise in GDP. The calculations in the text were made using a value for GDP in 1930 of £4,228 million. Since the volume (and foreign currency value) of imports is thereby held constant the additional revenue to the Exchequer is simply the original sterling value of imports, taken as £1,100 million in 1930, times the increase in the tariff.

3 The expression for the percentage devaluation necessary to keep the balance of payments surplus constant as a proportion of the import bill is derived in Hatton [130, *appendix 3*]. It is based on similar assumptions about elasticities and price changes used above and referred to in Note together with a marginal propensity to import of 0.21. Using export price elasticities of -1, -1.5 and -2.0 the percentage devaluation required to accommodate a 1 per cent increase in national income is calculated as -2.09, -1.29 and -0.93 respectively (the middle estimate being used in Table 7.2). This implies percentage increases in exports of 1.26, 1.16 and 1.15 respectively. Expressed a different way these figures give a 'marginal propensity to export' of about 0.2, and incorporating this into the three alternative multiplier values gives the result in Table 7.2 (b).

Part 2

The Policy Debate

8

Keynes

G. C. PEDEN

Introduction

Down to the early 1970s, it was possible to believe that the Keynesian revolution in economics was the one cause above all others of full employment after 1945 [257, *13*]. This belief implied not only that the publication of Keynes's *The General Theory of Employment, Interest and Money* in 1936 was a decisive step on the road to full employment, but also that earlier acceptance of Keynes's ideas would greatly have reduced the scale of interwar unemployment. Recently, some economic historians have emphasized the importance of political and administrative barriers to acceptance of Keynes's ideas [for example, 199; 200; 223; 224; 252; 253; 272], but this emphasis does not imply that Keynes's approach was wrong in principle. There has also recently been renewed recognition of structural aspects of interwar unemployment, which would not have been easily dispelled by an increase in aggregate demand alone [26; 105]. This recognition has helped to restore the reputation of those interwar economists who, unlike Keynes, were primarily concerned about the high levels of real wages in relation to productivity, and also about lack of labour mobility in response to structural changes in demand [52]. The fact that there were structural causes of unemployment does not, however, in itself mean that Keynes's macroeconomic approach was wrong; although it may have been incomplete. Experience since 1945 suggests that greater aggregate demand encourages greater mobility of labour, and also increased willingness on the part of businessmen to invest in areas where labour is available [139, *271–2*].

97

Keynes himself does not seem to have supposed that macro-economic measures alone would create full employment in the sense that everyone who wanted a job would have one. Keynes was interested in removing unemployment which was due to deficiency in aggregate demand but he accepted that some of the unemployed were virtually unemployable, some were out of work because of seasonal factors, some were moving between jobs and some could not find employment because of lack of mobility between trades or locality. In 1930, Keynes regarded unemployment amounting to 6.5 per cent of the NIS workforce as 'normal', a figure which he revised in 1942 to 5 per cent. He did not, however, think in 1944 that there would be any harm at aiming at an average level of 3 per cent, although he doubted whether this could be sustained [152, *29–30*].

Keynes's own interests as an economist were largely confined to monetary economics. It is difficult to summarize his thought, since his views changed, at least in emphasis, over time. However, the four main areas in which he contributed to theory and policy were as follows: first, from the early 1920s he believed that a country's currency should be managed so as to ensure stability of domestic prices rather than to maintain a *fixed* exchange rate, although he did see merit in *stable* exchange rates, as these benefited international transactions in trade and finance. Secondly, from the later 1920s he challenged the pre-Keynesian assumption that all savings would find their way into investment through the mediation of interest rates and he advocated state borrowing for capital expenditure to ensure that no savings remained idle. Thirdly, from the 1930s he argued that changes in interest rates alone could not offset great changes in businessmen's expectations and, in particular, that a 'cheap money' policy of low interest rates could not in itself be effective in ending a depression. Fourthly, in *The General Theory,* he arrived at the macroeconomic concepts which, together with the development of national income accounting by other economists, made possible measurement of the community's flow of income in the now familiar terms of private consumption *plus* private investment *plus* government expenditure *plus* exports *minus* imports. Using this analytical framework, governments could, at least in principle, ensure that no unemployment would arise from a deficiency of aggregate demand.

While there is reason to believe that Keynes and his followers were too optimistic about what could be achieved through macroeconomic policies, there is a danger that there will be too great a reaction among economic historians to past overemphasis on Keynes. A number of solutions to unemployment were offered in the interwar period, but Keynes's approach was outstanding for the intellectual rigour of its theoretical basis. 'Planning' was in vogue, but it proponents tended to confine themselves to vague generalities [29]. Moreover, the fact that Keynesian policies foundered in an age of stagflation does not prove that they would have been inappropriate to the solution of unemployment at a time when prices were falling or were stable. In any case, Keynes's historical importance is not solely dependent upon the validity of his economic theories. He occupied a unique position as someone who could influence economists, politicians and administrators, and public opinion. As an economist, he wrote two major theoretical works, *A Treatise on Money* (1930) and *The General Theory*. He had served with distinction as a civil servant in the Treasury during the First World War, and he was consulted by politicians and Treasury officials from time to time throughout the interwar period before returning to the Treasury as an economic adviser in 1940. He was also a prolific writer of polemical articles and pamphlets which sought to mobilize public opinion behind the policies which he advocated. Whatever may have been the success of these essays in persuasion on contemporaries, Keynes's work has been widely read by economists and economic historians, who have relished his controversial style, and consequently Keynes has had a considerable impact on the historiography of employment policy. That alone would be sufficient reason why this volume should include a study of the development of his thought in the interwar period, together with some speculation as to the extent of his influence by the later 1930s.

The Gold Standard

Much of the debate on the decision in 1925 to return to the gold standard has focussed on the effects of an overvalued exchange rate on industry and employment (see Chapters 7 and 10). Keynes was certainly concerned with this issue, but his initial concern was with the stability of prices. He believed that monetary policy should be designed to avoid violent price fluctuations, both inflation, which had occurred in Britain between 1914 and 1920, and deflation, which had occurred since. The Bank of England and the Treasury hoped to achieve stability by returning to the gold standard, which fixed the value of sterling in relation to a given weight of gold, and which therefore fixed the sterling exchange rate with all other currencies whose value was defined in terms of gold. In his *Tract on Monetary Reform* [154], Keynes argued that the gold standard would not guarantee stability in the value of money, except in the unlikely event of prices abroad remaining stable. There was no reason, he said, to suppose that the quantity of newly-mined gold which would become available for monetary purposes would be equal to the amount required by the world's economy. Gold was likely to be either too dear or too cheap in terms of goods and services [154, *132–3*]. For this reason, Keynes advocated a managed currency, in which the value of money would be held stable in relation to an index of the price of commodities, weighted in accordance to their relative importance in the economy.

The stability of prices was important for employment policy. As Keynes pointed out, when prices fell, the real rate of interest rose, as did the value of money relative to fixed assets. In these circumstances, a businessman might do well to delay new investment [154, *23*]. Indeed, Keynes believed that the gold standard worked through the mechanism of unemployment. Under the gold standard, there was no restriction on the import or export of gold, and the Bank of England reacted to outward gold flows by raising Bank Rate. Higher interest rates not only checked the flow of gold abroad, but also discouraged investment at home. As domestic demand and employment fell, so, in theory, did prices and wages, checking imports and stimulating exports until the desired external balance was restored. It had been possible to keep the monetary system out of politics before 1914 because no large-scale adjustments of prices had been required. Matters were different in the 1920s, when the level of price-and-wage adjustments which Bank Rate was expected to effect were very much greater than the unions were prepared to tolerate. Keynes himself did not anticipate fully in 1925 how 'sticky' the level of money wages would be [246; *vol. 3, pp. 179–80*]. Money wages were stable from 1923, but prices were falling and, unsurprisingly, British employers reacted by shedding labour.

In the 1920s, Keynes still held to the pre-Keynesian assumption that changes in financial variables did not affect the long-term equilibrium positions of real variables in the economy. However, as he remarked in the *Tract*, in one of his most famous phrases (which is still apt in an age of monetarism):

> this *long run* is a misleading guide to current affairs. *In the long run* we are all dead. Economists set themselves too easy, too useless a task if in tempestuous seasons they can only tell us that when the storm is long past the ocean will be flat again. [154. *65*]

It was Keynes's concern with current affairs which led him to give increasing priority to the problem of unemployment, even before he had escaped from the influences of pre-Keynesian theory which stated that unemployment was a short-run phenomenon which would automatically be corrected by market forces.

From the *Tract* to the *Treatise*

While the *Tract* had contained much that was novel in its advocacy of active monetary management, the framework of the analysis did not differ from that of other Cambridge economists at the time. In the earliest drafts of the *Treatise on Money*, dating from late 1924, Keynes seems to have held beliefs similar to those which he later characterized as the 'Treasury view' (see Chapter 9). He wrote that public works, which were financed by borrowing, could do nothing to improve matters in a slump, and might do actual harm by diverting existing working capital away from production goods [159, 22–3]. His focus was on businessmen's expectations, and, even in its published form, the *Treatise* contained passages which suggested that Keynes assumed that changes in short-term interest rates would normally be sufficient to set the economy on the path to recovery. He did note that in the depression of the 1890s a reduction in Bank Rate had not been sufficient to prevent deflation, and that probably only loan-financed public works could have absorbed surplus savings on that occasion [156, *150–2*], but the implication was that such circumstances were exceptional.[1] Nevertheless, in the *Treatise* Keynes moved to an analysis of savings and investment which underlay his proposals for public works in 1928–30.

Established economic theory held that savings and investment were kept in equilibrium by changes in the rate of interest. However, Keynes's Cambridge colleague, Dennis Robertson, had recently drawn attention[2] to the importance of the distinction between decisions to save and decisions to invest, meaning by the latter the acquisition of fixed capital or stocks of goods. Keynes believed that if the public increased its holdings of financial assets by more than the amount which businessmen required for investment, prices would fall and excess savings would result in business losses, which would lead businessmen to reduce output and employment. The monetary authorities should try to prevent this by lowering the rate of interest and by making credit freely available, but these measures might be inadequate since businessmen would also be influenced by costs of inputs, such as raw materials and labour, and the prices of their products. Moreover, domestic and international monetary policy might be in conflict. If Britain tried to maintain a rate of interest more than marginally below the rate in New York or other leading financial centres, gold would tend to flow out of the country. In Keynes's view, the rate of interest necessary to maintain the gold standard might be too high for a mature economy like Britain to find profitable outlets at home for the whole of its savings. Excess savings must then run to waste in business losses, or be invested abroad.

Keynes arrived at a practical solution to this problem even before he had worked out his theoretical position in the *Treatise* (a fact which suggests that there can be no simple relationship between economic theory and policy). In 1924, Keynes took part in a debate in the Liberal journal, *The Nation*, about Britain's immediate economic future. He suggested that the government should finance public works, such as housing, roads and electrical transmission lines, partly by using revenue currently earmarked to pay off the National Debt, and partly by borrowing funds which would otherwise have been invested abroad. Although lacking a theory of the multiplier (see Chapter 7), Keynes noted that 'prosperity is cumulative', and he believed that a 'jolt' in the economic system would provide businessmen with profits and confidence, which in turn would lead to an increase in private investment and a reduction in unemployment [160, *219-23*]. In terms of the *Treatise*, Britain was a special case of a mature economy with an overvalued currency where monetary policy could reduce money wages only through a long, economically and socially wasteful, deflation. Loan-financed public works, which absorbed surplus savings, Keynes believed would enable employment to increase at the existing rate of interest.

This 'special case' argument lay behind Keynes's contributions to the Liberal Industrial Inquiry of 1928,[3] which proposed loan-financed public works, and his support for Lloyd George's claim in 1929 that loan-financed public works could reduce unemployment to 'normal' proportions within a year. In *Can Lloyd George Do It?* [158, *88-125*], a political pamphlet written with fellow Liberal economist Hubert Henderson, Keynes expanded on his arguments of 1924. He also tried to show that the Chancellor could expect to be able to pay off the loans, since in addition to the direct money returns on capital expenditure, tax receipts would rise with increased economic activity, while the cost of unemployment relief would fall. He took the Treasury to task for its opposition to public works, claiming that if it were true that public investment could not create employment, the same must be true of private investment – although in this would seem that he did less than justice to the qualitative argument in the Treasury view (see Chapter 9). Subsequently, in 1930, as member of the Macmillan Committee on Finance and Industry, he was able both to cross-examine the Treasury's witness, Sir Richard Hopkins,[4] and to give him his own views. In his own 'evidence' Keynes showed himself to be willing to consider a range of policies to cope with the deepening depression – even tariffs, although as a Liberal he had been a lifelong free-trader. Interestingly, in view his earlier criticism of Britain's return to the gold standard at an overvalued exchange rate, Keynes was not in favour of devaluation in 1930. He recognized that such an act by Britain would disturb the international financial system. He was aware also of the need for increased efficiency in industry, through rationalization. His favourite remedy, however, was loan-financed public works. He believed that business confidence was so low that it was only with a restoration of profits through increased economic activity that private investment would recover [29, *170–7*; 161, *38–157, 166–269*].

Once Britain had been forced off the gold standard, in September 1931, Keynes concentrated upon monetary matters. There was no longer, in the logic of the *Treatise*, a special case for public works in Britain. In theory, the exchange rate could be adjusted to whatever was desirable from the point of view of lowering domestic interest rates, and depreciation of sterling would also restore profits by making British goods competitive at existing levels of money wages and productivity. Keynes also withdrew his support for a tariff, since, again in theory, the exchange rate could be adjusted to whatever was necessary to give British industry protection. His main concern at the end of 1931 was with the need to reverse the fall in prices.

From the *Treatise* to *The General Theory*

Keynes started work on *The General Theory* in 1932, the worst year of the slump. He had been disappointed by the reception of the *Treatise* from fellow economists, and *The General Theory* was an attempt to win professional acceptance of his ideas. He used a single-country model, which assumed that either the economy was a closed system or that equilibrium with the rest of the world could be secured by means of fluctuating exchange rates [157, *270*]. Subsequent expositions of Keynes's economics have tended to concentrate on domestic macroeconomic management, a perfectly legitimate emphasis so far as the issues between Keynes and pre-Keynesian economists were concerned, since these issues related to the way in which the economic system worked. Nevertheless, it is as well to remember that Keynes was in favour of international co-operation, whenever such co-operation was likely to bear fruit.

In his evidence to the Macmillan Committee, Keynes had advocated international action by central banks to raise world prices to the level of money incomes and money costs of production, so as to cut business losses and encourage private investment. Subsequently, in his pamphlet *The Means to Prosperity*, he advocated international co-operation whereby loan-financed public expenditure would be begun in different countries simultaneously, so as to remove the fears of each government about consequences for the balance of payment [158, 356]. However, he did not think that governments should postpone measures to deal with the slump while awaiting agreemen on international measures. Thus, in 1933, when other commentator criticized President Roosevelt for torpedoing the World Economi Conference in London, when Roosevelt rejected an agreement on stabilizing exchange rates, Keynes published an article stating tha 'President Roosevelt is magnificently right' [162, 273–7]. Keyne hoped that America's refusal to co-operate with European countries which were still on the gold standard, would lead to a managed currency, whereby prices would be raised, then stabilized. In this however, he was to be disappointed. Later in the year, he wrote to Roosevelt that, while the monetary and exchange rate policy of government should be dictated by the need to raise output and employment, 'the recent gyrations of the dollar have looked to m more like a gold standard on the booze than the ideal manage currency of my dreams' [162, 294–5].

In 1933, Keynes was once more pushing hard for public works. In *The Means to Prosperity*, he tried to explain his ideas at a level which the reader of *The Times* could understand, making full use of th concept of the multiplier. Likewise, in his 'Open Letter' to Roosevelt, published in the *New York Times* at the end of the year he put 'a large volume of loan expenditure under governmen auspices in the forefront of recovery policy' [162, 296]. The fact tha he advocated loan-financed public expenditure in Britain and America, even though both countries had floating exchange rates suggests that he had gone beyond the special case of the *Treatise* to the gloomy vision of *The General Theory*, where he suggested tha there would be a chronic tendency for a mature industrial society' savings to exceed what was required for investment.

In *The General Theory*, Keynes focused primarily on output an employment. In his view, given that money wages and prices wer 'sticky', at least in the short run, the economic system was likely to respond to changes in demand by changing the volume of output an employment. He stressed the importance of uncertainty as a influence on investment decisions. Writing at a time when prices ha until recently been falling, and were still well below their 1929 level Keynes took the view that individuals, when faced with uncertainty were more likely to hold money or financial assets than industri securities. The effect of the demand for money might be that th economic system could be at equilibrium at less than full employmen Indeed, Keynes's claim to have formulated a general theory rested o his claim to have replaced the pre-Keynesian assumption that the economic system tended automatically to return to full employment, with a model which suggested that it was full employment, not the existence of unemployment, which was the special case. The implication for policy was that governments must accept responsibility for ensuring that aggregate demand in the community was sufficient to secure full employment.

Keynes did not, of course, overlook the importance of supply conditions, but his interests as a monetary economist may have led him to neglect other factors. For example, while he made much of the fact that wages were 'sticky' in a downwards direction, he did not ponder sufficiently the possibility that trade unions might respond to increased demand by pushing up wages for those in employment, rather than by allowing output and employment to expand. Again, there was no reference in *The General Theory* to regional aspects of unemployment, although the uneven distribution of unemployment in Britain was one of the most obvious features of the time. However, at the beginning of 1937 Keynes did address this issue in an article in *The Times*, in which he admitted that 'the economic structure is unfortunately rigid and . . . (for example) building activity in the Home Counties is less effective than one might have hoped in decreasing unemployment in the distressed areas'. By 1937, NIS unemployment was at about half the level at which it had been when Keynes had begun work on *The General Theory* and he now believed that 'we are in more need . . . of a rightly distributed demand than of greater aggregate demand' [162, 385]. Subsequently, he stated that, while it was easy to reduce unemployment, from 20 to 10 per cent, a reduction of unemployment to the range of 5 to 0 per cent would led to inflation unless managed with care [162, 409]. It would be wrong, therefore, to suggest that by 1937, at least, Keynes believed in a simple comprehensive solution to the unemployment problem, even if some of his polemical writings, such as *Can Lloyd George Do It?* or *The Means to Prosperity* suggest that he did so.

Keynes's Influence in the 1930s

How much influence did Keynes have before the Second World War? As I have argued elsewhere [222], it is easy to exaggerate his influence on the Treasury, the department with which he was primarily concerned, even in the later 1930s. However, in contrast to the 1920s, when his suggestions for a managed currency made no perceptible impact, Keynes did play a part in the development of monetary policy in the wake of Britain's departure from the gold

standard. His advice was sought by the Treasury at the end of 1931
and his arguments were used by officials who were opposed to
return to the gold standard [136, 82–9, 173–9]. On the other hand,
cannot be said that monetary policy in the 1930s was wholly i
accordance with Keynes's views. In particular, the Treasury though
at the end of 1936 that the best precaution against a renewed slum
would be a rise in interest rates to check expansion once prices wer
back to their 1929 level [136, 128–31], whereas Keynes believed tha
interest rates should be held low even in a boom. He argued that de
money, joined with other factors, would make another slum
inevitable, and that it was better to find other means of preventin
excessive investment [162, 388–91]. In 1937, the government seem
to have accepted, in a limited way, Keynes's suggestion of holdin
back public investment in a boom, so as to have public works i
reserve to mitigate a slump [140, 141–2, 147], but the scale of th
proposed counter-cyclical measure was small compared with Lloy
George's programme, which Keynes had supported in 1929 [22
176–8]. Moreover, there is evidence that Treasury officials had yet
accept the macroeconomic concepts of *The General Theory* or th
need to compile data for national income accounting [222, 7–9
Recently, Middleton has produced evidence to show that by 193
Treasury officials recognized that loan-financed rearmament wa
stimulating employment, and that in consequence tax increases wer
being delayed until full employment had been achieved [20
118–21]. However, as Middleton argues in Chapter 9 of this volum
this was not evidence of official acceptance of Keynesian principles
demand management.

There are major difficulties in separating Keynes's influence
policy from the influences of public opinion and events. Keyn
himself, through his press propaganda, was in no small wa
responsible for the growing belief amongst the electorate th
governments could do something about unemployment, and experien
of the way in which loan-financed rearmament was reducir
unemployment by 1939 seemed to provide evidence for this belie
By 1938 it was argued in the Treasury that, in the next depressio
pressure would be irresistible for loan-financed road works to crea
employment [224, 178]. It was certainly to be expected that if ev
unemployment became a decisive political issue – as it did during th
war, when a high proportion of the electorate was in the services
munitions industries and faced the prospect of finding new jobs
peace – then the political parties would make such use of Keynes
ideas as suited their purposes. In the 1930s, however, even in th
worst of the slump, the greater part of the electorate had jobs an
largely as a result of the fall in prices between 1929 and 1933, we

njoying higher real income than before the slump. It is not wholly surprising that in these circumstances there was only limited electoral pressure in support of Keynes's ideas (see also Chapter 4).

There were a number of avenues through which Keynes could try o influence opinion. His own political contacts and sympathies were with the Liberal Party, and, thus, he tended to find himself treated as an outsider by the Conservatives, who were in power for most of the interwar period. His advice was sought by Ramsay MacDonald during the short-lived Labour government of 1929–31, but Keynes's influence on thinking in the Labour Party in the 1930s seems to have been slight [29]. MacDonald made Keynes a member of his Economic Advisory Council, which brought together ministers and economic experts. However, the council was moribund from 1932 and Keynes had to rely thereafter upon one of its subcommittees, the Committee on Economic Information, to raise his ideas in Whitehall. The fact that there was no minister in charge of the committee meant that its reports were not discussed in Cabinet, and Keynes could only hope that Treasury officials on the committee would take up his ideas as one of them, Sir Frederick Phillips, sometimes did) [140]. Nevertheless, as will be shown in Chapter 13, the Treasury was far from being Keynesian even by the time the 1944 white paper on *Employment Policy* was being drafted.

Keynes had a considerable impact on the younger generation of economists, including James Meade, who played an important part in formulating employment policy in the 1940s [29, *143–4*]. Moreover, although Keynes's theoretical works were critically reviewed at the time, even those economists, like Pigou, who disagreed in part with Keynes's analysis, found that they had been affected by it in their own thinking [209, *73*]. This may help to account for the fact that Keynes's ideas enjoyed considerable support from fellow economists in the Committee on Economic Information, despite theoretical differences [140]. However, in the short run, this mattered less than his impact on Treasury officials, since it was not until the Second World War that economists were fully integrated into the Whitehall decision-making process [27].

The effects of Keynes's attempts to influence public opinion may have been mixed. If he was to get his ideas across to the average reader of a newspaper, he had to state his case boldly, without qualifications about practical problems or ulterior consequences. However, this sort of article was likely to go down badly with those who were responsible for policy, who might well feel that Keynes's arguments were not merely simple but simplistic. Keynes's political journalism, like his economic theories, probably found its most appreciative audience amongst the younger generation. This would not have surprised Keynes, who observed in *The General Theory* that 'in the field of economics and political philosophy there are not many who are influenced by new theories after they are twenty-five or thirty years of age' [157, *383–4*]. Keynes himself, thus, seems to have expected his influence to have its full impact only after the young men of the interwar years had risen to positions of power and responsibility in the academic and political worlds.

Notes

1 In this he did not differ greatly from R. G. Hawtrey, the only Treasury official at the time to enjoy a reputation as an economist [see 224, *16*, *172*].
2 In his book, *Banking Policy and the Price Level*, 1926.
3 Popularly known as 'The Yellow Book' [176], this exercise in party political propaganda was reissued, with an introduction by David Steel, in 1977.
4 For Hopkins and employment policy see [223].

9

Treasury Policy on Unemployment

ROGER MIDDLETON

Introduction

The history of interwar Treasury policy on unemployment has hitherto been largely a Keynesian history [see, for example 257; 293]. Such has been the dominance of this Keynesian historiography and of Keynes's personal standing in the interwar fiscal policy debate, that for over half a century Keynes's ridicule of the Treasury has prevailed. For Keynes, the infamous 'Treasury view' on deficit-finance, which formed the essential foundation of all Treasury macroeconomic policies, was 'obviously the work of persons who are not familiar with modern economic thought' [160, *820*].

Recently, however, this condemnation of the Treasury view as theoretically untenable, easily discredited and unworthy of further serious study, has undergone revision. Two developments have been responsible for this. First, in the early 1970s there became available in the Public Record Office the Treasury's internal papers, making possible a proper study of Treasury thinking. Second, the end of the Keynesian era, with the current crisis in Keynesian economics and policy, initiated an increasingly comprehensive process of questioning the Keynesian filters through which the interwar period has traditionally been viewed.

From these developments there has arisen a rejection of the simple Keynesian historiography, that the key to the fiscal policy debate lay in the gradual refinement of Keynes's theoretical position, and in the concomitant process whereby the Treasury eventually succumbed by the force of reason to the theoretical correctness of the new economics. Instead, while the theoretical dimension has not been dismissed from account, the debate has increasingly been viewed in terms of certain compelling political and administrative constraints to the adoption of the Keynesian solution for unemployment between the wars, and which need also to be taken into account in any explanation of subsequent, wartime developments [199; 201; 239; 224; 271; 272]. A very different specification of the Treasury view has resulted, important not just for an understanding of interwar Treasury policy, but also for the current crisis of economy and policy.

This chapter, however, will focus on the theoretical foundations of the Treasury view [for a fuller treatment, see 201, *chs*. 5, 8], and the impact of Treasury thinking on policy during the 1930s. We begin with the policy debate generated during the 1929 general election with the Liberal Party's pamphlet *We Can Conquer Unemployment* [177], which proposed an ambitious two-year £250 million (approximately 6 per cent of 1929 GDP) public works programme to reduce unemployment to normal levels within one year.

The Treasury View 1929–30

Without undue characterization, the orthodox Keynesian view has it that the Liberal programme was rejected because of the dominance and stultifying influence of an obscurantist Treasury, rather than the programme's technical deficiencies and the widespread mistrust of it as a mere electioneering stunt. The Treasury view has been interpreted as deriving from classical economics with its implicit (Ricardian) assumption of full employment and a fixed fund of savings [160, *819–24*; 158, *350*; 239, *71*; 250, *25*]. Furthermore, it has been criticized because it ignored both the multiplier effects of, and social rate of return on, public investment.

To substantiate our case that this Keynesian historiography is misfounded, we need first to discuss certain broad characteristics of the Treasury and its economic thinking.

Two central points should be established from the outset. First, the Treasury did not consider that its primary responsibilities included the levels of production and employment. Rather its traditional functions were those of budgetary control and debt management. While the First World War, and immediate postwar administrative reforms [39], broadened Treasury functions, and there developed a wider conception of its responsibilities for economic policy, this development was always seen as secondary. The integration of the secondary with the primary functions – this, of course, being the essence of the Keynesian revolution in economic policy-making – was not to be fully realized between the wars. The Keynesian historiography, which has assumed that the Treasury should have been primarily concerned with full employment, is therefore guilty of anachronism.

Second, the Treasury view was not a narrow Treasury departmental view, but a broader and more general Whitehall view. The infamous *Memoranda on Certain Proposals Relating to Unemployment* [107], the Baldwin government's reply to the Liberal proposals, and the principal document upon which all accounts of the Treasury view have been founded, contained contributions from all the principal departments concerned. The Treasury view in fact mirrored opinions widely held within government, the financial and business communities, and the general public who saw much elementary wisdom in its emphasis upon sound finance. This orthodoxy can be decomposed into six essential elements.

First, note needs to be made of the balanced budget rule, the cornerstone of the Treasury view. While this rule was to be denigrated by Keynes and others as 'some unthinking Victorian moral code which had nothing whatsoever to do with the rational conduct of government affairs' [37, 46–7], it was perceived by Whitehall and a wider opinion as an essential constraint upon the otherwise inherent biases of the fiscal system to over-expenditure and deficit-finance. These biases or weaknesses in the fiscal constitution centred on fears of profligacy of politicians in a democratic, pluralist setting. The balanced budget rule acted as the ultimate constraint on the growth of expenditure, since it moderated and tempered the natural demands of politicians and sectional interests for new expenditure, and provided a 'neutral' framework within which competing demands were reconciled. Of course, the balanced budget rule is more usually associated with the Treasury's conception of the crowding out of private expenditures that would follow from deficit-finance, but its perceived function as a constitutional discipline must not be left out of account.

Secondly, the political dimension of the balanced budget rule made the Treasury prefer monetary to fiscal instruments. With monetary probity secured by the independence of the Bank of England, monetary instruments were perceived as in a sense politically neutral, providing less scope than fiscal instruments for politicians to interfere with the operation of market forces for the benefit of particular groups, and guarded against the situation in which politicians, for electoral purposes, pursued expenditure and tax policies against the long-term public interest.

Thirdly, the state of confidence, both domestic and foreign, was crucial. Apprehension (later made legitimate by the 1931 crisis) that the government's financial policy would be viewed abroad a[s] 'unsound', with the risk of an outflow of sterling (with grav[e] consequences for the domestic credit base) and upward pressure o[n] short-term interest rates, imposed an external constraint upo[n] policy-making. The strict standards required to act as a leadin[g] financial centre imbued economic policy with a moral dimensio[n] which, by the interwar years, acted to Britain's disadvantage becaus[e] it made imperative more exacting standards of financial conduct tha[n] those adhered to by other countries.

Fourthly, there had developed a strong and apparently irration[al] fear of inflation by those who had witnessed the continental inflation of the early 1920s. This was to influence many of the policy decision[s] of the period, notably the return to the gold standard in 1925 and th[e] heroic efforts made to remain on gold in 1931. While Treasur[y] officials saw no automatic or theoretical connection between defici[t] finance and inflation, the two were strongly associated in the publi[c] mind and a risk-aversive Treasury did all that it could to avo[id] arousing public fears.

Fifthly, the business community in particular objected to larg[e] scale public works on several grounds. They viewed them [as] undesirable politically, because their successful execution woul[d] necessitate greatly increased state powers and interference i[n] industry. On economic grounds, it was believed that fiscal operation[s] were incapable of permanently raising the level of employment because they did little to improve the economy's productive base and thus the policy would flounder on fears that the increased de[bt] charge would eventually have to be financed by higher taxation. Th[e] *prospect* of such an increase in taxation might anyway itself ensure th[e] failure of such a policy as a result of businesses (and consumer[s]) revising their expectations and adjusting their spending downwar[d] to meet the future higher taxation.

Finally, however serious the unemployment problem, no remedi[al] action should be taken which might entail disbenefits for tho[se] remaining in employment, always the majority of the labour forc[e]. Thus there was an embargo on policies which might impair curre[nt] income or future growth prospects. Similarly, businessmen shou[ld] not be encouraged to seek state assistance, for this would threaten[a] debilitation of entrepreneurial independence with consequent adver[se] effects for growth. It was within such a spirit that public works we[re] rejected, their possible disbenefits being particularly marked relati[ve] to unemployment benefit payments which could be easily presente[d] as quite the most economical response to mass unemployment.

With this backcloth we can now proceed to specify the Treasu[ry] view, to show that properly defined it was very different from t[he] orthodox Keynesian view of it. We begin with certain practical difficulties associated with the Liberal programme. These were not a mere screen for more fundamental, and largely indefensible, theoretical objections. Rather, they formed an essential part of the Treasury's conception of the crowding-out process.

To Whitehall, the Liberal programme (and other similar programmes of the 1930s) completely understated the technical and administrative problems of large-scale public works. They ignored or underplayed the crucial requirements of adequate planning machinery, effective central co-ordination of spending agencies (especially local authorities which undertook the greater part of public investment) and pre-prepared unemployment plans. The British administrative system, in particular the relations between central and local government, was quite unsuitable – without major and politically highly contentious reforms – for what would have been required of it [200; 201, 51–6, 152–3, 179–80]. The Liberals had pledged that on the basis of their detailed plans, the programme 'would begin to absorb Labour within three months of the adoption of policy, and would before the end of twelve months reduce the numbers of unemployed workers to normal proportions' [177, 9]. This was particularly contentious, for upon closer inspection there were no detailed plans [107, 22–3]. This was hardly surprising since opposition parties were denied Whitehall's access to information and were not in a position to compile such plans and accordingly laboured at an immense disadvantage. All subsequent programmes in the 1930s suffered from a similar problem of credibility over the time-scale of their execution. This was important because it affected the public's perception of such schemes, which, in turn, through a confidence effect, diminished their effectiveness.

There was an additional set of problems with the Liberal programme. It did not analyse the state of the labour market, but merely assumed that the 1.4 million unemployed in the spring of 1929 were permanently unemployed and available for employment on public works (essentially road programmes). The dynamics of the labour market, the flows on to and off the unemployment register, were ignored; the Liberals overstated the cyclical character of unemployment; and failed to appreciate the difficulty of matching labour (both occupationally and geographically) required for the schemes to the available labour supply.

These points bring us to the heart of the Treasury view and to the notion of crowding out. It is the Keynesian orthodoxy that because there were over one million unemployed in 1929, then the Treasury could only argue that a deficit-financed demand stimulus crowded out a comparable volume of private investment, if they also, consciously or unconsciously, adhered to the Ricardian full employ ment assumption 'that all factors of production are normally and inevitably utilized by private business, [and] . . . that the State can obtain the use of such factors only by preventing private business from using them' [248, 86].

In discussing the crowding out issue it is first necessary to distinguish between real productive resources and financial resources, a distinction not always made evident in the literature. Our concern here is with the latter, although the Ministry of Labour's objection to the Liberal programme centred upon real resources, in the form of labour supply.

Financial crowding out may be described in the following manner: with a given money stock, an increase in bond sales to the non banking sector (to finance a budget deficit and/or public works programme) would have little or no impact on aggregate demand because the rise in interest rates required to sell the additional bonds would crowd out an equivalent volume of other expenditures (private investment and consumption, in so far as they are interest-elastic). In its most extreme form, therefore, it would be held that fiscal operations could not affect the level, only the composition, of aggregate demand.

Unfortunately, the use of such arguments during the interwar period was characterized by a failure to specify clearly what factors were operating to raise interest rates and the channels through which they operated. Two main alternatives suggest themselves.

(1) That with a fixed money stock and at a position of full employment, the financing of a deficit purely by bond sales crowds out private expenditure because extra transaction balances are required for a higher level of incomes and these will be released from asset balances only as interest rates rise.

(2) Also with a fixed money stock but at a position of less than full employment (or, indeed, irrespective of the pressure of demand in the labour market), a deficit financed by bond sales would crowd out private expenditure if there was sufficient opposition to, and apprehension about, the government's policy that there was an increased demand for cash balances (a change in liquidity preference) which prevented idle balances from taking up the additional bonds without raising interest rates.

The first case represents what is commonly termed crowding out and has been taken as a description of the Treasury view. However it is the second case, which can be viewed as a form of psychological crowding out, which in fact best represents the Treasury view. Thus for the Treasury, much of the Liberal Party's case for public works was misdirected and irrelevant. For example, the Liberals and Keynes expended much effort in arguing that borrowing for public works would not impinge on the supply of capital available for private investment, because it would be financed from idle balances existing in a depression, a reduction in net overseas lending and the savings to the budget (reduced outlay on unemployments benefits, etc) consequent upon the higher level of employment generated by the fiscal stimulus, whereas the Treasury's real concern was its ability to market government debt without a crisis of confidence.

From this there has resulted a complete misspecification of the Treasury view. One myth in particular needs to be dispelled immediately. At no time did the Treasury doubt, *ceteris paribus*, that in the short-term state expenditure could raise aggregate demand and employment. The Treasury were not, as Keynes accused them, 'trying to solve the problem of unemployment with a theory which is based on the assumption that there is no unemployment' [158, *350*]. Rather, they contended that, largely irrespective of the pressure of demand in the labour market, a number of constraints – disruptive intermediaries – would operate to neutralize the favourable effects of state expenditure if it was on the 'huge' scale envisaged by the Liberals (objections not applicable to smaller-scale projects). In any case, such a policy was undesirable because it failed to offer a permanent solution to mass unemployment.

The Treasury's case was founded upon the difficulties of the staple industries, where approximately one-half of the insured unemployed were concentrated [3, *146*]. The cause was seen as high production costs; the problem was how to reduce them. While, by 1929, unit wage costs in UK industry had fallen by 5 per cent since Britain returned to the gold standard at an overvalued exchange rate in 1925 [208, *table 8*], the Treasury were extremely cautious about future developments. The atmosphere following the 1926 General Strike was not conducive to an attack upon real wage resistance. Thus, constrained by the gold standard and its professed faith in the efficacy of free market forces, the Treasury promoted rationalization in the hope that the long-term employment so generated would more than compensate for the short-term labour shedding (see Kirby's Chapter 10 on the rationalization movement).

From this standpoint, two objections were advanced against large-scale public works. First, even assuming that the schemes were feasible, they 'would concentrate employment in a marked degree upon individual trades which [were] neither unsheltered nor unprosperous . . . and while increasing employment and profit making there would be little or nothing for the depressed basic trades'. Secondly, this concentration of employment would result in supply bottlenecks, generating cost pressures, which would then b transmitted throughout the economy. The final effect would be worsening of the already diminished competitiveness of the expo sector, and perhaps also increased import penetration: seriou consequences given the then prevailing gold standard, and th precarious external balance.[1]

In turn, these objections followed from two central tenets interwar Treasury thinking. First, the Treasury were antipathet towards the notion, implicit in Keynes's and others' writings, of th homogeneity of demand impulses – a reflection of their essentiall microeconomic or structural diagnosis of the unemployment proble and of the way in which they viewed income generation. The concep of 'industry', in the aggregate, was rejected as a mere abstraction one that led to potentially destabilizing policy actions.[2] Secondly and not unconnected, was the belief in what might be termed th 'normal channels of trade', the policy implications of this being tha public investment was a complement to that of the private sector, n a substitute for it. It was held that public works on any substanti scale distorted the course of economic activity from its norm channels (determined by relative prices), made the ultimate transitic to normal employment patterns more difficult, and forced period reflationary stimuli in order to permanently sustain the higher lev of employment.[3]

The reasons for the Treasury's dismissal of Keynes's contentic that a public works programme gained additional justification fro its positive social rate of return should by now be clear. Whi accepting the logic of this argument at the level of the individu project, its validity was questioned at the macro level where a gener reaction against the programmes might be expected, this leading the establishment of forces which acted to neutralize at the nation level any local benefits accruing from the schemes. We should no properly specify this neutralizing mechanism – the disruptiv intermediaries.

We noted earlier that the Treasury accepted that small-scale publ works programmes would generate employment. Why then did oppose large-scale programmes? In essence because the init expansion of demand would be neutralized if it did not flow throug the 'normal channels of trade' (or even through a rearmame programme). Two Treasury judgements were involved at this poin First, that 'Keynes, with all his brilliance, appears frequently misunderstand the psychology of the markets' in assuming th public works should be warmly welcomed because of their theoretic potentialities.[4] Second, that 'the atmosphere in which [public work schemes may be undertaken will itself condition the immedia consequences which they produce' [108, 20]. These disruptive intermediaries that neutralized the potentialities of public works (or budget deficits) assumed two forms.

First, account needs to be taken of a deflationary reaction to the announcement of the introduction of the public works programme, a reaction composed of two distinct elements. The first relates to the adverse confidence effect upon the business community, whereby entrepreneurs view the programme as creating a highly artificial situation, this resulting in a revision of their perception of future profitability and thus a contractionary shift in their investment demand schedule. The second, to the fact that the programme was concentrated upon a narrow range of industries (facing upward-sloping marginal cost schedules) and that this would, in aggregate, generate shortages and price rises which would tend to cause some curtailment of private, and perhaps even public, sector investment.

Secondly, this deflationary reaction to the initial fiscal stimulus was compounded by deflationary monetary consequences – higher interest rates which would have jeopardized the Treasury's other, *prior* objectives by making debt management more difficult and expensive and by adding to industry's debt burden. As Hopkins, a senior Treasury official, put it:

> I should have thought that a scheme of this kind so far from setting up a cycle of prosperity would produce a great cry against bureaucracy . . . and so far from it producing a general willingness to invest in these vast Government loans I should have thought that the loans would have to be put out at a very high price. [108, *18*]

From this Treasury judgement upon the state of confidence, it follows that the monetary consequences of the introduction of the public works programme were also deflationary: the initial fiscal stimulus inducing a change in liquidity preference (a lessened preference for bonds), the operative intermediary here being the fear of inflation. As earlier, this reaction was also composed of two distinct elements. The first relates to the adverse confidence effect on the financial community noted above, whereby bond-holders viewed unfavourably the government's departure from fiscal orthodoxy, doubted the logic of the Keynesian case, and judged that unbalanced budgets could not be indefinitely financed from bond sales to the non-banking sector without an inevitable crisis and resulting inflation. The second relates to an increased preference for equities relative to gilt-edged, this is a response to the inflation expected to be generated (by real causes) as a result of the pursuance of the Liberal programme.

Thus, the Treasury view might have been administratively

conservative, but it did not stem from some unthinking adherence to classical economics. The Treasury view was founded upon a firm and logical model of crowding out which was crucially dependent upon confidence. By virtue of its intangibility confidence cannot be accurately specified or measured; that fact, however, hardly questions its existence or potency. As we shall see, the maintenance of confidence was to dominate the policy-making stage for the whole of the 1930s, there being no discernible lessening of business and financial opposition to the Keynesian solution.

The Treasury View and Employment Policy in the 1930s

To begin with, we should briefly note the 1929–31 Labour government's experience of actually conducting a large-scale public works programme. Such were the technical and administrative problems that by June 1930, a full year after taking office, schemes approved only totalled £110.1 million, while even a year later, at their peak, schemes actually in operation totalled but £107.7 million on an annual basis [201, *165*]. These results were criticized by Lloyd George, Mosley and others as totally inadequate, a reflection of the government's conservatism, obstructionism and lack of real commitment to the policy. Within Whitehall, however, where it was believed with some justification that the policy had been pursued to the fullest extent possible, the conclusion drawn was that the programme's poor results vindicated Whitehall's earlier objections to such policies. This experience confirmed the Treasury view, and influenced the public works debate for the remainder of the 1930s.

The Labour government's public works programmes terminated with the budgetary and gold standard crisis of August–September 1931. The experiment was not to be repeated, this despite both widespread opposition to the apparent embargo on public works and the regained freedom afforded by the abandonment of the gold standard. The latter might have been expected to lead to a major reorientation of policy thereafter. And in a sense it did. For within nine months the Treasury had adopted a cheap money policy and protective tariffs, and the Bank of England was actively (but covertly) managing the sterling exchange to Britain's competitive advantage [136, *86–9*; 138]. While under the gold standard regime there had been no essential divergence of views between the Treasury and the Bank [290], the abandonment of gold did allow the Treasury to regain effective control of monetary and exchange rate policy. The Bank, like the Treasury, had long favoured cheap money; the low and floating exchange rate after 1932 was more a Treasury initiative, being conceived *inter alia* as an alternative to wage cuts [138, *32–3*] (which were politically unacceptable), as a means of breaking the political and economic impasse of the gold standard years. Specific intervention at a microeconomic level and a regional policy were also to develop in the following years. However, Britain almost alone of the major Western countries refused to promote recovery by deficit-finance.

The National government's unemployment policy came under serious and concerted attack in 1933 and 1935, as represented by the reflationary programmes proposed by Keynes in *The Means to Prosperity* [158, *335–66*] and Lloyd George in his 'New Deal'. On both occasions, the government's response was to allow a limited expansion of public works, whilst rejecting the general case for large-scale loan-financed expenditures. The relaxation of Treasury opposition was thus more apparent than real: it was largely a response to certain political pressures. There was a need to mollify the more progressive government back-benchers, pacify the opposition, and be seen to be taking account of the change in public opinion since the 1931 crisis measures. It was an acknowledgement of the opportunities afforded by gradually improving economic conditions, where public investment might play a supporting, not initiatory, role. There was no discernible lessening of the theoretical objections to public works.

A new factor had intervened: that of cheap money. This policy had long been a Treasury objective, a means of promoting industrial recovery (assuming the interest elasticity of investment expenditures) and of relieving budgetary pressure (by reducing the interest charge on the National Debt); and once instituted it was to become – with tariffs – the centrepiece of domestic recovery policy [136; 203]. However, cheap money was not without its costs. While recent research has reaffirmed the traditional view that cheap money underlay the strong recovery of 1932–7 [78, *338–40*; 136, *ch. 5*; cf. 2, *3–64*], it was also to inhibit the adoption of other, less orthodox policy instruments. In particular, the authorities' fear that cheap money would be threatened – via adverse confidence effects – by a policy of deficit-finance and/or resumption of large-scale public works programmes acted to reinforce the commitment to an orthodox budgeting policy. Thus a trade-off existed, that between an active monetary policy and an expansionist fiscal policy.[5]

Orthodoxy was also assured during Chamberlain's tenure as Chancellor (November 1931 to May 1937). His belief that unemployment constituted a long-term problem, one not susceptible to non-market solutions or palliatives like public works, was combined with adherence to a hair-shirt philosophy of economic management which saw virtue and economic salvation in the moral courage to rejec 'easy' policies such as those offered by the Keynesian solution [201 *114–5, 186–7*].

This professed orthodoxy, however, should not obscure certai important features of budgetary policy. While the fiscal stance di not support the recovery, and owed little to the influence of Keynes the Treasury cannot be accused of financial orthodoxy in an nineteenth-century sense. The period saw a number of majo departures from orthodoxy: the virtual abandonment of sinking fun payments and the use of fiscal window-dressing to conceal deficits both of which lessened the deflationary consequences of the balance budget rule. However, in a wider sense the influence of th nineteenth-century fiscal constitution on policy formulation is clearl discernible, in the refusal to countenance deliberately unbalance budgets and in the reliance on 'normal channels' to promot recovery. The Treasury was only to have recourse to deficit-financ with the advent of rearmament.

Indeed, it is with the later 1930s and rearmament that a change i Treasury thinking has been identified; the view of its continue theoretical orthodoxy being challenged, and substantially modifie first by Howson, and later by Howson and Winch [136; 140]. Such revision can be taken too far. While the evidence does not suppo Hutchison's sweeping statement 'that both the Treasury and th Bank were largely converted to "Keynesian policies" . . . *at least year before the publication of The General Theory*' [143, *155*], there sufficient evidence for the more limited conclusion, that in the real of monetary policy, Treasury economic thinking was increasingl influenced by Keynes and other economists.

As regards fiscal policy, and public works in particular, Howso and Winch have established that by the later 1930s, the Treasury w prepared to countenance public works as a stabilization instrume in any possible future recession, a change they attributed to Keynes growing influence [140, *134–48*]. By contrast, Peden's researches le him to conclude that before the Second World War 'the Treasu remained sceptical about the use of public works as a cure f unemployment' [222, *6*]. In fact, there is no necessary contradicti between these two views. The case rests on the motives for, a permanence of, the change in Treasury policy.

On the basis of *a priori* logic a change in official attitudes towar public works at this time would appear perfectly plausible. Economi had become more united in their support for, and more convinci in their theoretical justifications of, public works, while t favourable effects of rearmament expenditures on employment cou be taken as a demonstration of the legitimacy of the general case f deficit-finance. The empirical basis of these influences has been well documented [293, *ch. 9*], but their *actual* influence on the course of events has by no means been proven. Indeed, when subject to closer examination, it becomes clear that the Treasury's support for what appears to be a Keynesian policy measure (a policy in fact never pursued because of the war) was actually a development of no particular long-term significance.

The operative forces were rather less theoretical developments or Keynes's influence than the interaction of changing political and economic circumstances occasioned by the finance and management of the rearmament programme. First, the decision to finance rearmament partly by borrowing had created a precedent with serious political repercussions for the issue of loan-financed public works in peacetime. Secondly, as the growth of defence expenditure accelerated in 1938–9, there developed the first tentative attempts to actively manage demand – in a Keynesian sense – using the budget as an instrument of economic policy. By the time of the April 1939 budget the Treasury was awaiting the achievement of full employment – induced by the greatly expanded military outlays – for only then could taxation be significantly increased. Full employment, with its accompanying higher level of savings, would also permit greater borrowings from the non-banking sector. These were important changes in fiscal policy. They were, however, partially (and deliberately) obscured from public view as the Treasury sought to maintain the appearance of orthodoxy. As with earlier periods, the objective at this time was to maintain confidence. The Treasury felt that the size of borrowing in 1939/40 was such that it could be financed, without inflation, only by raising aggregate demand. While defence expenditure would, *ceteris paribus*, ensure this end, a collapse of confidence with its consequent adverse effect on private sector demand would jeopardize this increase and therefore the increase in current savings felt to be necessary. The question of confidence thus assumed a new meaning.

Conclusions

It has been shown that by 1939 fiscal and other instruments were being used to actively manage aggregate demand, but that this was not evidence of official acceptance of Keynesian principles of demand management. While 'increased public expenditure, albeit not the kind advocated by the economists, did indeed combat the slump' of 1937–8 [136, *139*], government was still far from accepting as one of its 'primary aims and responsibilities the maintenance of a high and stable level of employment' [117, 3]. Thus we need to acknowledge that rearmament engendered rather special circumstances in the later 1930s, ones in which a retrospective assessment may lead us to infer erroneously that the effects of a policy were actually intended at the time of its inception. Deficit-finance after 1937 may well have created a precedent for later peacetime economic management, but that was not the authorities' intention.

Indeed, the rearmament phase was seen as but a temporary lapse from orthodoxy. Had war not intervened the Treasury intended imposing balanced budgets in 1942/3, when the rearmament programme was completed and borrowing powers terminated. Nor did the observation that rearmament expenditures were directly stimulating employment give validity to Keynes's policy prescriptions or his theoretical position. Rather, it highlighted and reinforced what the Treasury had always maintained: that public expenditure could only be used, and would only be effective, as an employment measure in special circumstances, these dependent upon a favourable concatenation of political, economic and psychological factors.

Although axiomatic that any commitment to 'full' employment still lay in the future, there had none the less occurred important changes in official and ministerial thinking about unemployment since the early 1920s. For example, the belief in the market's efficacy, constantly alluded to in the 1920s, had by the mid-1930s definitely been superseded by a more pessimistic philosophy which ascribed a much enlarged role to government and recognized the case for stabilization.

Such progress is vividly illustrated by a comparison between the recessions of 1920–1 and 1937–8, the former being exacerbated by government financial policies, the latter eventually overcome by fiscal policy, albeit under the guise of rearmament. In the intervening period the authorities had become much more self-confident about their ability to influence the economy. This was essential if they were ever successfully to assume a full demand management responsibility. Similarly, the political preference for monetary rather than fiscal instruments had also to be overcome. This was to prove a more intractable problem, since it was contingent upon a demonstration that politicians could use Keynesian budgetary instruments in responsible manner.

After 1931 economic nationalism pervaded the thoughts and actions of British policy-makers, which although tempered by imperial reality was nevertheless very different from attitude prevailing in the 1920s. Moreover, if we interpret Keynesian economic management as requiring that the needs of the domestic economy be acknowledged as paramount, then the 1930s witnessed wo important developments. First, the increased independence of he British economy from the vagaries of the world economy was iirrored by a monetary policy which now directly served the needs f the domestic economy, not the external account as under the gold tandard. Secondly, there was a strengthening of the controls over oreign investment, a course of action long sought by Keynes as a uttress for an active domestic recovery policy.

While the Treasury view was undoubtedly responsible for the light on adopting the Keynesian policy alternative, the broader onfidence issue must also be taken into account. With the advent of he new classical macroeconomics it is now accepted that the private ector response to a change in taxes or transfer payments will depend pon expectations of the duration of the income change, whether ransitory or permanent. More fundamentally, when economic ehaviour depends upon expectations of economic behaviour, the ffects of policy in one period and economic structure cannot utomatically be applied to another age or structure [184]. Thus, ven if Keynesian stabilization policies were successful in maintaining ull employment until the late 1960s, no useful guide is offered to the ossibilities for successfully applying such policies in interwar ritain – the earlier age being marked not just by a different conomic structure but also by pre-Keynesian expectations of the ehaviour of the public and private sectors.

In the early 1930s, when fiscal policy was founded upon the alanced budget rule, the appearance of a deficit during the epression led to expectations of higher taxation which exacerbated epression through its effect upon private sector expenditures. onversely, in the postwar period, during the phase when fiscal olicy was the central instrument for securing full employment, tax acreases were not expected in recessions and private sector xpenditures supported the policy stance. In a study of the postwar JS economy, Baily has shown how the behaviour of the corporate ector was quite different in the mid-1960s, when it was expected nat an active stabilization policy would secure full employment and igh growth, from earlier periods, when other objectives prevailed; nd that rational expectations of monetary and fiscal policies not only o not nullify the intended influence of these policies but actually einforce their effect upon economic stability [8]. On this reasoning, is clear that, for example, the case of the US economy in the 1930s, here the 'New Deal' and deficit-finance failed to stimulate full ecovery, had an important demonstration effect for business and olicy-makers alike. Without a positive demonstration of fiscal olicy's potency – in the context of a largely unregulated market conomy, rather than in, say, Nazi Germany – it is difficult to

conceive of the creation of expectations which would so moul
private sector expenditure behaviour as to allow fiscal policy
effectiveness. Hence the importance of the Second World War as
demonstration of a successful, responsible Keynesian fiscal policy.

Notes

This chapter is drawn from my recently published study of the Treasury an
economic policy in the 1930s, *Towards the Managed Economy* [201]. I shoul
like to thank the ESRC, Houblon-Norman Fund and the University o
Durham for financial support; the Controller of HM Stationery Office fo
permission to cite Public Record Office documents; and my colleague Phili
Williamson, and the editors of this volume, for their helpful comments on a
early draft.

1 Public Record Office (hereafter PRO) T175/26, R. V. N. Hopkins, 'Th
   Liberal Plan. Draft notes for evidence', undated (but internal evidenc
   suggests early May 1930), pp. 6–7.
2 PRO T175/26, F. W. Leith-Ross, 'The assumptions of Mr Keynes', 2
   February 1930; F. W. Leith-Ross, 'Note on Mr. Keynes' exposition to th
   Committee on Finance and Industry. Discussion of 20/02/30', 28 Marc
   1930.
3 PRO T175/89, Note by F. Phillips, 31 January 1935, para. 4.
4 PRO T175/104, pt. 1, F. W. Leith-Ross, 'Twenty-sixth EAC report', 2
   December 1938.
5 See Neville Chamberlain's 1933 budget speech – *Hansard* (House
   Commons), 5th series, vol. 277, 25 April 1933, col. 61.

10

Industrial Policy

M. W. KIRBY

n a wide-ranging survey of the relationship between economic hought and policy between the wars, Donald Winch concluded that >y 1939 British governments had assembled the essential ingredients f the postwar mixed economy [294; 293, *223–9*]. Such legislative nactments as the enforced amalgamation of the railway companies n 1921, the creation of the Central Electricity Board in 1926 and the artelization of coal and agriculture after 1930 bear witness to the ncreasing penetration of government into the internal affairs of ndustry. Whilst the pre-1914 British state had made progressive nroads into the principle of non-intervention as it sought to create an nstitutional environment conducive to the efficient functioning of rivate enterprise, it is legitimate to argue that the interwar period ʋas notable for an extension of state power of such magnitude that he ideal of *laissze-faire* in the peacetime economy was irrevocably ndermined [16, *279*]. There is a danger, however, that an account f government industrial policy which highlights the antecedents of he mixed economy will convey the impression that the movement ɔwards state collectivism was elevated to a conscious strategy for conomic progress. Once the focus of attention is broadened to nclude the manufacturing sector in addition to those industries ʋhich were to be transformed into public utilities, government olicy can be viewed as vacillating and ambiguous. Circumstances ıay very well have been forcing the pace of intervention throughout he industrial economy but there is ample evidence that the redominantly Conservative administrations of the interwar period ʋere concerned to resist the collectivist trend in order to preserve the ıstitutions and mechanisms of capitalist free enterprise [123, *51–2*]. he purpose of this chapter is to analyse the record of government-ndustry relations between the wars with a view to explaining the

inconsistencies in the state's response to the collapse of prosperity fo
those industries which had provided the dynamics of expansion fo
the Victorian economy, Why, for example, was intervention in th
cotton textile industry to achieve desired organizational change
delayed until the later 1930s whilst the coalmining industry, whos
market conditions were no more adverse, was subjected to a highly
restrictive scheme of central action involving a statutory carte
system and powers of compulsory amalgamation at the outset of th
decade? Why, too, did the state act to establish centralized contro
over the electricity supply industry as early as 1926 but delay th
attempt to impose a form of national co-ordination on the iron an
steel industry until the mid–1930s? The answers to such question
will serve to underline the manifold influences on policy-makers
from technocratic and commercial considerations to motives c
political expediency (reinforced on occasion by ideological rigidities
and social amelioration. It is also pertinent to ask whether at the en
of the interwar period the state had fashioned a set of interventionis
instruments which could be termed an industrial policy *per se*, or wa
the record of intervention too haphazard and pragmatic for th
emergence of clearly defined principles? Finally, it is worthwhil
paying some attention to the effects of government policy: in othe
words, was the general movement towards state collectivism o
balance beneficial or harmful to the industrial sector?

The Effects of the First World War

Any analysis of government-industry relations between the wai
must begin with the legacy of the First World War. It is, of course,
commonplace to emphasize that although the state assumed unpre
cedented powers over the industrial sector, the abandonment c
wartime controls after 1918 was inevitable [263]. Thus, the wartim
economy may have been a remarkable achievement, not least i
terms of the impetus it gave to the introduction of standardized mas
production techniques and automatic machinery in the munition
related industries, yet 'It left Britain with an unfamiliar econom
organisation devoted to unfamiliar ends' [7, *284*]. Although it ha
been argued more recently that, but for a reprehensible degree c
financial parsimony on the part of the Treasury, reformist influenc
were as strong as those in favour of reaction in the immediate postwi
years [180], the image of a state anxious to divest itself of th
apparatus of intervention remains substantially intact. Nowhere wi

this more evident than in the coalmining industry where the postwar controversy over nationalization and decontrol served to politicize the issue of industrial reorganization to the extent that dispassionate consideration of the merits or otherwise of state intervention was virtually precluded for the whole of the 1920s, if not beyond [169, *80*].

The lack of an intellectual conversion to the merits of a greater degree of government participation in economic affairs and a politically charged labour relations crisis in the coalmining industry were not the only factors impelling the state towards decontrol. Equally important were the postwar boom and the rise of the Treasury as the most powerful Whitehall department. In the former case, the need to restock and reconvert industrial capacity for peacetime purposes created a business outlook in which state controls were regarded as a serious impediment to economic recovery, especially in view of the straitened economic circumstances confronting Germany, Britain's powerful prewar competitor [62]. The boom was, in fact, of critical importance in creating structural rigidities which were to plague large sections of British industry throughout the 1920s. The buying and selling of iron and steel, shipbuilding and cotton textiles firms at vastly inflated prices, often on the basis of borrowed money from a highly liquid banking system, was justified by expectations of an increase in market demand which failed to materialize due to the onward march of the American and Japanese economies, and the resurgence of Germany after 1924. As export markets were lost, therefore, high-cost, under-capacity working came to be the norm in the staple industries such that by the end of the 1920s many firms were dependent for their survival on the willingness of the clearing banks to accommodate mounting overdrafts. As for the Treasury, it is important to note that it emerged from the war not only with enhanced powers and duties in the areas of external finance and exchange policy, but also with a determination to curtail public expenditure and to impose centralized control over the Civil Service establishment. Financial orthodoxy, therefore, was to prove a powerful brake on any industrial policy initiative which entailed subventions from public funds [40].

For all these reasons, a war in which the state had forged new links with the industrial sector placed major impediments in the way of closer government–industry relations in peacetime. It is true that the policy of the Ministry of Munitions in encouraging mergers and the adoption of best practice techniques over wide sections of the engineering industry can be regarded as an important progenitor of the rationalization movement of the later 1920s (see below) and that many of the businessmen who were to support the movement

towards large-scale amalgamation in British industry first became
alerted to the possibilities of scale economies as a result of their
experience as administrators in wartime production departments
[300, *48–9*; 274, *13*; 236, *241*], but these are hindsight observations.
The fact remains that the majority of contemporary businessmen and
politicians regarded bureaucratic controls as anathema in the context
of a peacetime economy. In any event, the Ministry of Munitions was
hardly likely to be viewed as a suitable model for the postwar world
when its very real achievements in the area of production were
entirely dependent upon the abandonment of cost constraints and the
overruling of vested interests at a time when the nation was fighting
for survival [214, *760*].

Thus, by the mid-1920s, government-industry relations had
reverted in most respects to their prewar pattern of regulation,
notably with regard to company law and statutory obligations in the
area of employee safety. The principal exception was the Safeguarding
of Industries Act of 1921 which endowed a small number of
strategically important 'key industries' with a degree of tariff
protection. The issue of a general tariff was raised explicitly by the
Conservative Party in the general election of 1923 when the Baldwin
government attempted to persuade the electorate that protection
would make an important contribution to the resolution of the
unemployment crisis ushered in by the collapse of the postwar boom
in 1920. The Conservative defeat and the evident divisions among
industrialists themselves, even within the tariff-conscious iron and
steel trades, merely served to reinforce the arm's-length nature of
government-industry relations. On returning to office in 1924, the
Conservatives, having promised not to introduce a general tariff
without consulting the electorate, were obliged to concentrate their
energies on attempting to revive the level of British staple exports by
resurrecting the pre-1914 international economic infrastructure. The
focal point of government endeavour in this respect was restoration
of the gold standard.

As early as 1918, the Cunliffe Committee had reported that a
return to gold was 'the only effective remedy for an adverse balance
of trade and an undue growth of credit'. By the mid-1920s, fear of
inflation was still a prime consideration in determining the course of
monetary policy, but with the emergence of the 'hard-core million'
unemployed in the staple export trades both the Treasury and the
Bank of England had come to accept that the establishment of a fixed
currency and stable exchanges would provide 'the essential framework
for a sound and permanent revival of trade and industry' [290, *106*].
As such, the restoration of the gold standard at the prewar sterling-
dollar parity in April 1925 can be viewed as part of a clearly

perceived strategy for industrial revival even though the underlying rationale for the decision was provided by a narrowly conceived interpretation of Britain's economic interests which accorded primacy to external finance [293, *92–8*; 272, *92–105*].

The debate on the effects of the return to gold on industry has focused on the issues of overvaluation as it affected the level of exports and also on the deflationary impact of the restrictive monetary stance that the gold standard policy entailed. According to Keynes, the adoption of the prewar parity led to an overvaluation of 10 per cent in relation to the dollar, but recent calculations, using a 'basket of currencies' approach, have pointed to a rate of overvaluation approaching 20–25 per cent in 1925, with the rate still above 10 per cent in 1930 [237]. It would appear, therefore, that the return to gold was a serious handicap for British exporters. Moggridge, for example, has suggested that a 10 per cent lower exchange rate in 1928 would have boosted employment by 729,000 [208, *98–112, 245–50*], while Pressnell has stressed the employment-creating effects of an imperial devaluation of the pound which would have raised the competitiveness of sterling in third markets and also within sterling markets themselves [234]. It has also been estimated that a 10 per cent higher value of sterling in 1924 could have raised unemployment in the workforce by 1.3 per cent, a figure which masks the disproportionate loss of jobs resulting from overvaluation in those regions with an industrial structure dominated by the staple export trades [149]. Whilst it is likely that sterling devaluation would have been countered by competitive devaluations with the added possibility of raised tariff barriers against British goods, there can be little doubt that an overvalued currency exacerbated the problem of localized unemployment in a situation where labour markets were subject to rigidities arising from a marked degree of geographical immobility, the product in part of industry-specific skills. On the subject of domestic monetary policy, it is generally accepted that it, too, had an adverse effect on industry. Although interest rates in the 1920s fluctuated far less than in the period before 1914, this hardly compensated for the increased cost of borrowing; credit restriction increased the cost of servicing the National Debt and therefore penalized industry with a heightened tax burden which was all the more onerous in the context of mounting interest liabilities incurred during the postwar boom [4, *93*; 225, *73*].

Whatever the views of economic historians on monetary policy in the 1920s, it is incontrovertible that it created a climate of opinion within government and industry which stressed the vital necessity for cost, and therefore wage, reductions. This is exemplified in Baldwin's reported statement to a miners' delegation in July 1925 that 'all the workers of this country have got to take reductions in wages to help put industry on its feet'. These remarks were made during the opening stages of the most traumatic episode in Britain's industrial history between the wars – the General Strike and miners' lockout of 1926, an occurrence which was the inevitable outcome of an irreconcilable conflict between capital and labour centring on the issue of national versus district wage negotiations [169]. It matters little that the exporting difficulties of the coalmining industry pre-dated the return to gold and were intimately linked with the rise of competing sources of energy, overseas competition and, more especially, the resumption of German coal production in the aftermath of the Ruhr evacuation in 1924. The true significance of the crisis in British labour relations in the mid-1920s is that it marked a decisive challenge to the restoration of prewar 'normalcy' and presented the Baldwin government with an industrial policy dilemma which was to remain unresolved until the end of its period of office. Briefly, it was generally agreed at the highest levels of government that the coalmining industry contained too many units of production in view of the collapse of overseas demand. It was also agreed that the survival of any significant exporting capability in coalfields such as Northumberland and South Wales was dependent upon wage reductions. But the prospect of a Conservative administration forcing unwilling colliery owners to amalgamate their concerns in order to reduce surplus productive capacity raised political issues of first-class importance. Both Baldwin and his Minister of Labour, Sir Arthur Steel-Maitland, were aware that a programme of large-scale amalga-mations would seriously exacerbate the industry's existing unemploy-ment problem, whilst the spectre of nationalization, supposedly destroyed in 1921, could reappear and a precedent be established which, if it were applied to other ailing industrial sectors, would undermine the private enterprise system. Similarly, the alternative to wage reductions – a long term Treasury subsidy – was rejected on financial grounds and because it too could create a general precedent as well as providing a lever for nationalization [169, 82–5, 90, 102–6]. It has been argued that the government's muted response to the reorganization issue (permissive legislation in 1926 for the encouragement of amalgamation under private auspices) demonstrated a lamentable failure of imagination to grapple with the problem posed by the precipitate collapse of a major staple industry [226, 131–3]. The validity of such a view receives some confirmation from the fact that the state was simultaneously establishing a national co-ordinating authority in the electricity supply industry. But this is to ignore the essential point that the Central Electricity Board, although a public concern, enjoyed a large measure of political independence and was designed to be operated on commercial lines 'by practical men closely in touch with the industry'. This was 'government by subcontract' in a new sector of the economy unencumbered by a legacy of politically-motivated labour unrest and where technocratic considerations loomed large. Conservative politicians could, therefore, legitimately claim that the Electricity Supply Act of 1926 made no concessions to 'socialization' and the principles of public ownership [121, *207–26*; 122, *100–2*].

The events of 1926 provide a watershed of sorts in the evolution of interwar industrial policy. The General Strike itself demonstrated the excessively high cost in social and political terms of the imposition of wage reductions alone as a solution to the economic difficulties confronting exporting industries. This was openly admitted by Baldwin himself when he stated after the strike that he would 'not countenance any attempt on the part of employers to use the present occasion for trying in any way to get reductions in wages'. Employers in general heeded this injunction and the search began for less painful means of achieving cost reductions in order to regain export markets. It is against this background that the rationalization movement in British industry in the later 1920s should be considered.

Rationalization

'Rationalization' was to become a vogue word in the years after 1926 and although it was undoubtedly a 'cloak for confused ideas and sometimes . . . a badge of respectability for processes of doubtful value' [*Economist*, 7 Dec. 1929 cited in 123, *29*], it came to be synonymous with the movement towards amalgamation in British industry as a panacea for the loss of competitive efficiency endemic in the existence of surplus productive capacity. If horizontal integration was a direct means of overcoming the slowness of market forces in securing the elimination of marginal concerns in structurally fragmented industries, vertical integration could be viewed as essential for the achievement of large-scale economies in industries such as cotton textiles, and more especially, iron and steel. Rationalization owed its popularity, therefore, to increasing dissatisfaction with market mechanisms and a growing belief in the efficacy of large-scale business organization. It was conceded that amalgamations would have the immediate effect of increasing unemployment, but in the longer term, as industrial efficiency improved in response to technical and commercial economies, lost export markets would be regained and rationalized industries would begin to recruit more workers. The idea that rationalization was part of a structuralist solution to the unemployment problem appealed strongly to Conservative politicians in the late 1920s, notably to Cunliffe-Lister, at the Board of Trade and Steel-Maitland at the Ministry of Labour. By 1929, both ministers were in favour of an 'active' industrial policy and Cunliffe-Lister, disappointed at the slow rate of voluntary amalgamations in coalmining, had begun to prepare a scheme of state financial incentives to accelerate the process of integration. If the government had remained in office, however, it may be safely assumed that such initiatives would have foundered on the rock of Treasury opposition, even though they were not necessarily in conflict with the private enterprise system [169, *120–1*].

Superficially at least, the iron and steel industry provided a more promising field for rationalizing endeavours. It too was structurally fragmented, with a haphazard mixture of old and new plant operating at well below optimum capacity thus raising overhead costs to the detriment of competitive ability both at home and abroad. Cunliffe-Lister, Steel-Maitland and Baldwin were eager to see the industry rationalized and after 1924 the steelmakers themselves were increasingly in favour of a defensive tariff. Was a trade-off possible between these positions? The short answer is 'no', for the Baldwin government held to the view that protection, far from accelerating the pace of integration, would act as a decisive barrier to structural change in a ruggedly individualistic industry, bedevilled by entrenched vested interests and virulent boardroom animosities [221, *163–210*, 31]. For a Conservative government, the problem of precedent was yet again a critical consideration; how could a tariff for iron and steel be justified, even under the guise of safeguarding, when the industry's linkages with the rest of the economy would concede the general principle of protection [49, *61–76*]? After 1929, the succeeding Labour government shared the view that a tariff would delay reorganization and powerful elements within the Cabinet were opposed to protection on ideological grounds. In these circumstances, neither government had any effective means of forcing the industry in general to reorganize, with the result that attention was concentrated increasingly on individual firms which were vulnerable to the coercive power of bankers as a result of their inability to meet debt obligations incurred during the postwar boom. It was hardly surprising, therefore, that both the Conservative and Labour governments came to regard the clearing banks and the Bank of England as the most appropriate vehicles for industrial regeneration. The banks as proxy rationalizers, however, proved to be a broken reed. The clearing banks in general were unwilling to foreclose on loans as long as there was the prospect of trade revival, and enforced liquidations would inevitably lead to disputes over priority of claims [270, 94–5]. Even the Bank of England, which was favourably disposed towards rationalization on account of its deep involvement in the affairs of particular firms and its desire to strengthen the export trades [61, 318–59; 246, *vol. I, 314–30* and *vol. II, 546–51*], was not prepared to act as a cat's-paw for government. The Governor, Montagu Norman, was concerned to avoid 'the charge of domineering over industry through money trusts' [269, 60]. In this respect, it is ironic that the Bank's most ambitious forays into the business of rationalization via its own specially created institutions – the Securities Management Trust and the Bankers Industrial Development Company (BIDC) – were occasioned by Norman's fears that the Labour government would embark on a programme of nationalization for the iron and steel and cotton textile industries [270, 95–6]. These fears were grossly exaggerated in view of the Cabinet's rejection in 1930 of Mosley's radical proposal for compulsory industrial reorganization on the basis of state finance. Thereafter, the Labour government was obliged to perpetuate the policy of its predecessor – to support rationalization publicly as a structuralist unemployment policy and to act as a bridge between industry and finance.

The major exception to the general rule was the Coal Mines Act of 1930 which imposed a state-sponsored cartel system on the industry and established the Coal Mines Reorganisation Commission (CMRC) as a statutory body charged with the task of bringing about amalgamations, compulsorily if need be.[1] The measure, which was passed with Liberal support, was opposed by the Conservatives on the predictable grounds that it interfered with the principles of private enterprise, but there can be little doubt that it reached the statute book precisely because coalmining was perceived to be a special case in view of its uniquely disastrous record of labour relations and the general political consensus in favour of compulsory reorganization which had emerged after 1926 [170].

Thus, with the advent of the predominantly Conservative National government in 1931 industrial policy had yet to advance beyond the general exhortations to rationalization which had characterized the later 1920s; industrial reorganization was perceived to be a desirable objective but in the iron and steel industry, for example, there was no consensus on the form that it should take and politicians in general were incapable of producing informed judgements on such technical issues as desirable plant size and capital equipment. Whilst the Bank of England, drawing on expertise within the BIDC, possessed firm and realistic views on reorganization, favouring a series of regional amalgamations suggested to it by the American consulting engineers H. A. Brassert and Co., Norman was determined to avoid becoming a coercive agent of government, as indicated already. In this light, it was probably inevitable that following the inauguration of a general tariff under the Import Duties Act of 1932 the iron and steel manufacturers were able to circumvent governmental pressures for reorganization. It is true that in conformity with the policy of the Import Duties Advisory Committee (IDAC), the body created under the terms of the Act to liaise with the Treasury and the Board of Trade on tariff levels, the industry as a whole reluctantly came to accept the need for a national co-ordinating authority – the British Iron and Steel Federation, established in 1934 with the progressive Andrew Duncan, protégé of Montagu Norman and former head of the Central Electricity Board, as chairman. But a lack of consensus ensured that the powers of the new body were severely limited. As the industry's most recent historian has concluded, 'the final scheme was not one of reorganization but solely of price maintenance' and until 1939 'the state sponsored a cartel over which it had little control' [269, *69*, *74*].

The long-running saga over the tariff is indicative of the power of vested interests and their ability to resist governmental and other semi-official pressures for reorganization. The dominant element in the iron and steel industry, the heavy steelmakers, were determined to adopt a defensive posture behind a tariff wall buttressed by the suppression of internal competition. In the face of their intransigence the National government was obliged to accept the industry's view that amalgamations could only be secured by 'natural market forces'. Radical state-sponsored programmes were therefore ruled out by the government's desire to avoid *direct* involvement in industrial affairs for fear of falling into a policy morass which would lead very quickly to the undermining of private managerial prerogatives. The approach of interwar governments to industrial affairs, therefore, was *indirect*, or at one remove, as evidenced by the creation of quasi-official bodies such as the CMRC and IDAC. In the former case, although the National government remained committed to compulsory amalgamations in coalmining throughout the 1930s, the CMRC and its successor (from 1938), the Coal Commission, did not possess the necessary authority for decisive action. They were therefore ignored by the majority of colliery owners who, like their iron and steel counterparts, preferred to operate within an increasingly restrictive cartel. In this, they received the sustained support of government which saw in the cartel system a device to maximize employment levels [169, *145–6*]. As with the state's attitude to IDAC, it was again the line of least resistance which was followed. In iron and steel on the other hand, the National government was committed to fundamental reorganization but found that the tariff, once enacted, enabled the industry to dictate the course of events. It is important to note, however, that contemporary understanding of the effects of the tariff was limited by a failure to distinguish between nominal and effective rates of duty. In contradistinction to the nominal rate which is imposed on the final values of goods imported, the effective rate applies only to the value added in the production process in the competing British industry. Whilst date limitations have prevented an assessment of the extent to which the effective tariff structure of the 1930s was instrumental in promoting a misallocation of resources within the industrial sector, a recent study has concluded that the iron and steel industry was relatively disadvantaged by the tariff, with an effective rate lower than the nominal rate [49, *113–28*].[2] It must remain a matter for conjecture but it is reasonable to presume that had such calculations been available to IDAC officials after 1932, they would not have been unduly concerned.

Industrial Diplomacy

A further perspective on governmental antipathy to direct and open involvement in the affairs of private industry is provided by the growth of informal contacts between senior civil servants and industrialists. As the chronic nature of the exporting difficulties confronting the staple industries was confirmed after 1929, the need for a more interventionist policy stance was conceded in Whitehall. The problem for civil servants, however, was that their desire to offer assistance to depressed industries was inconsistent with the prevailing ideal of the neo-classical market economy which accorded the state a minimal role in the conduct of economic affairs. According to Richard Roberts, this ideological conflict was reconciled by 'a careful distinction between the short and long run' [238, *98*] in which the tenets of neo-classicism were accepted as the norm but with permissible *ad hoc* deviations. The latter were the product of what Roberts chooses to call 'industrial diplomacy' and an excellent illustration of the process is to be found in the cotton textile industry. The creation of the Lancashire Cotton Corporation under BIDC auspices in 1929 was an explicit attempt to recover lost export markets by the achievement of scale economies and the elimination of weak selling [123, *65, 75–6*], and when the Labour government came to office it endorsed this general strategy of horizontal integration. The technical re-equipment of the industry was also canvassed as a means of reducing costs in order to boost exports. A third strategy was to reduce the surplus productive capacity which had plagued the industry throughout the later 1920s; amalgamations, therefore, were the key to the kind of fundamental reorganization of the industry which current market conditions demanded. It was this pessimistic approach which won the day in 1930 and from then until 1935 Whitehall officials conducted an informal dialogue with cotton entrepreneurs with a view to securing agreement on the elimination of marginal concerns. These discussions eventually bore fruit in the Cotton Spinning Industry Act of 1936 which instituted a compulsory levy for the scrapping of redundant spindles. The legislation was presented as nothing more than the industry itself desired, but this was to deny the critical role of the Board of Trade in securing private agreement for its preferred strategy. Similar 'behind the scenes' diplomacy was evident in the shipping and chemical industries and it serves to underline the commitment of civil servants to the ideal of minimum state interference. But equally important was the fact that 'industrial diplomacy' was an eminently suitable means of preserving the integrity of established parliamentary procedures during a period of sustained economic difficulty. In this context, Keith Middlemas has advanced the controversial view that in the years after 1911 the 'British system' of government was being transformed by an emergent 'corporate bias' in which employers' and employees' organizations were raised to the status of 'governing institutions' [195]. Whilst this interpretation receives some support from the corporatist experiments of the 1960s and 1970s, it ignores the fact that in the 1930s the policy of manipulating industrialists *covertly* served to inhibit the growth of corporatist tendencies by preserving existing constitutional relationships [238, *100*]. The inevitable result of the growth of informal contacts, however, was to encourage fragmentation and imbalance in the policy-making process; in their determination to avoid formulating general principles which could be applied across the industrial spectrum Board of Trade officials succeeded in devising an 'industrial policy for each industry with which informal discussion had been held' [238, *101*]. Thus, the conservatism of civil servants reinforced that of politicians in resisting the collectivist trend. At no time was this more evident than in 1935 when a Conservative back-bench proposal for a general enabling bill to permit industrialists to reorganize themselves with statutory authority to coerce recalcitrant minorities was rejected by the then President of the Board of Trade, Walter Runciman, on the grounds that there was no general requirement for legislative assistance since industry could not be reorganized by 'any one cut and dried method' [cited in 169, *167*].

Conclusion

In analysing government-industry relations, this chapter has concentrated on the issue of rationalization. In the later 1920s, amalgamations were favoured as an active response to foreign competition and it is by no means coincidental that the industrial economy in general was subject to a significant merger movement at that time [123, 90–100]. The alternative to amalgamations, however, was the cartel or marketing scheme and it was perhaps inevitable that after 1930, with the revival of the export trade an ever diminishing prospect, industrialists aided and abetted, albeit reluctantly, by governments took refuge in defensive organizations whose primary purpose was to preserve the existing structure of an industry. To the extent, therefore, that interwar industrial policies encouraged the consolidation of producers' associations it is legitimate to question their long-term effects on industrial performance. There can be no doubt that the social costs of rationalization in the guise of amalgamation were potentially high in conditions of localized mass unemployment, but an industrial structure increasingly subject to a plethora of price controls was hardly conducive to economic growth [183, 317–36]. In so far as price cartels in coalmining and iron and steel subsidized the more efficient producers and permitted the less efficient to remain in business, they promoted ossification of the industrial structure. The legacy of the 1930s producers' associations – enhanced by the needs of government output planning during the Second World War – was highlighted by the 1944 white paper on employment policy when it drew critical attention to the possibility that governmental attempts to stimulate aggregate demand might be frustrated by the pricing policies of collusive selling organizations. In a similar vein, it has been argued that 'the cartelization of England' bred attitudes of complacency which served the British economy ill when an outmoded industrial structure was exposed to a renewed upsurge of international competition after the mid-1950s [279, 19–37]. On the other hand, it must be conceded that statutory marketing schemes in coalmining contributed to an improvement in profit margins during a period of great trading difficulty, thereby providing some of the financial resources to sustain substantial mechanization. There is also the question of the extent to which industries burdened by over-capacity would have benefited more from exposure to the full blast of market forces or from collective schemes for the reduction of capacity. In the case of cotton spinning, as Hannah has emphasized, the financially weak firms were often those which had suffered from speculative promotions and not necessarily those with uneconomic equipment; in this industry, therefore, the competitive process working through bankruptcy might have had adverse effects on overall productive efficiency, had it not been tempered by planned scrapping of the uneconomic equipment' [123, *138*]. It is impossible therefore, to offer anything but an agnostic conclusion on the 'efficiency' effects of state intervention in industry. In the face of large-scale unemployment and commensurate levels of social distress defensive postures were understandable. It is also worthwhile re emphasizing that a vigorous policy in favour of amalgamations could have raised the problem of monopoly control and, in the context of the later 1920s, any favourable effects on competitive efficiency overseas could well have been negated by retaliatory action on the part of foreign producers.

It should be clear from this brief account of government–industry relations between the wars that the principle of *laissez-faire* in the peacetime industrial economy had been abandoned by the mid 1930s. But as the views of Walter Runciman well illustrate, the National government was very far from subscribing to the notion of an active and generalized industrial policy. In part, this can be explained by the relative strength of Britain's recovery from the depths of the slump in 1932 but far more fundamental was the determination of ministers and civil servants to preserve the integrity of the free enterprise system. Moreover, the pressure from business interests for a more active policy was uneven and subject to the changing perspectives of vested interests. This is exemplified by the debate over the tariff in the 1920s. In industries such as fuel oil and dyestuffs, where a core of influential employers formulated clear plans in highly specific circumstances, the state was prepared to lend active support to the process of reorganization [148; 63]. Similarly in electricity supply technological factors virtually dictated national co-ordination, and in any event the state was endowed with the centralizing weapon of the national grid. Elsewhere, as in coalmining powerful political and social considerations impelled the state towards an interventionist stance, but in iron and steel and cotton textiles the full force of structural fragmentation and entrenched positions conspired to prevent or seriously delay the emergence of a industry-wide consensus on the need for structural reforms; amalgamations would come about in response in 'natural market forces', not unreasonable view in the light of the demonstrable failure of such multi-plant mergers as the Lancashire Cotton Corporation [12 75–6; 168, *150–1*]. Nevertheless, the vacillations and inconsistencies in the record of state intervention should not be allowed to mask the dramatic change which was taking place in government-industry relations during the interwar years. It is salutory to remember that on the eve of the First World War, up to the passing of the Munitions of War Act in 1915, the integrity of private enterprise was regarded as sacrosanct and it is surely correct to draw attention to the rush to decontrol after 1918 and the defining of an explicit neo-classical orthodoxy with its emphasis on cost and wage flexibility. The collapse of the staple export trades, however, eroded faith in market mechanisms such that from the mid-1920s onwards the foundations of the close interpenetration of government and industry which had come to be the norm by the early 1970s was being laid. Slowly, but surely, the state was being drawn into the affairs of the boardroom just as industrialists were becoming accustomed to and dependent upon state direction and support.

Notes

1 The Labour government's Agriculture Marketing Act of 1931 similarly provided for the establishment of statutory marketing schemes if they were desired by a majority of farmers. Until the legislation was re-enacted in 1933, only one enforceable scheme (in hops production) had been introduced.
2 For a critique of Capie's analysis, see the article by Foreman-Peck [91] and the response by Capie [48].

11

Labour Policy

RODNEY LOWE

From the 1870s to the 1980s, with their common experience of trade
union legislation and economic recession, labour policy has been a
major concern of central government. Except in wartime, however,
there has been little agreement over what the exact nature of such a
policy should be. Given the economic realities of international
competition, should it be concerned with the efficiency of labour as
an impersonal factor of production; or, given the political realities of
parliamentary democracy, should it be concerned more broadly with
the accommodation of organized labour and the social aspirations of
the mass electorate? Should the focus of labour policy, in other
words, be manpower (the quality of the labour force, its mobility and
productivity) or industrial relations and social policy (the level of
wages, industrial harmony and social stability)? Clearly, these
alternative approaches – which might be termed the 'economic' and
'social' approaches – to labour policy can overlap. Good industrial
relations, for example, by minimizing strikes and restrictive practices,
can increase productivity. Likewise, social policy (be it health,
education, housing or income maintenance) can improve the quality
of the labour force. Equally clearly, however, they can conflict. An
attempt to increase productivity by the removal of restrictive
practices can upset a delicate power balance on the shopfloor and
thereby generate both industrial unrest and psychological resistance
to increased productivity. Similarly, improved social services can
reduce industrial competitiveness by increasing costs (directly
through taxation or indirectly through their influence on wage levels)
and undermine the quality of the labour force (by discouraging
mobility and the 'work ethic').

As was increasingly recognized in the 1930s, this inherent conflict
in labour policy reflects a political tension common to most advanced

industrial societies: the problem of how to correlate the economic facts of international competition with democratic electoral demands. It is a tension which British governments have traditionally failed to resolve – not least because of an administrative vacuum in Whitehall. Before the First World War, labour policy had been primarily the responsibility of a comprehensive 'ministry of labour and industry' – the Board of Trade. Divergent economic and social interests could therefore be reconciled within one department. During the war, however, the Board of Trade was dismembered. Administratively, the responsibilities of central government had expanded so greatly that it was logical – as the 1918 Haldane Committee on the Machinery of Government (Cd. 9230) recognized – to create specialist ministries of production and of employment. Politically, the board's paternalism had also antagonized labour. Its responsibilities for industrial relations and social policy were therefore transferred in December 1916 to a new Ministry of Labour which, as its name implied, was intended to be more sympathetic to the trade unions. As a consequence, the 'economic' and 'social' approaches to labour policy came to be institutionalized in two separate departments; and to a political disinclination to raise contentious issues there was added a bureaucratic reluctance to trespass upon another's preserve. Rather than being administered by one ministry, labour policy became marginal to two.[1]

In the gradual evolution of the popular and political commitment to full employment in 1944, labour policy and the tensions it reflected played a small but nevertheless significant role. It can be most effectively analysed in three periods (1916–22, 1923–39 and 1940–44) and through the focus of the Ministry of Labour which, throughout the interwar period, was not only responsible for the 'social' half of labour policy but was also officially regarded (much against its will) as the 'employment' department. [182, *ch.* 6] This latter assignation had two important consequences. First, ministers seeking to deflect criticism by proving that 'something was being done' acquired a vested interest in pioneering new legislation; and it was through this legislation that traditional cures for unemployment came to be discredited and public acceptance for novel remedies fostered. Secondly, in implementing these policies, ministry officials rapidly developed both a commitment to and an expertise in the alleviation of unemployment. This administrative expertise greatly increased their authority in Whitehall with the result that, in 1943, three of the eight members of the Committee on Postwar Employment, which first drafted the Employment Policy White Paper were officials who had had lengthy apprenticeships in the interwar ministry – Sir Thomas Phillips (the permanent secretary and an expert on unemployment insurance) and two officials recently transferred to the Treasury, Sir Alan Barlow (who had been responsible for industrial training and industrial relations in the 1920s) and Sir Wilfrid Eady (who had made one of the first surveys of structural unemployment in 1926 and had been the secretary of the Industrial Transference Board and the Unemployment Assistance Board). This influence of the ministry, and thereby of labour policy, on the final drafting of full employment policy has been noted in the past and ascribed to either Bevin's leadership or the success of the ministry's wartime manpower policy. Both undoubtedly contributed to the political weight of the ministry's views but, as will be shown, the substance of the ministry's contribution to policy was squarely based on peacetime expertise and experience.

Wartime Reconstruction, 1916–22

A 'labour problem' was first identified in the late 1870s when a growing awareness of unemployment and poverty combined with an increasing number of strikes aroused within government circles a fear of social instability and economic retardation [71, *ch. 2*]. Unemployment and poverty were seen to be breeding grounds for an ideological attack on prevailing capitalist values, whilst labour militancy (resulting in industrial disruption and high wages and thus in the discouragement of entrepreneurial initiative and investment) was identified as a major cause of Britain's decreasing competitiveness. A labour policy was duly developed, centred on the Board of Trade and embracing both industrial relations and social reform. In 1896, the Conciliation Act was passed to provide government with the expertise and opportunity to intervene in industrial disputes. Then, after 1906, a series of famous reforms including Labour Exchanges (1909) and National Insurance (1911) was introduced both to alleviate the major causes of poverty and to increase 'national efficiency'. These reforms had clear political advantages for the Liberal government and social benefits for manual workers, but they were also deliberately designed to be compatible with industry's international competitiveness.

A latent authoritarianism, however, characterized the board's policy and this proved to be its Achilles' heel. Even in peacetime it aroused employers' concern for traditional managerial prerogatives and trade unions' fear of a 'servile state'; and in wartime, when the need to maximize production fully exposed this authoritarianism, it provoked the threat of public non-compliance. Shop-floor unrest escalated and, in 1916, both sides of industry rejected the government's

142

attempt to extend unemployment insurance [128, *chs. 9–10*; 285]. After 1916, therefore, labour policy – although it by no means abandoned the prewar ideal of 'reasoned progress' – had to become more conciliatory, seeking to encourage and foster (rather than impose) good industrial practice.

The main objectives of this new labour policy were greater consultation with and the better organization of industry [182, *ch. 4*]. The creation of the Ministry of Labour was a token of government's greater willingness to consult organized labour, whilst the summoning of the National Industrial Conference (1919–21) and the establishment of the International Labour Organization in 1919 were serious attempts to construct industrial consensus. At a less rarified level, both sides of industry were encouraged to co-operate at national, district and local levels through joint industrial (Whitley) councils; and the number of trade boards was rapidly increased to establish minimum wages and thereby to encourage better organization and the more efficient use of labour. The Industrial Court was also established in 1919 in the hope that its judgements in major industrial disputes would provide a set of rational criteria for pay awards. Industry's needs were not always predominant. For rational political reasons, the government passed the industrially irrational Restoration of Prewar Practices Act (consensus, it was felt, could not be built on broken promises, whatever the short-term consequences for productivity). To alleviate unrest, the government also increased public expenditure on social services such as housing and unemployment insurance far beyond the immediate industrial need for the greater mobility, health and general 'employability' of the labour force. The critical issue of productivity, however, was not evaded. Various training schemes were inaugurated to make good wartime losses and in 1920 the Ministry of Labour summoned both sides of industry to a Committee on Increased Production. 'Notwithstanding the fact that possibly some home truths have got to be said about both parties', minuted one official, 'the menace to the welfare of this country by a continuance of present methods is too great to allow susceptibilities to stand in the way of a searching inquiry.'[2]

The complete failure of this committee symbolized the collapse of postwar idealism. Conventional constitutional and economic opinion (as represented by the Treasury) increasingly questioned the legitimacy of state intervention and the expenditure of tax-payers' money in such areas of policy. The National Industrial Conference and the International Labour Organization demonstrated the absence, not the existence, of effective industrial consensus. No major industry, moreover, could be persuaded to reform itself in accordance with Whitley principles. The conservatism of both sides of industry was simply too ingrained. The naivety of the assumption was also exposed that the Industrial Court could 'apply principles of justice to what is in effect a conflict of forces'.[3] As for the Committee on Industrial Production, trade unionists (especially after the onset of depression in 1920) declined to discuss productivity for fear that it would increase unemployment and reduce still further labour's share of industrial profits whilst employers were highly suspicious, as before the war, of any outside inquiry into managerial methods and levels of profit. Consequently, the representatives of both sides of industry failed to appear and the Ministry of Labour, to force the pace, had to join the Board of Trade in a request to Cabinet for a more authoritative inquiry. Eventually, the Balfour Committee on Industry and Trade was appointed; and, with its surveys of oversea markets and industrial relations and its two-volume appraisal of 'factors in industrial and commercial efficiency', it may be seen as the last flowering of the comprehensive prewar approach to labour policy (Cmd. 3282). Its recommendations, however, were largely ignored by politicians and industry alike.

Peacetime Pragmatism, 1923–39

This rejection of an active labour policy, of both an 'authoritarian' and a 'consensual' nature, had a profound long-term influence on civil servants' perception of what was politically practical. For most of the interwar period they tended to retreat into a 'stoical realism' which was further encouraged in Whitehall by the increasingly divergent interests – and vested interests – of the Ministry of Labour and Board of Trade. Policy superficially remained the same – home rule for industry; but within this policy government became far less active in the promotion of good industrial practice. As a Ministry of Labour official, during the reversion to a more positive policy in the 1960s, recalled: 'The traditional attitude of the Ministry has been that, while it has a general concern for industrial relations and good industrial training, both these matters were primarily the responsibility of the "two sides of industry". The Ministry's place was on the sidelines, making encouraging noises but only entering the field when things went wrong and then only by invitation and with the intention of getting out again as soon as possible' [292, *112*].

In industrial relations, the ministry's stoicism was dictated by the reduction of its conciliation staff to less than thirty and by the administrative divorce from both the Factory Inspectorate (which remained attached to the Home Office until 1940) and other related agencies, such as the Industrial Fatigue Research Board. The simply was not the opportunity to promote, as Bevin was later to wish, a 'new code of conduct, inspection, enforcement and welfare' in order to change shop-floor attitudes.[4] More significantlly, there was also no radical expansion of industrial training, although many economists at the time considered training to be a potential cure for unemployment. There were four main reasons for this failure. First, the Treasury as ever was reluctant to enter into long-term financial commitments. Secondly, the case was considered unproven that increased expenditure on education and training would either reduce the general level of unemployment or, in a period of excess labour supply, increase an individual's employment prospects. Economists' assertions were merely 'an act of faith' [86, *141*]. Thirdly, there was the problem of non-compliance on the part of industry and the unemployed. Craft unions were hostile to any increase in the supply of skilled labour and employers equally resented increased public expenditure, feared for their supply of cheap labour and remained highly suspicious of both technical skills learnt in universities and manual skills acquired elsewhere than on their own shopfloor. Making training a condition of unemployment benefit was also adjudged to be politically unacceptable for all but juveniles, at a time when no promise of an ultimate job could be made. The second Labour government did indeed introduce such a condition, but it was rarely enforced and was rapidly dropped by the National government. Finally, ministry officials doubted whether the state had the ability to predict accurately future labour shortages. The majority of training centres that were established were consequently either Juvenile or Transfer Instruction Centres, offering three-month courses and concerned only with the physical and mental demoralization of juveniles and the unemployed in the depressed regions. Government Training Centres, providing six-month courses and a sound grounding in semi-skilled work, never – even in the skill shortage occasioned by rearmament – produced more than 10,761 trainees per year [41, *373*]. The real-world constraints on the interwar training programme are perhaps most graphically illustrated by the fate of the official directly responsible for policy in the late 1930s. In 1939, on a complaint from the engineering unions, he was reprimanded by his permanent secretary for surreptitiously expanding training places for engineers. In 1940 he was reprimanded again and transferred to other duties by Bevin for not having had the foresight to expand training faster.

The ministry, however, could not long remain above the contemporary debate on the causes and cures for mass unemployment. As the department responsible for industrial relations and unemployment benefit, it attracted the attention of orthodox economists and industrialists. As the 'employment department', with a political interest in and an administrative commitment to experiment, it was also unable (despite the increasing power of the Treasury in Whitehall) to rest content with orthodox policy. Consequently, it, and the practical realities of labour policy with which it was concerned, played their part in the gradual evolution of a public and political commitment to full employment.

Consistent with the prewar critique of the 'labour problem', both classical economists and industralists condemned the ministry's twin responsibilities of conciliation and unemployment benefit for high wages, and thus the high industrial costs, which they identified as the main cause of mass unemployment. Conciliation, they argued, maintained wages above 'market' levels by recognizing trade unions, raising workers' expectations and obscuring the economic criteria on which wage settlements should alone have been based. Unemployment benefit inflated industrial costs by both increasing taxation and acting as an effective minimum wage for low-paid workers – and hence as a rigid base for hallowed 'relativities'. Further, they argued unemployment benefit sustained 'uneconomic' wage rates by permitting the unemployed to refuse any job below the 'standard rate' without forfeiting their right to benefit; by eradicating the pools of blackleg labour which had depressed prewar wage levels; and by relieving trade unions of their 'friendly society role'. If unions no longer had to care for the welfare of their unemployed members, it was inevitable that they would be less wary about pricing worker out of jobs. Finally, unemployment insurance was held to reduce both geographical and industrial mobility [52, *ch. 3*]. Thus although government strove to have no direct influence on wage levels, abandoning the extension of minimum wage legislation in 1922 and seeking always to follow the market in the pay and conditions of it own employees, the consensus of 'expert' opinion was that th indirect consequences of its social policy were catastrophic.

The ministry had the practical expertise to reject many of these assertions – just as its records today contain evidence to refute th unrealistic assumptions on which much econometric analysis i based [182, *ch. 6*]. Rather than demoralizing recipients, ministr officials argued, unemployment benefit maintained their physica fitness and thereby their 'employability'. By maintaining demand, also created employment. At the margin, it was admitted, unemploy ment benefit might affect the mobility of individual workers and th strength of trade unions, by relaxing the urgency with which alternative employment had to be sought and by relieving trad unions of their friendly society role. The ministry's extensiv enquiries, however, consistently confirmed that there was littl general preference for idleness over work – and, after 1928, the Industrial Transference Board did exist to expedite the search for work. Moreoever, ministry officials insisted that trade unions had shown a marked reluctance to strike against wage reductions after 1926, owing to their loss of members and fears about their ability to recruit new ones (in no small part because government had now assumed their friendly society role). Where employers were sufficiently determined, therefore, money wages could be – and had been – reduced. The real crux of the ministry's beliefs, however, was that conciliation and unemployment benefit were but symbols of a far larger and irreversible political change. Increasingly since the 1870s, manual workers had become politically articulate and in 1918 universal suffrage had been granted, revolutionizing the whole electoral basis of politics. These political changes had effectively foreclosed the traditional option of consistently sacrificing workers' living standards to correct market forces. They had thereby also invalidated many of the assumptions underpinning classical economics. Industrial costs would inevitably be inflated by higher taxation and wages; and they could now only be realistically reduced by technical innovation and higher productivity. Similarly, in the real world, trade unions should no longer be attacked but encouraged, through conciliation, to act 'responsibly'.

The ministry was equally impatient with the negativism of orthodox government policy. Having identified the existence of structural unemployment in the mid-1920s, it secured the appointment of the Industrial Transference Board to assist the movement of surplus workers from the 'derelict' areas. In 1929, it also challenged the Treasury in Cabinet over the efficacy of the gold standard and, for its pains, was requested to collate the official rejection of the Liberal Party's programme of loan-financed public work, *We Can Conquer Unemployment*. Although its own contribution to the white paper [107] duly exposed the impracticalities of the Liberal proposals (in particular the assumption that the unemployed were a uniform body of people who could be instantly moved to prepared work in any part of the country with no adverse effect on either business confidence or wage rates in other industries), it did not reject the provision of public works, in excess of normal government contracts, for a smaller body of men. Public works were supported, not as a single cure for unemployment, but as a means to improve the country's economic infrastructure and as a strategic boost to demand in order to increase business confidence.

It was in the late 1930s, however, that the ministry really started to challenge orthodox policy successfully, particularly in relation to regional policy and public capital expenditure. In the Special Areas

(Amendment) Act of 1937, the fundamental objective of regional policy was changed from the simple improvement of the social infrastructure (in order to reduce the disincentives for investment) to the use of financial inducements to attract private industry into the depressed regions in order to diversify permanently their industrial structure. This change in policy was actively defended against later administrative attempts by the Treasury to negate it. Similarly on the Phillips Committee on Public Capital Expenditure, the ministry secured the commitment of government to a counter-cyclical programme of public works – not just to relieve inflationary pressure in 1937 but also to reserve useful works for the expected downturn in the early 1940s. An agreement to prepare and to keep under constant review a programme of specific proposals for immediate implementation was again secured as a vital bulwark against Treasury bad faith [182, *ch. 6*].

The practical achievements of the ministry's alternative programme may have been slight. An estimated 280,000 workers and 35,000 households were transferred after 1928, of whom approximately 2 per cent returned home. This represented an estimated third of total internal migration [218, *335–8*]. Even allowing for the multiplier effect, it has been estimated that the Special Areas Commissioners' expenditure created fewer than 150,000 jobs – although in the light of the late introduction of financial inducements, the concurrent impact of rearmament contracts and the fact that policy was essentially concerned not with immediate relief but the long-term health of the depressed regions, these figures should not be taken as conclusive evidence of the 1937 Act's failure [232, *tables 32 and 34b*]. The counter-cyclical public works programme also amounted to little more than £50 million over two years. What was really important, however, was that by the late 1930s traditional remedies for unemployment (such as emigration and land settlement) had been tried and found wanting; and that, before the 1938 Barlow Commission, the irrationality of many business decisions and the inability of the market to provide public goods had been exposed [114, *q. 2651, 2779*]. Involvement in the practical realities of labour policy may not have enabled the ministry to define a theoretically rigorous 'alternative' philosophy; but at least it had encouraged legislative experiments which, in the pragmatic tradition of British policy-making, theorists could later legitimize. A key feature of these experiments was a renewed attempt to correlate economic and social policy. Given government's unavoidable commitment to the electorate's welfare, and its unavoidable repercussions on the market, the ability of the market to function efficiently without some measure of active government intervention was being seriously questioned.

Wartime Reconstruction, 1940–4

Labour policy in the Second World War was a resounding success. More effectively than in other combatant nations, manpower was mobilized, trained and distributed with a minimum of compulsion whilst wage inflation was checked by a mixture of exhortation and price controls [106]. The political credit for this success was attributed rightly to Ernest Bevin as Minister of Labour and National Service and his consequent prestige made him a major force in the formulation of full employment policy. He attended all but six of the ninety-eight meetings of the Reconstruction Committee, at which policy was finalized, and, as the government's main spokesman, introduced both to Parliament and the public the controversial principles of the 1944 white paper far more effectively than his colleagues had introduced the Beveridge Report [38, 313–22]. His commitment was based on a determination that there should be no return to the mass unemployment of the interwar years and on his optimism that wartime manpower budgets could be successfully translated into peacetime 'employment budgets' which could predict, and therefore help to prevent, unemployment. His success as minister, however, was heavily dependent on the expertise of his officials; and they used their experience of interwar labour policy both to restrain his optimism and to question the realism of economists' 'abstractions'.

Practical experience of interwar labour policy had its greatest impact on policy, outside Bevin's direct control, in the Treasury. Here, Sir Wilfrid Eady demonstrated the extent to which labour policy had liberated him from strict orthodoxy by admitting (to the continuing consternation of certain Treasury colleagues) that unemployment should not automatically be countered by deflation and that resort might be had to both public investment and temporary budget deficits. He also welcomed the compilation of national income statistics as a major technical advance to facilitate the management of the economy. He remained adamant, however, that the success of macroeconomic demand management was strictly conditional upon the stability of wages and prices, the mobility of labour and a healthy balance of payments; and on occasions, he argued, unemployment might be the 'only practicable corrective' to either a balance of payments deficit or the non-cooperation of either side of industry. Furthermore, he feared that – in the light of prewar experience – macroeconomic solutions to unemployment might be frequently frustrated by microeconomic, structural impediments. He seriously doubted also the speed and effect with which demand could

be managed by the two main instruments proposed in the whit
paper: public investment ('which is now the polite term for publi
works') and variations in social security contributions. To the ver
end and with considerable success, therefore, he submitted substanti:
amendments to the white paper. 'Because of my many years o
unemployment', he wrote, 'this is a subject on which I feel mo:
deeply and I don't regard it as satisfactory that a State Paper of thi
importance should contain two major proposals on the variation (
public expenditure and on the variation of insurance contribution:
which all the officials concerned believe impractical or at best far le:
effective for their designed purpose than is claimed for them.'[5]

Within the Ministry of Labour, officials questioned the optimis:
of Bevin and the 'abstractions' of economists on three major issue:
training, regional policy and wages. On the assumption of fu
employment, Bevin wished the ministry's training service 1
discharge the dual function of determining whether an individu:
was permanently redundant and of providing him with the necessar
skills for redeployment. In the light of interwar experience, howeve
officials doubted both the efficacy of 'employment budgets' as
means of 'economic intelligence' and their own ability to predic
more successfully than employers, future skill shortages. The
doubted also the compliance of both individuals and trade unio
with an extended and perhaps compulsory training programme. I
contrast to Bevin, they feared that restrictive practices – develop∈
by trade unions over long years of unemployment and unde
employment – could not be wished away on the mere promise ar
temporary achievement of full employment. Postwar reality was
justify their scepticism.

Bevin and his officials were far more united on the issue of region
policy; but, again significantly in the light of postwar development
they failed to have their principles fully endorsed in the white pape
Both advocated regional policy as a cure not for mass unemployme
but for localised unemployment in an otherwise buoyant economy
a problem which many economists and even Keynes himself (exce
briefly in 1937) were reluctant to acknowledge. In 1943, indeed, tl
Economic Section still assumed that any such potential proble
could be eradicated by the mobility of labour – despite the interw
evidence that, whilst many were prepared to move (especially tl
young, fit and single), many others could not. Nor, as minist
officials continued to argue after the 1938 Barlow Commission, wa:
in the national interest that they should do so [114]. The moveme
of workers to jobs, they argued, added directly and indirectly to tl
costs of industry which far outweighed the economic advantage
individual firms of being nearer their markets. Public services (su

s houses and schools), for example, which were abandoned in the
depressed regions, had to be reproduced in the expanding areas; and
as the regional multiplier went into reverse in the depressed regions,
unemployment for non-migrants intensified and their relief became
an even heavier burden on the national tax-payer. Conversely, in the
expanding areas congestion directly increased industrial costs by
ultimately raising rates and wages. The ministry based its final policy
advice on three assumptions. First, the market did not automatically
safeguard the public interest. Secondly, many entrepreneurial
decisions on location were made with imperfect knowledge and for
economically irrational, personal reasons. Thirdly, many light
industries were highly mobile and could provide each region with a
healthy, diversified structure which would minimize the danger of
mass unemployment in the future. Either by compulsion (the
banning of new factories in certain conurbations) or financial
inducements, therefore, the ministry argued strongly that the
distribution of industry should be made to match the existing
distribution of the population. Such arguments, however, were
never fully accepted by the Cabinet and Bevin's demand was flatly
rejected that, where private enterprise had failed, the state should
open factories. Even worse, for a policy which depended for its
success on the vigour of its implementation, responsibility for
regional policy was transferred in 1944 from the ministry to the
Board of Trade. The conflict between the 'economic' and 'social'
approaches to labour policy had reasserted itself.

The third major area of the ministry's influence, and in the light of
subsequent events the most important, was wages policy. Economists,
such as Robbins, recognized by 1942 that the limitation of wage
increases to those justified either by increased productivity or by
changes in terms of trade was the 'sine qua non of anti-depression
policy'. Little scientific thought, however, had been given to the
rational – or irrational – way in which, in the real world, wages were
determined. Keynes was amongst the most culpable and eventually
admitted that the solution to wage inflation could only be political
and not theoretical [150]. This being the case, the ministry, with its
unrivalled experience of the realities of wage bargaining and its
proven success both in helping to develop 'responsible' industrial
relations in the 1930s and in controlling wartime inflation, found
itself in an extremely influential position. Its advice which was
ually, if reluctantly, accepted by the Economic Section, was clear-
at.[6] Free collective bargaining should be maintained, supported by
a policy of greater education (to encourage an awareness of national
and not just sectional interests), increased conciliation (to anticipate
and speedily settle strikes) and improved welfare (to demonstrate

151

that living standards could be improved through political and no
just industrial action). In contrast to the economists' panaceas o
labour controls, compulsory arbitration or centrally determine
wage norms, the ministry argued, such a policy was the only trul
democratic one. Moreover, it was the one most likely to succeed
Free collective bargaining provided the flexibility with which th
wage structure of each industry could be adapted to changin
economic circumstances. It also provided trade union leaders wit
the opportunity to consider the national interest and the incentive t
keep in touch with their rank and file. If, on the other hand, th
results of wage bargaining were effectively determined by goverr
ment norms, trade union leaders would be personally relieved of th
need to define the national interest and pressurized by the
membership to turn maxima into minima. The spectre of nor
compliance would also be raised. In short, the ministry (if not th
Treasury and academic economists) had learnt the simple fact tha
freedom constrained trade union leaders, while constraints free
them from having to act 'responsibly'. In the given circumstances
the 1940s, with the voluntary suspension of the right to strike unt
1951 and voluntary wage control after 1948, the ministry's advic
proved to be not pessimistic but highly realistic.

Conclusion

Labour policy lies uncomfortably astride conventional economic an
social policy and, ever since the First World War, has enjoyed
political or administrative unity. In the 1930s and 1940s, however,
might justifiably be said to have approximated to the policies of th
newly established Ministry of Labour. In the 1930s, these polici
appeared 'progressive', with their defence of increased soci
services, the pioneering of regional policy and their commitment
government to a policy of counter-cyclical public works. In t
1940s, by contrast, they appeared 'regressive', with their questionir
of the optimism of both the politicians and the economists wl
supported a policy of full employment. In reality, however, t
nature of labour policy did not change; it only appeared to do
because of the revolution in theoretical perceptions of what w
economically practical. In the 1930s, labour policy was an effecti
avenue through which to challenge the perceived negativism
classical economics. In the 1940s, it was again an effective means
which to question a perceived lack of political and administrati
realism in Keynesian economics.

If the impact of labour policy on the final commitment to f

employment is to be criticized, it might be on the grounds of its excessive concern for the past rather than for the future: its respect, in other words, for history. Such a criticism, were it to be admitted by a historian, might – especially in the present political climate – bring a charge of serious professional misconduct and so fortunately, on two grounds, it can be rejected. First, events since the 1960s have placed the wartime forebodings of those responsible for labour policy in a new and more favourable light. Secondly, in the real world, government policy is always a fortuitous mixture of decisive political leadership (to make the choice between available options), theoretical clarity (to raise perceptions of what is possible) and administrative experience (to suggest what is practical). The formulation of full employment policy was undoubtedly an example of good policy-making in which justifiable risks were taken. In seeking through their caution to minimize these risks, officials long-experienced in the practical realities of labour policy played an important, if somewhat unglamorous, role.

Notes

Long-standing tensions were but brought to the surface in the late 1960s by the transformation of the Ministry of Labour into an agency for economic planning, the Department of Employment and Productivity, only for 'productivity' to be hastily returned to the Board of Trade on a change of government three years later.

I. Mitchell in PRO, Lab 3/1.

PRO, Cab 24/105/CP 1232.

PRO, Lab 10/248.

PRO, T 161/1168/S.52099. Letters of 3 March and 26 April 1944.

PRO, Lab 10/160 and 248.

12
Real Policy Options

SEAN GLYNN

Influences on Economic Policy

Many influences combine to make economic policy which i
essentially a range of priorities set against a view of the real world
theory, ethics, politics, ideology and administrative convenience ma
all play some part and any discussion of policy must inevitably be ar
attempt to distil essentials from a complex brew. To say that policy i
determined by politicians or administrators is, indeed, simplistic bu
it may serve our purposes.

The contemporary view of the time between the world wars wa
that it was a bleak period beset with economic difficulty and disaster
This view was shared by most historians until, in the late 1960s, nev
estimates of economic growth revealed a different story. The perio
is now seen a time of historically respectable growth with marke
rises in consumer incomes. Even during the crisis years of 1929–33
British product only fell by about 5 per cent. In retrospect, ther
unemployment is the main reason for continuing to hold advers
views about the period and it has become the major benchmar
against which policy is measured.

Of course, to contemporaries, and especially those with power, th
perspective was rather different. The main concern was n
unemployment as such and no interwar government thought i
terms of solving the unemployment problem as a first priority ove
all other aims. The main concern throughout was with Britain's ro
and position in the world economic and political order. This shoul
not be taken to suggest that unemployment and the unemploye
were matters of little or no concern. The State Papers clearly indica
that, as the unemployment problem persisted through the interw
years, there was an increasing tendency to measure all aspects

154

policy against it and to judge them in employment-creation terms. This applied not simply to policy items which were clearly within the economic sphere, such as interest rates, but also to social and political items such as immigration and colonial policy [100]. This reflected official concern and the political pressures created by and on behalf of the unemployed. The policy-making processes were placed under heavy pressure which affected politicians and administrators in almost every activity. While few saw the removal of unemployment as their first concern, the problem was never entirely off-stage. By the end of the interwar period it had filtered into almost the entire range of policy-making at least as the enduring backcloth against which events were staged. Only great actors like Churchill could carry the audience while ignoring the scenery, and this required the smoke of war.

Unemployment had been an important issue in British politics before 1914 and various measures to deal with the problem had been introduced [127]. It had become clear that unemployment was a major cause of poverty and discontent which could be politicized, especially by the Labour Party. Old Age Pensions and National Insurance were, in part, measures to deal with unemployment. Of course, the pre-1914 concern was essentially with two specific types of unemployment – casual and cyclical. By the eve of the First World War answers were being developed. Attempts to improve the labour market were being made through the establishment of Labour Exchanges (1909) and the notion of counter-cyclical public works, which had long been advocated and was most clearly propounded in the Minority Report of the Royal Commission on the Poor Laws, was beginning to gain acceptance.

The policy measures of the pre-1914 era were comparatively ineffective after 1920 in the face of massive unemployment with heavy structural and long-term components. Nevertheless, it is impossible to understand the interwar policy debate without reference to these Edwardian developments. Labour Party policy throughout the interwar period owed much to the pre-1914 campaign for counter-cyclical public works and Keynes, to many of his opponents at least, seemed to be part of the same tradition.

In Chapter 1, it was emphasized that the interwar unemployment problem had some important long-run aspects. In particular, the continued dependence on a relatively narrow group of staple industries from the Industrial Revolution onwards exposed Britain to changing world market conditions. There appears to have been very little growth in the economy between the late 1890s and the end of the First World War, and the level of economic activity during the interwar years was well below long-run trends. These long-run aspects of the problem may be taken to suggest that the scope for short-run policy solutions to unemployment was limited.

It was clear that the First World War had brought major changes, most of which were unwelcome to a generation of leaders who viewed the pre-1914 situation as something between the norm and the ideal. Some of the economic policies of the 1920s, and not least the return to gold, were undoubtedly influenced, if not dictated, by nostalgia. During the 1930s it was accepted that the world had changed irrevocably and serious attempts were made to find a new role for Britain. There are major policy differences between the 1920s and the 1930s and the essential division is between a decade when policy-making looked backwards and one where it was finally accepted that pre-1914 conditions were gone for ever.

Politically the interwar years represent a long period of Conservative dominance for reasons which are examined in Chapter 4. The party had replaced the Liberals as the political representative of British business and finance and the belief in *laissez-faire* had been rendered obsolete by new circumstances. The long-intended return to protection was achieved in 1931 and this and other measures indicate quite clearly that Conservative economic policy was not bound and gagged by the dictates of classical economics. Indeed, it is clear that the needs of economic pressure groups in business and finance were more important. The interests of business and finance were not usually thought to be in conflict. While the return to gold in 1925 may have favoured the City at the expense of export industries, this was not intended. Business was more powerful and important to the party than finance but the City was much closer to the policy-making process and was forcefully represented by the Bank of England.

On the Labour side it is possible to distinguish between party policy and what Labour governments actually did when in office. However, it is probably true to say that up to the 1931 crisis over cuts in public spending, some attempts to implement party policy were made. The essential flaws were in the policies as such rather than a failure of leadership. Labour policy on unemployment owed little to socialist theory or left-wing intellectuals beyond the late-nineteenth century demand for 'work or maintenance'. Essentially the latter had been achieved by the early 1920s with the establishment of National Insurance and other benefits. Clearly the party accepted a brief to maintain or improve this system, but by the time Labour assumed office, the need was for work rather than maintenance. The party had no effective policy for large-scale work creation. The policy proposals of Keynes and Mosley were rejected for political and personal reasons which are examined in Chapter 4. While it is clear that MacDonald, by default, and Snowden, through strong personal conviction had an impact, Labour policy on unemployment was dictated by the larger trade unions. the unions favoured some provision of public works to create jobs but did not entertain great hopes for a solution by this means and only Bevin among Labour leaders openly advocated budget deficits along Keynesian lines. The unions were more concerned to maintain and improve the benefits system as a support for wages and union power and organization. When a Labour government threatened the system in 1931 they were prepared to withdraw their support [249].

By coming into office in 1929 Labour reaped the economic whirlwind and was ill-prepared and inadequate in the circumstances. More fortunate timing might have produced a very different outcome and more effective policies might have developed during a longer period in office. However, Labour did not have a full employment policy and the leadership accepted that they could only reduce rather than remove the problem. Then as now Labour lacked confidence in their own policies while seeking to make political capital out of the unemployment issue and concern for the unemployed. Radical policies at home and abroad were viewed with suspicion and distaste by the Labour leadership and much energy was devoted to purging 'extremists', including Hannington and others who represented the unemployed, from party and trade union ranks. Only Lloyd George, a spent political force, sought to make unemployment the major electoral issue, and Mosley ended by wasting his energies on the extremist fringes.

Interwar governments did not create the unemployment problem in Britain. While government policies such as the return to gold, budgets, tariffs, cheap money and rearmament had an influence the main indictment of interwar political leaders is essentially for sins of omission. Given what amounted almost to a policy vacuum at the political level, those responsible for the implementation of policy were able to play a crucial role.

The Implementation of Policy

The two main agencies of policy implementation were the Treasury and the Bank of England. The precise demarcations of power and influence between these two institutions are not always clear but here are some grounds for suggesting that the Bank was in the ascendancy during the 1920s but with the abandonment of gold in 1931 the initiative passed to the Treasury [260]. However, there is no evidence of major conflict on matters of principle between the two.

Both were dominated by much the same kind of people, though the Treasury had no equivalent to the eccentric Montagu Norman, Governor of the Bank throughout the period. In the late 1920s Sir Otto Niemeyer, second in seniority in the Treasury, moved to Norman's right hand at the Bank. Such moves were unusual but clearly possible.

In the years before 1914 neither the Bank nor the Treasury accepted responsibility for management of the economy in the modern sense. The Treasury was concerned primarily with the supervision of the national accounts and running the Civil Service. The Bank's public role relating mainly to National Debt management and supervision of the gold standard was less clearly defined but equally functional and routine. (It remained, of course, a private institution and had other functions.) The interwar years were a period of transition between nineteenth-century *laissez-faire* and the modern managed economy. While the First World War was a major turning point in this transition, both institutions adapted slowly.

The First World War was inefficiently financed with heavy public borrowing leaving what appeared to be a massive legacy of debt to be managed by the Bank and the Treasury. At the same time there had been a sharp increase in public expenditure which had to be matched by increases in taxation. Budgets became larger and more difficult to manage on orthodox lines. As a result of these changes the basic tenets of Victorian public finance were strained and the tasks of the Bank and Treasury became less routine and much more difficult. In discussing policy in relation to unemployment it is important to remember that official attitudes were conditioned and constrained by concern about difficulties in these traditional areas of operation. Debt servicing and budgetary problems produced a Treasury which advised against further increases in public spending on public works to relieve unemployment and welcomed expenditure cuts. Unemployment caused the Treasury problems in itself by reducing revenue from taxation and increasing expenditure through unemployment benefits [102]

The war also led to Britain's departure from the gold standard and sterling became a managed currency. Inflation during the war and postwar boom caused prices to rise rather more in Britain than in competitor countries, especially the USA. Returning to gold at the 1914 parity meant reducing Britain's relative price level compared with other countries and unemployment was an essential tool in this process. After the war British exports were about 20 per cent below the prewar volume and imports had risen by a similar proportion. During the interwar years Britain was faced with a balance of payments constraint which senior officials were continually concerned about. This also influenced their attitudes towards the unemployment problem.

Economic Policy during the 1920s

During the immediate postwar years there was considerable concern even at cabinet level about political stability and it was feared that heavy unemployment, especially of ex-servicemen, might have serious and possibly revolutionary consequences. For a time the canons of orthodox public finance were abandoned and both public and private sector borrowing were encouraged as the Lloyd George government pursued an expansionist policy. Against a background of rising unit costs in British industry, accelerating inflation and a depreciating exchange rate the Bank and the Treasury began to urge retrenchment through reduced money supply [136, *11–22*]. At the end of 1919 the government accepted the recommendation that the gold standard be restored at prewar parity as soon as possible. Reduced public borrowing and expenditure and a deflationary budget followed in 1920 and there was a sharp increase in Bank Rate. These measures coincided with the end of the fragile postwar boom, intensifying the downturn and producing heavy unemployment. However, the policies continued and under the so-called 'Geddes Axe' of 1921–2 there were more cuts in public expenditure. The general policy drift of the 1920s was deliberately deflationary – first, in order to get back to the gold standard and, after 1925, in order to maintain it.

The driving motivation behind economic policy during the 1920s was a determination to restore Britain's international economic and financial role as far as possible to something approximating the pre-1914 situation. The paranoid fear of inflation shown by British leaders and officials resulted partly from the threat to the international system posed by hyperinflation in various European countries [225, *63*]. However, the fear also derived from the belief that British war and postwar inflation had undermined the nation's international position. There was a determination not only to 'beat inflation' but also to purge the effects of the damage done during the war and postwar boom. As Middleton suggests, for the officials of the Bank and the Treasury the gold standard was a welcome disciplinary device which could be used to convince politicians, and the electorate, of the need for 'sound money', restraint and retrenchment.

Full employment was deliberately sacrificed during the 1920s out of consideration for the external account. Controls were removed from British industry and the main aim was to restore competitiveness to the staples. This clear commitment to restore the pre-1914 system of external trade and finance left little scope for manoeuvre in policy terms. Dear money and restrictions on public spending and borrowing followed automatically. By 1924 fears of revolution had given way to a willingness to confront organized labour on the issue of wages. The gold standard was restored at the prewar parity with the US dollar in 1925. This move was debated at the time and seems to have been under debate by historians ever since. It is generally agreed that sterling was overvalued against the US dollar and that this probably caused some damage to British exports (see Kirby, Chapter 10). However, the major damage caused by the gold standard policy came from a decade of dear money and deflation rather than the overvaluation against the US dollar which resulted in 1925 and competitive devaluation by some European powers. The fact remains that Britain's export staples would still have faced severe difficulties even without gold standard policy. If Britain had abandoned free trade and currency stability during the early 1920s this must surely have encouraged even more trade barriers. While the gold standard policy caused some damage to the British economy during the 1920s, it is difficult to see how some unemployment and adjustment problems could have been avoided after 1920, and the events of the 1930s do not suggest that all might have been well in a world without a gold standard.

The attempt to restore the pre-1914 international payments system during the 1920s failed because major adjustments in national economies were required and these failed to take place. In simple terms it can be said that British prices should have fallen more than they did and/or American prices should have risen more. Either or both carried sufficiently far might have restored equilibrium. The adjustment failed to take place for essentially political reasons. The authorities in each country either prevented adjustment or failed to promote it effectively. In Britain the sharp price reductions required could only be achieved by drastic reductions in wages. Some of such reductions might have been nominal, with real wages being maintained by falling prices, but individual workers and trade unions tended to view all wage movements as real and opposition was naturally vigorous. During the nineteenth century such adjustments did occur although Britain's strong and stable balance of payments ensured that the most drastic adjustments took place in smaller countries on the periphery of the system such as Australia, New Zealand and Canada. Nevertheless, there was clearly a degree of wage flexibility in the British industrial economy before 1914 which was absent after 1920.

There are many problems in relation to interwar wage data but the overwhelming evidence is that, from the early 1920s until the Second World War, nominal wages were reasonably steady while prices were falling. Between 1923 and 1937 average weekly earnings remained almost constant at about £3.00 while retail prices fell some 15 per cent. [179, *table E*, *p. 8*]. Of course, there were changes in relative wages and earnings and there is ample evidence of cuts in some industries especially in the early 1920s, in 1926–27 and during the early 1930s. Also, earnings were affected by the number of hours actually worked so that changes in earnings may have been much greater than fluctuations in wages and wage rates. It is on these grounds that Whiteside questions interwar wage data in Chapter 2. As Capie suggests in Chapter 5, there were real wage effects and wages could have and probably did influence employment to some extent. However, as Garside shows in Chapter 6, there must be considerable doubt that real wage effects could explain the major part of interwar unemployment. Also, the suggestion that wage variations account for the main fluctuations in employment, particularly during the early 1930s, remains controversial. In Chapter 5 and 6 Capie and Garside come to opposing conclusions about the importance of real wage effects on variations in the level of employment [see also 14; 79]. It is also worth noting that Benjamin and Kochin [17] have argued, in effect, that wages were too low – giving rise to a major work disincentive and a preference for unemployment benefit. As Whiteside in Chapter 2 indicates, benefit was by no means generous and the official poverty line was based on destitution criteria. Several interwar poverty surveys make clear that those living on benefit alone were living in poverty. This should suggest that the scope for real wage adjustments in a context of political stability was limited. As indicated in Chapter 6, this seems to have been widely accepted by the 1930s. The wage (and price) adjustments which did occur were clearly insufficient to solve Britain's problems on external account and, more particularly, to revive the flagging export industries. Of course, it is unlikely that cost reductions could have entirely solved the export problems of industries which were threatened by substitution, trade barriers, synthetics and technical obsolescence as well as competitive prices. However, most economists during the 1920s, including Keynes, seem to have accepted that wage reductions could solve the problem. It is therefore important to look more closely at the failure of wage flexibility.

Wages failed to adjust in regional as well as national terms with wage rates (but not, of course, actual earnings) being well-maintained even in areas of very heavy unemployment such as South Wales [266]. As Garside has suggested in Chapter 6, this is in part attributable to the maintenance of trade union strength in the face of mass unemployment. While total membership fell after 1920 it remained high as a proportion of those actually in work and compared with the situation before 1914. Although there was a problem of organization in the new industries, such as motor vehicles, and in the expanding areas in the Midlands and South-East, and some skills were being eroded, unions remained powerful in the export sector and only the miners suffered a devastating defeat. During the war and postwar boom organization and unity probably improved and the quasi-independent shop stewards who had emerged during the war were either removed or absorbed into official structures. By the 1920s most wage bargaining was on a national basis with comparatively little account being taken of local conditions including the level of employment. The unions struggled to preserve the improved wages and shorter hours gained before 1922 and, in general, they succeeded. Most of the major unions were concerned with wages, rather than employment and were not prepared, officially at least, to trade wages for employment. Even in the most depressed circumstances they struggled to maintain the 'rate for the job', even when jobs were very few. Rates for skilled workers were often highest in the depressed regions. The miners' leaders during the first half of the 1920s were prepared to fight on the slogan 'Not a penny off the pay, not a second on the day' even though they must have realized that at prevailing costs and prices for coal this must result in many miners being unemployed. Perhaps justifiably the unions have been accused of ignoring the unemployed in order to ensure improvements for the employed, but of course they were offered very few clear assurances that lower wages would mean higher employment [104].

During the 1920s the British authorities were prepared to push for wage reductions in so far as political circumstances allowed. An open campaign for wage cuts was ruled out and the essential device employed was unemployment promoted by dear money, public spending cuts and deflationary budgeting. When prolonged and heavy unemployment failed to promote wage adjustment and a return to equilibrium the policy was judged to be a failure. However this judgement was delayed at least until the 1929 down-swing. During most of the 1920s it could be said that the authorities had reasonable grounds for hoping that things were moving in the desired direction. Such hopes were blown away by the depression of 1929–33.

Wages failed to adjust in a situation of prolonged and heavy unemployment. This may owe something to union strength, national bargaining and the reluctance of government to confront wage earners. Clearly this reluctance was overcome in 1925–6 in the event leading to the General Strike. It is perhaps insufficiently understood and emphasized that the essential point at issue in the General Strike was wage cuts. Other unions and the TUC supported the miners for historical reasons and through feelings of class solidarity but it was also the case that the miners were seen as a test case in relation to wage cuts. While it suited the government to turn the strike into a constitutional issue, the unions were essentially concerned with wages rather than politics. Although the miners suffered a major defeat which was translated into wages, the General Strike was a victory for trade unions on the wage issue which was not pressed subsequently. At grass-roots level the strike was well supported and organized and it was clear that if confrontation continued the moderate leadership in the TUC might be swept aside by more radical elements. In the 1920s it was established that government had to find a *modus vivendi* with organized labour and, in the process, economic policy had to be sacrificed in the interests of political survival. In many ways this development was a harbinger of the situation which prevailed after the Second World War. Major unions such as the miners and the engineers could be defeated, but wage earners maintained a bargaining power which flew in the face of economic reality and policy. This power rested ultimately on the ballot box rather than industrial might.

Of course the wage issue was ground out at the micro rather than the macro level. Individual employers and employers' associations were either unwilling or unable to force wage adjustments. In some industries reductions in non-wage costs helped to maintain profitability. Individual workers and the unemployed in particular were generally unwilling to undercut existing rates. This cannot be simply ascribed to union power which applied directly to only about half the workforce. Unorganized workers maintained their wages almost as well as those in trade unions. The unemployed, in general, were not prepared to price themselves into work. While union power and a sense of wage justice played some part in this, the essential explanation for the failure of wage adjustment must lie in the system of unemployment relief which had evolved by the early 1920s. Without relief from National Insurance, unemployment benefit or what was left of the Poor Law system, economic necessity must surely have promoted wage adjustment. In short, economic policy was sacrificed in favour of social and political considerations. While the dole in various forms was below the least generous poverty lines defined in various interwar poverty surveys, it was enough to prevent a general shattering of wage rates. We should remember that some workers in full-time employment were also living in poverty. In the absence of unemployment relief wages might have adjusted but the risks in social and political terms were too great to be contemplated. This is not to suggest any possibility of armed insurrection or revolution. Major political changes in modern industrial society are rarely effected through such crude devices. Fascism assumed power in Germany and Italy through more or less democratic means and the obscene violence of those regimes was prepetrated not in gaining power but in exercising it. In Britain the dole, which was a conscious item of policy, had a crucial role in underwriting political stability but in the process it may have been the essential barrier to a restoration of economic equilibrium which the authorities believed was possible. If they were correct, then one branch of policy destroyed another.

During the 1920s Britain's unemployment problem emanated essentially from a cost-contrained export sector. Adjustment failed to take place in part at least because the desirable degree of wage flexibility was not forthcoming and could not be enforced by the authorities. For social, humanitarian and political reasons Britain established in the 1920s a new system of unemployment relief which served to take the edge off desperation and acted as a support for the existing wage structure. (There remains the possibility that lower *rates* of unemployment benefit might have promoted some wage adjustment without destroying the social fabric.) On the domestic front social policy, in effect, cancelled out the main thrust of economic policy. In these circumstances the only real hope for economic success lay in a rapid growth of exports. The authorities might have promoted this either by a competitive devaluation of sterling or by encouraging international expansion. There was failure on both fronts. Even if devaluation had been attempted there must be serious doubts that it could have been achieved on an effective scale. International reflation was even more elusive and was clearly beyond the depleted power of Britain in the world economy.

Economic Policy during the 1930s

With Britain's enforced departure from the gold standard in 1931 the policies of the 1920s were seen to be in tatters. Sterling became a managed currency and there was some marginal depreciation in order to stimulate export industries. Interest rates were no longer so important to the currency and external account and this made 'cheap money' possible. There must be some doubt that the cheap money policy was initially the result of government decision or that it was intended to stimulate investment, output and employment. The Treasury, of course saw, in lower interest rates an opportunity to reduce the burden of public debt servicing. Later in the 1930s the policy was promoted as a recovery measure and some commentators believe it played a major role in recovery [193]. There is little clear evidence that cheap money induced higher investment in British industry. It may have produced a greater degree of flexibility in the public accounts and possibly gave some stimulus to building which was a labour-intensive activity [136]

In 1931-2 Britain formally abandoned free trade and introduced tariff protection and Imperial Preferences. This had long been Conservative policy but the party had failed to convince the electorate which, in particular, feared a rise in food prices. By the early 1930s there were compelling practical arguments for this step although to many economists and those in the Liberal tradition it was anathema and a further blow to world trade. By the early 1930s protection was very much the rule and Britain the outstanding exception. In a world where trade was increasingly regulated and subject to bilateral bargaining Britain's considerable commercial bargaining power could no longer be sacrificed to the principle of free trade. Some British industries such as textiles urgently needed a measure of protection in the home market. Also, without protection it was impossible to establish Empire preferences. The Ottawa Agreements of 1932 took the form of a series of bilateral agreements giving mutual preferences on specific items. British goods gained preferential entry to the increasingly valuable Dominion markets and there was some diversion of trade towards the Empire. However, British gains from the Ottawa system extended beyond trade into debt repayment and the protection of sterling [43]. The effects of protection are difficult to evaluate [49] but they were probably positive in employment terms, especially in textiles, and there were important indirect effects especially in relation to business confidence.

As Kirby has shown in Chapter 10 industrial policy also changed during the interwar years. The bonfire of controls and new faith in competition after the First World War had not restored British industry in world markets and the faith in competition gradually gave way to a search for alternatives. Tariffs were one alternative but clearly they could not solve the problems of ailing export industries which were only able to rely to a limited extent on a protected home market. The answer which came most readily was 'rationalization', a process which sounded rather better than it worked in practice. Ideally it meant the orderly reduction of the least efficient capacity in order to retain the viable parts of manufacturing industry. It was not, of course, an employment policy as such and this can be most readily appreciated if we recall that the acute unemployment crisis in Jarrow during the mid-1930s was accentuated by a rationalization scheme which closed Palmer's Shipyard, the town's principal employer. Rationalization schemes which commenced during the 1920s were usually voluntary and compulsory schemes were only undertaken with widespread support in the industry. In general they sought to reduce capacity and competition in order to maintain prices and profits, and maintaining employment was not usually a first consideration. In other industries market control was encouraged by public policy in order to retain capacity. In agriculture, for example, producers were given the opportunity to control prices as a means of encouraging output and employment, but above all market control was intended to protect and enhance profits. By the 1930s British government was prepared to ignore and in some instances to encourage an alternative to free market pricing. Far from being hidebound by the principles of classical economics government was prepared to accept and sometimes to legalize collusion and price controls in a variety of forms. Industry was slow to take advantage of these opportunities and remained suspicious and wary of government involvement.

Industrial policy abandoned a basic faith in competition but never gained new faith in planning as an alternative. The 'planning movement' of the 1930s (see Chapter 4) ignored detailed industrial planning and failed to grasp an important opportunity which changing attitudes to industry and competition presented. During the 1940s under wartime emergency circumstances the inclination to interfere with basic industrial matters lost all inhibitions but the interference which occurred during the 1940s took the form of control rather than planning. When such controls were removed once again, Keynesian economics provided a substitute for detailed industrial planning. British industrial policy in peacetime moved from *laissez-faire* market capitalism to Keynesian macroeconomic control and detailed industrial strategy as practised in postwar Japan was never seriously contemplated despite Britain's industrial problems.

The nearest interwar exception to this came with rearmament in the later 1930s where a good deal of attention was paid to microeconomic and regional matters. Some declining areas and industries gained in the process and the fiscal stance became mildly expansionist. However, it would be quite wrong to elevate rearmament into an industrial or employment policy. The employment effects of rearmament are considered by Middleton in Chapter 9.

During the 1930s there were major changes in economic policy and some important contrasts with the 1920s emerge. Monetary policy was relaxed in 1931 with the departure from gold and the beginnings of cheap money. From 1934 budgetary policy also become less rigid and the need for rearmament made some fiscal stimulus not only possible but acceptable. These measures may have caused some very modest reductions in the incidence of unemployment but the problem tended to be even worse than during the 1920s and, while some changes in official attitudes can be detected, there was no question of a sustained assault on the unemployment problem. The most we can say is that attitudes were becoming a little more flexible. But it required a national emergency such as the need to combat Nazism to produce this and major changes had to await full-scale war.

With the failure of previous policies not in doubt the National government which came into office in 1931 had to favour the expansion of British industry, but the preference for a private sector solution remained strong. The measures taken were designed to bolster business confidence rather than to increase public sector employment. Budgets were balanced, tariffs imposed and interest and exchange rates brought down (in the latter case, temporarily). To a large extent, however, the changes were imposed by circumstances beyond government control. The effects of these changes on employment, if not on business confidence, seem to have been rather limited. The aggregate effect of balancing budgets was to reduce economic activity, since cuts in public spending far outweighed any boost to demand from increased private sector investment, and fiscal policy remained very restrictive until 1933–4 [198]. Cheap money and changes in money supply did not have a major impact and the effects of tariffs is debatable. It is clear that the interventionist implications of tariff policy were largely ignored. The main positive effort of the 1930s, the Special Areas legislation, was very small-scale and remained a political gesture devoid of economic faith [22].

Real Policy Options

It is perhaps worth asking how much choice interwar governments really had. There was very little difference between Conservative or Labour governments, though it is true that the latter tried to do more in terms of public works and were inclined to be more generous to the unemployed, but these were differences of degree. As in the 1980s, electoral pledges aside, the parties of government had little faith in their ability to solve the unemployment problem. While administrators in the Civil Service and the Bank of England certainly had strong views it would be difficult to prove that they dictated policy to politicians. In general, the politicians and, to a large extent, the general public were carried along by the prevailing opinion. Like the weather, unemployment was bad but had to be accepted with as much dignity as possible.

A classic example here is to be found in the return to the gold standard in 1925. The policy was generally accepted by all shades of opinion with varying degrees of enthusiasm but largely without criticism. Only Keynes and a few others really understood the issues involved and were prepared to support an alternative policy. Churchill as Chancellor in 1925 could see major disadvantages in deflationary policies and had no particular axe to grind in terms of economic theories or beliefs. He was prepared to consider alternatives and the Public Records show that he made some attempt to do so [208, 64–79]. As a practical politician Churchill came to accept that the alternative, however attractive and despite the advocacy of Keynes, had no adequate political and administrative base.

It can also be shown that where governments were clearly committed to economic policies the Bank and the Treasury were prepared to implement these policies even where the principles of classical economics or traditional budgetary practices were offended. This was the case, for example, with tariffs and rearmament. If Lloyd George had been elected in 1929 there can be little doubt that some attempt would have been made to implement the 1929 manifesto even though the Treasury had some major reservations and would not have anticipated a very successful outcome. The events of the 1940s show that political changes could direct economic policy even where prominent figures in the Treasury remained sceptical about the theoretical foundations.

In general then, the Treasury cannot be blamed for rejecting political programmes which might have solved the unemployment problem. Such policies were not being proposed by interwar ministers for reasons which are considered in Chapter 4. It is of course the case that the Treasury rejected Keynesian views and the reasons for this are examined in Chapter 9 by Middleton who shows that the rejection was less irrationally dogmatic than may have been suggested. Viewed in the light of British economic problems and policies since 1975 the interwar Treasury stands on stronger ground than it appeared to do during the post-1945 Keynesian consensus. Interwar notions of 'crowding out' appear to be rather more robust than they did a decade ago and the rational expectations hypothesis may give the 'Treasury view' a new lease of life.

Also, it is now much more widely accepted that the scope for a unilateral Keynesian solution to Britain's interwar unemployment problem was indeed questionable. Few people now challenge the view that multipliers were low and especially regional multipliers in the depressed areas [103]. It is hard to reconcile the apparently massive budget deficits and exchange depreciations which a Keynesian solution would have required with the need to maintain political and business confidence. Of course, moderate reflation might have produced some short-run benefits but even measures of this kind faced real difficulties.

Apart from the crisis years of 1929–31 when Labour was rattled from office the trend in unemployment during most years of the 1920s and 1930s was downwards. Politicians were able to claim that their policies were succeeding slowly but that the process would inevitably be painful. During the 1920s they were able to point to hyperinflation and economic crisis abroad and in the 1930s Britain's heavy unemployment was by no means unique or the most severe. Also, as Deacon has shown in Chapter 3, Britain had a national system of unemployment relief which was generous by previous standards and looked rather better than what was available abroad. Britain's unemployed may have been poor but they did not starve and it was possible to retain some dignity. The view that unemployment was a curse which had to be borne with dignity may have had some appeal to an electorate which was mainly Victorian born and bred and mildly masochistic. Of course, there was the eventual hope that 'sound money' and a period of deprivation would, in the 'long run', give rise to a restoration of prosperity for all. Such feelings together with the perceived lack of a political alternative go some way towards explaining the remarkable level of support for National government during the early 1930s. The truth was that politicians were not prepared to apply effective policies for dealing with unemployment and any reductions which did take place were usually fortuitous rather than the result of policy.

While some contemporaries may have hoped and believed that policies were working it is clear in retrospect that there was policy failure. This was not necessarily because policies were wrong in the sense of being incorrect or illogical. As Middleton shows Treasury thinking was more sophisticated and flexible than has often been supposed and it is clear from Lowe's Chapter 11 that there were progressive attitudes in the Ministry of Labour. We have to remember that there were major constraints on government power both internally and externally. These constraints defeated policy.

For example, in the 1920s Britain was attempting to run an open economy although both internal and external circumstances were against this. Vested interests and indeed public opinion strongly favoured restoration of the open economy on pre-1914 lines and the electorate pronounced itself against protection in 1923. The problem of unemployment appeared to emanate largely from an export sector which was constrained by high costs and external trade impediments.

In these circumstances the only logical policy was to attempt to promote internal deflation and international liberalism. On the domestic front policy success was blocked by the failure of wages to adjust. The rigidities in the labour market have been analysed by Garside in Chapter 6. Wages also remained inflexible for political and social reasons and it has been suggested that the system of unemployment relief may have been an important influence. Social policy and political circumstances created an economic policy impasse.

In this situation a stimulus to exports could only be provided by devaluation or through expansion in world markets. The issue of devaluation appears to have been avoided on repeated occasions and especially in 1919, 1921 and 1925, and this constitutes a major Keynesian criticism of policy. Devaluation would certainly have assisted the export industries but it was, in a sense, contrary to the object of the exercise which was to restore the pre-1914 system. There can be little doubt that a British devaluation would have set a bad example and would have given rise to a competitive round. There must be a good deal of doubt about Britain's ability to force an effective and lasting devaluation. The record of the 1930s suggests that devaluation was a very limited remedy to unemployment and that the scope for making devaluation effective was severely constrained.

Britain simply did not have the power to promote an expanding international economy. Some economic and financial power and influence had been lost, particularly to the United States, and America failed to assume the international role which Britain had lost. During the 1920s the expanding American market remained largely closed to European manufactures shielded by an undervalued US dollar and protectionism [87; 101]. As Svennilson has indicated, there were important long-run influences making for secular stagnation in the international economy during the interwar period [261]. Britain's external strategy was baulked in part by continued disagreements with the United States over economic and financial policies.

After the sharp international downturn in 1929 the policy impasse was clearly revealed and circumstances dictated new policy departures. Devaluation, cheap money and protection in the early 1930s can all be seen as the products of economic crisis. As cures for unemployment in the circumstances of the 1930s they were clearly ineffective. Devaluation was inevitably limited and short-lived. The price of money was not the major factor governing industrial investment. Some British industries, as Kirby suggests in Chapter 10, may have gained from high rates of effective protection but gains from trade had little influence in the 1930s recovery. The most important influence in the upswing of 1932–7 appears to have been rising consumption which owed much to favourable terms of trade and very little to changes in government policy.

In the 1930s also it is possible to defend policies in logical terms while at the same time pointing to blockages which amounted to impasse. Kirby shows that industrial policies were baulked by the resistance of business to government interference and the unwillingness of governments to set precedents for nationalization and planning. Middleton's analysis of Treasury policy reveals the institutional barriers to reflation and Lowe's chapter indicates how progressive attitudes in the Ministry of Labour were largely stifled. In academic terms, of course, it has been the fashion to look behind these mundane influences for some great failure in concept. In Chapters 6 to 8 Garside, Hatton and Peden have examined some of the prospects for a Keynesian solution to unemployment.

In the post-1945 Keynesian consensus it was easy to portray the policy problem as a legendary confrontation with Keynes as St. George and the Classical View as the Dragon. Of course, the real conflict was much more complicated and remains to a large extent hidden from view today. Essentially it related to the question of market equilibrium and the role of the market in achieving economic aims. This question remained unresolved and remains the central issue today.

At the end of the interwar period most British economic policy-makers and most economists had probably come to accept that there was something like an irreducible minimum of 9 per cent (NIS) unemployment in Britain. There is some evidence to suggest that Keynes himself may have accepted this view which suggested a 'natural rate' of about 10 per cent below which the economy became 'overheated' [103]. This rather high 'natural rate' may have rested on serious structural rigidities in the economy which began to disappear after 1940. Keynes and his close followers were, in effect, saying that measures could be taken to reduce the peaks of unemployment which occurred during the troughs of trade cycles and, in particular, during major downturns such as 1929–32. But they were not, and this must be emphasized, putting the view that anything approaching the 'full employment' of the period following the Second World War could be attained. Also, and this is more important, Keynes did not fundamentally challenge the private enterprise, market economy, though some of his followers did. Meanwhile, in other industrial economies, non-market corporatist states had emerged in spectacular forms in Russia, Italy and Germany. These regimes were politically repugnant to the British political mainstream even though they had solved the unemployment problem as such. Less prominent and extreme alternatives in Sweden and perhaps New Zealand were given little attention. To Britain in the late 1930s these models did not seem very relevant. Indeed, the British economy had performed well during the 1930s on all economic measures except unemployment

While a number of new economic models had emerged in different parts of the world by the end of the 1930s, the real choices were far from clear to contemporaries. As a simplification, and with the advantage of hindsight, four main possibilities can be suggested.

First there was the free market model where government intervention was kept to an acceptable minimum and being mainly confined to regulatory devices such as control of the money supply balanced budgets, gold standard or exchange mechanisms and with direct involvement only where the free market was unsatisfactory or appeared to have failed. This approach, based on neo-classical economic views, which happily coincided with vested interests dominated British economic policy during the interwar period and from 1979, the Thatcher government attempted to apply a modernized version.

Secondly, there was the neo-Keynesian manipulated market economy which became established in Britain between 1950 and the 1970s. Keynesian and classical views were partially reconciled in belief in long-run market equilibrium (the 'neo-classical synthesis') It was accepted that the economy was basically free enterprise and the role of government was essentially confined to macroeconomic regulation. By the 1970s this model was being increasingly questioned both in theory and practice.

Thirdly, there was the choice of a planned economy where the economic interests and activities of companies and individuals were to some degree influenced and controlled by non-economic consider ations. Planned economies may take many forms and 'planning' can be interpreted and applied in many different ways. In essence however, the notion of a planned economy is based on a view that the free or manipulated market is in some way inadequate. Such views were quite naturally common during the 1930s and they gave rise to flourishing 'planning movement' which extended across the political spectrum. In questioning the classical concept of market equilibrium and stating the case for government intervention Keynes gave planning some intellectual support. Many Keynesians supported planning although Keynes himself appeared to stop short a macroeconomic control. By the 1940s Beveridge, the arch-mandarin clearly favoured planning and grafted Keynesianism on to h scheme of things at a fairly late stage. Full employment was a *sine qu non* of the Welfare State and Keynesian policies provided a means t full employment. However, the essential contribution of Keynesian policies was in their ability to neatly reconcile economic control with political democracy. Beveridge was concerned about ensuring 'full employment *in a free society*'. During the 1940s the British public was prepared to accept heavy state intervention, deprivation and sacrifice. As the following chapter shows, by the end of the 1940s, the Conservative Party was able to take advantage of a different mood which coalesced into a neo-Keynesian compromise in the 1950s. When this appeared to succeed the remarkably successful economic control of the 1940s was confined to history.

The fourth model was the corporatist state which was manifested in Russia, Italy and Germany during the interwar years, attracting much attention and some admiration in Britain. Mosley presented such an option in Britain and the Mosley alternative and the reasons for its rejection are examined in Chapters 4 and 6. Fascism and other forms of corporate control were repugnant to the British political tradition and economic and social circumstances in Britain were not sufficiently extreme to provide political scope for extremist alternatives. Mosley, Lloyd George and others failed to find political support for alternative economic policies and in the crisis of the early 1930s the National government obtained massive electoral support for orthodoxy.

In the absence of political alternatives and democratic pressure the only hope for an employment policy lay with the established authorities who were continually impressed with the disadvantages of any employment policy. Kirby in Chapter 10, for example, details that while government had industrial policies there were real barriers to industrial planning and indeed to any kind of coherent strategy. The plain truth appears to be that vested interests and those in control were happier with the *status quo* than they would have been with any feasible employment policy. Unemployment was the product of self-interest rather than stupidity.

The policy options have not been resolved by economic theory and economics is as much a divided profession now as during the late 1930s. The essential division in economics, then as now, rested upon attitudes to the notion of long-run market equilibrium. Keynes himself was ambivalent on this – subscribing, on the one hand, to a sceptical attitude towards equilibrium but, on the other, refusing to accept the policy implications of his belief. Keynesian economics continued to operate and to be articulated in quasi-classical forms and, by the 1960s, the so-called 'neo-classical synthesis' had effected a Keynesian-classical reconciliation which satisfied those who yearned for it.

The next chapter explores how after the Second World War the controlled economy gradually crumbled in postwar prosperity and continued full employment bolstered a misplaced confidence in the belief that the Keynesian paradigm, suitably adapted, offered an easier and more acceptable alternative. Over several decades Britain's relative economic decline and deteriorating international competitiveness were masked by continued full employment and improving material standards. In the long run the basic problems evident during the interwar years re-emerged and fundamental policy choices became prominent once more, only to be temporarily submerged once again by North Sea oil which solved balance of payments if not employment problems.

Because of the Keynesian paradigm there has never been a serious policy debate in Britain about the choice between a market and a planned economy. This was largely absent during the interwar years just as it is from the policy debate during the 1980s. Some may doubt that the choice between Keynes and the classical view was real in the final analysis. In the interwar period the *real* policy option was never faced and a solution to the unemployment problem was never in sight. In this essential, at least, history may have repeated itself.

13

The War and the White Paper

ALAN BOOTH

The Second World War banished unemployment. Labour market conditions changed dramatically. At the outbreak of war, there were still obvious signs of excess supply; in early 1941, Britain entered a labour famine which endured at least until the armistice. In part, the change was caused by the special conditions of war. Over 4.5 million people entered the defence services and civilian employment actually fell by 8.8 per cent between 1939 and 1945 [225, *128–9*]. More importantly, wartime conditions gradually broke down many of the constraints which had so limited economic policy between the wars. After 1940–1, the importance of the balance of payments, the political power of the City and the Treasury-Bank axis, and *laissez-faire* attitudes to both industry and labour all diminished in strength as short-run influences over economic policy. For the first time in 20 years, the British government pursued an all-out production policy, and real output rose by 31 per cent between 1938 and 1942. The economic role and attitude of government also changed during the war; there was much greater willingness to intervene and control, though the extent to which these new ideas and policies could be translated into peacetime was disputed. For those willing to learn, however, this was a powerful demonstration of the economic potential of government and it stiffened the resolve of those who maintained that a full employment policy should be maintained as a deliberate goal for peacetime governments [21, *81*].

Wartime Economic Policy and the War Economy

The war brought three main changes of importance for the emergence of a commitment to peacetime full employment. First,

175

there were a number of significant changes in the machinery of economic policy. These changes partly reflected and were partly a consequence of the second major development, the rise in the status of organized labour. Finally, there were shifts in the balance of international economic power which had implications for the conduct of domestic policy.

Britain's economic war plan was to shift resources from the civilian to the munitions sector while retaining sufficient capacity to produce consumer goods to preserve morale at home and manufactures for export to pay for essential imports (especially from the USA). Britain hoped to achieve rearmament in depth over a period of three years. The principal tool with which government began to restructure the economy was its control over imports and its system of allocating raw materials [142, 85]. Through military conscription and the schedule of reserved occupations, the government also acquired enormous potential leverage over the labour market. The railways, shipping and agriculture also came under state supervision shortly after the outbreak of war, and controls over foreign exchange deals and the allocation of private capital were tightened considerably.

These were important steps, but they did not amount to a planned economy. Financial control continued as in peacetime, and the Treasury remained the key co-ordinating department. These arrangements could persist only as long as a pool of unemployed resources was available. The main priority in this first phase of the war economy was the creation of additional munitions capacity, some of it in the USA [284, 70], and domestic unemployment fell only slowly during the winter of 1939–40. To a nation at war, this appeared perplexing and demoralizing. Public attitudes to unemployment were changing rapidly.

The shortcomings of the three-year rearmament strategy were cruelly exposed in the spring of 1940, when Germany conquered most of continental Europe and devastated the Anglo-French war plan. With the Germans on the French coast bombing British cities and planning invasion, everything had to be sacrificed to immediate production, especially for air defence. Finance very quickly became much less important, and policy-makers began to plan in terms of physical resources. Shipping space, raw materials, industrial capacity and manpower were all major limiting factors on production, but increasingly manpower and materials, especially steel, were the chief constraints and consequently became the principal instruments of planning [240, 37].

There were two lasting consequences for economic policy. The first was a revolution in official statistics. Policy-makers clearly needed much more detailed information than had been available in the 1930s if they were to plan output in the wartime economy faced by a range of capacity constraints. University economists who had come into Whitehall during 1940 as temporary civil servants took the lead in collecting and processing data [45, 55]. Whitehall began to assemble reliable series on the major economic aggregates and began to base its decision-taking much more on quantitative information. The creation of the Central Statistical Office in 1941 was a major, if often neglected, step towards rational decision-making [120, 220–2]. Although problems remained with the coverage and speed of production of official statistics, policy-makers henceforward would have a much better idea of what was happening in the economy and had a reasonable basis for estimating the effects of policy changes.

A more temporary result of the rise of physical planning was the comparative eclipse of the Treasury. After the 1941 budget, the role of finance in the war economy was essentially passive; its principal role was to permit increased output and the reallocation of resources without inflation [244, *chs. 1, 3, 4*]. The influence of the Treasury declined as financial policy became less important [55, *17*]. The Treasury also suffered from the association of some of its members with appeasement and because Churchill believed that he had been badly advised by Treasury officials at the time of the return to gold. The downgrading of the Treasury was only temporary and marginal, but for a limited period the department lost both its role as sole internal adviser to governments on monetary and fiscal policies and its power to veto proposals on the grounds of cost. We shall return to these issues when discussing reconstruction planning.

It is perhaps ironic but financial policy, especially after 1941, was one of the great wartime successes. Since 1937, Treasury officials had been coping with deficit-finance and had become increasingly worried about the threat of inflation, especially as First World War experiences had taught how damaging inflationary forces could be to the domestic social fabric. Thus, Treasury officials and their economic advisers sought to push up taxes as rapidly as was politically possible during 1939 and 1940. Even so, in 1940–1, borrowing covered approximately 60 per cent of all government spending [233, *214*], and Treasury officials had no clear analytical insights into ways of neutralizing inflationary pressures. The favourite remedy of the Treasury's economic advisers was to propose wage controls.[1]

Keynes, however, did have an understanding of the inflationary mechanism by adapting the analysis of *The General Theory* to a situation of excess rather than deficient demand. Once again, he mounted a very public campaign criticizing the Treasury for its lack of economic understanding. In articles for *The Times* in November

1939 and in *How to Pay for the War*, a pamphlet published in February 1940 [163, *40–155*; 158, *367–439*], he argued that the essence of the wartime financial problem was that incomes would rise in the war economy, but that the supply of consumer goods would have to be held to prewar levels if government was to produce the munitions it needed. Government had to close the 'gap' between private spending power and the value of consumer goods produced or prices would rise and social disruption would follow [163, *41–2*]. He proposed much heavier taxation but suggested sweetening the pill by treating part of the burden as 'deferred pay', to be repaid after the war and preferably to prevent unemployment.

At first, the Treasury could not accept these arguments, but in the crisis of mid–1940 Keynes could not be ignored. He was given a room in the Treasury, and from this base he began to produce a stream of memoranda on wartime financial policy. The Treasury gradually came round to Keynes's national income approach and the 1941 budget was explicitly Keynesian in its framework [247]. For the first time, national income estimates were used to help determine the government's fiscal stance [259, *84–5*]. The Treasury's adoption of Keynesian techniques during the war did not imply a full-scale Keynesian revolution within Whitehall, as we shall see below, but the 'stabilization' budget of 1941 did have an important long-term impact. The stabilization policy (Keynesian budgetary policy, subsidies to the cost of living and co-operation with the unions) managed to contain inflationary forces. Wartime policy demonstrated that deficit finance could be so managed to give very full employment *without accelerating inflation* over a substantial period. For those willing to learn, here was a lesson of the potential of the informed and intelligent use of state economic power.

The military crisis of 1940 not only facilitated necessary shifts in economic policy, it brought a change of government in which organized labour played an important part. Relations between Chamberlain and the unions had always been uneasy and the friction almost certainly retarded mobilization [195, *262–5*]. However, the labour movement trusted Churchill and Labour leaders joined the new coalition. The most significant appointment was that of Ernest Bevin, the outstanding personality of the interwar TUC, as Minister of Labour with additional responsibilities for helping to organize production [38, *5*]. The unions now had an effective foothold in power, and Bevin did much to promote greater confidence between the administration and the labour movement. The military situation decreed that the government should take enormous powers over its citizens, and the Emergency Powers Act of 1940 gave Bevin the power to direct anyone over 16 years of age to do any work. He also introduced the Essential Works Order of 1941, under which he could schedule any factory as undertaking essential work, whereupon no worker could leave or be dismissed without the minister's consent. Bevin used these powers as sparingly as possible, and ensured that workers affected should receive adequate wages, working conditions and welfare. Above all, he tried to inform and consult the unions much more fully than had been the case hitherto [38, *44–5*]. TUC leaders were sucked into the policy-making process to speak for the labour movement and helped to forge a new, close relationship between government and the unions [10, *165*].

The rise in the status of labour owed much to Bevin's forceful personality, but also to the broad recognition that labour enjoyed enormous scarcity power, especially after 1940, but did not exploit its advantages. Britain entered a labour famine in 1941, with shortages of all grades of workers in most parts of the country. There were a number of schemes (concentration of production, utility goods and the tightening of material allocations) to accelerate the release of labour from the civilian economy and, at the same time, women were drawn into the workforce in massive numbers. The proportion of women over the age of 14 in employment rose from 27 per cent in 1939 to 37 per cent in 1943 [206, *219*]. The proportion of the population in employment and military service was higher in Britain than anywhere else; average hours worked per week rose dramatically. Labour dilution was accepted much more easily than in 1914–18. This was a prodigious achievement, but even these methods could not supply enough labour. From 1943 onwards, planners had to accept that total numbers in employment and employment in the munitions industries had to decline.

The fear that labour might exploit its scarcity, especially after the privations of the interwar years, troubled policy-makers from the beginning. Under the Chamberlain government, ministers discussed the imposition of centralized wage fixing, but decided against and turned instead in December 1939 to a policy of subsidizing the cost of living to help prevent general wage increases [244, *63*]. Despite the subsidies, the index continued to rise and, after the change of government, Bevin came under immediate pressure to accept wage controls. Bevin, however, fought for the retention of free collective bargaining and the development of the subsidy policy, arguing that such an approach was essential if working people were to accept the huge increases in direct taxes implicit in the Keynesian budgetary strategy gaining ground within the Treasury. The deal was formalized in the 1941 budget. The Chancellor agreed to peg the cost of living index and the TUC leadership, through Bevin, promised to act responsibly during pay negotiations. The TUC became, in effect, the agents of the government in pay policy, and achieved enormous success. Wage rates rose marginally more rapidly than the official cost of living index, but more slowly than the real cost of living.[2] Again, this 'responsible' behaviour reflected nothing but credit on the TUC in the eyes of government and enabled the TUC to achieve in wartime what it could not in the 1930s – its assimilation into the power structure of the state. Having achieved this position, organized labour was able, as we shall see, to make demands on postwar policy.

Thus far, we have concentrated upon domestic economic and political changes. It seems obvious, however, that for a nation as committed to international exchange as Britain, the international order is equally important. Previous chapters have argued that some at least, of Britain's interwar economic problems resulted from the dislocation of world trade and payments. Between 1920 and 1929 world trade grew by only 8.5 per cent and by 1939 the 1929 level had scarcely been regained [102, 59]. By contrast, in the nineteenth century volumes of world trade had frequently grown by 40 per cent per decade and had not increased by less than 25 per cent in any decade after 1830 [173, 306]. The causes of this disruption of the interwar international economy are clearly complex, but a convincing case has been made that the root of the trouble lay in the unwillingness of the USA and the inability of Britain to stabilize the system in important ways [167, 291–2]. In the war, however, the US economy surged far ahead of its rivals. The period 1940–4 saw a greater expansion of US industrial production than in any previous four-year period, and productivity grew apace [206, 64–7]. At the same time, there were changes in US opinion which made it more likely that the USA would become a more active and willing participant in international economic and financial affairs. The isolationist lobby was severely weakened by Pearl Harbor. Neutrality was no longer an option. The USA had to enter the conflict and having entered, exerted the decisive influence on the outcome. As we shall see, the USA did not shirk the responsibilities of the most powerful victor.

The war also reshaped Anglo–American relations. The 'special relationship' between Britain and the USA, which had been decidedly strained between the wars, was renewed in the close personal friendship between Churchill and Roosevelt. The clearest illustration of the relationship was the passage of the Lend-Lease Act, without which Britain's war effort would have foundered. Lend-Lease, in turn, encouraged the British to be less suspicious of US economic power, and, as we shall see below, there was close co-operation in the planning of the postwar international settlement.[3]

Thus, at both the domestic and international levels, the war helped to create a new environment for policy. The decisive issue for our purposes is to examine the extent to which these wartime changes helped to create a commitment by government to maintain full employment after the war. Thus, we need to measure the impact of these changes on reconstruction planning.

Reconstruction Planning

The most obvious signs of the increased status of labour during the war were the assimilation of the unions into the state and the distribution of ministerial portfolios (Labour leaders held almost all of the major domestic offices). However, organized labour wanted much more than recognition which might be only temporary. It wanted reconstruction. Labour ministers began to make a new postwar deal the main theme of their speeches from 1943 onwards [30, 325–9; 38, 277–8]. The Labour Party programme, under the guidance of Dalton, put full employment, improved social services and economic planning as its priorities [231, 393–407]. The TUC's *Interim Report on Post-War Reconstruction* demanded that the unions be given 'a decisive share in the actual control of the economic life of the nation' and made it clear that full employment was an absolute priority. For the British labour movement to demand in wartime extensive postwar reconstruction was not unprecedented. Similar demands, though involving more fundamental change, had been advocated towards the end of the First World War, but with minimal impact on postwar policy [6]. But there were very different conditions in the early 1940s. In contrast to the class conflict and polarization of 1916–18 [195, *ch. 4*], in the Second World War there developed a strong *national* consensus on the need for the postwar reforms [1, *17–21*]. Driven, on one side, by the ethos of 'fair shares for all' and 'equality of sacrifice' (evident in both rationing and industrial conscription) and, on the other, by the scapegoating of the Conservative leadership of the 1930s for the debacle of 1940, British public opinion shifted subtly but perceptibly leftwards to support postwar reform [1, *213–68*]. From the working class, the demand for reform was also based upon a profound detestation of the experience of unemployment and a growing fear that similar conditions would recur after the war [187, *179*]. Politicians became aware of this reformist sentiment and all parties came to adapt their programmes to the new mood.

Perhaps the most important stage in the building of this reformist consensus was the debate on the Beveridge Report in 1942–3. The details of the report have been discussed in Chapter 3, but wha concerns us here is the political storm surrounding its treatment b government. There was tremendous popular interest, in pa orchestrated by Beveridge himself [128, *241*], in the proposals an intense popular pressure for the government to implement th measures in full after the war. This seemingly irresistible force public opinion met two apparently immovable objects in Treasu worry about the cost and Churchill's determination that the coalitic should concern itself only with matters directly related to the wa leaving contentious postwar issues to a postwar general election. I the event, public opinion won the first round and the Cabin committed itself to the spirit but not the letter of Beveridge.

This decision opened up the debate on reconstruction policy Whitehall as Beveridge had created his scheme on the assumptic that there would be family allowances, a comprehensive heal service and the avoidance of mass unemployment. His pla depended upon the average rate of unemployment being no high than the lowest level of the 1930s – 10 per cent of the interw insured workforce or 8.5 per cent of the broader postwar N scheme. The Treasury, however, continued to oppose Beveridg Officials were reluctant to commit themselves to any one category postwar expenditure when the total demand and relative prioriti were unknown. They also doubted whether Beveridge's unemplo ment target would be attainable and they continued to worry abo the cost [128, *422–4*; 1, *220–1*]. This conflict brought to the attentic of ministers an already protracted debate within Whitehall postwar employment policy.

Leading the optimists was the Economic Section, a group university economists who had been drawn into Whitehall temporary civil servants in 1940 and had established a considerab reputation in advising the Cabinet's senior economic policy committe Among the Section's members were a number of prewar converts Keynesian theory and one of them, James Meade, had drawn up proposal for postwar Keynesian policies. He identified three ma types of unemployment (transitional, structural and general) a believed that general (demand-deficient) was the most serious. could be avoided by a series of policy instruments acting up aggregate demand. If unemployment threatened, interest rates cou be reduced to encourage private investment; central and loc government could expand their own capital spending; and priva consumption could be stimulated if Beveridge's social securi scheme were adapted as an automatic stabilizer with the level employee contributions varying inversely with the rate of unemplo ment. The latter two policies would supply a sizeable injection demand but would almost certainly drive the budget into deficit. Meade was keen to point out that the domestic industrial structure should be competitive and labour mobile to prevent demand stimulation from going simply to higher wages or profits, but, even so, there was a proposal for a wages policy to curb cost-push pressure. Finally great importance was attached to reform of the international economy to promote world trade and export growth [see 24, *107–8*].

The pessimists were led by the Treasury, whose 'view' had changed very little from that analysed in Chapter 9. The balanced budget rule was still held, though not inflexibly, and was still justified by a range of political and administrative arguments [223, *288*]. The external constraint was again a vital concern, not least because Britain's postwar external prospects already seemed dire. The opposition to public works also persisted though in a different form, reflecting the views of Hubert Henderson, wartime economic adviser to the Treasury. Henderson anticipated another postwar cycle of exaggerated boom and slump, after which the main problem would be to transfer workers from an over-expanded capital sector to consumer industries. Public works, obviously, aimed to shift workers in the opposite direction [135, *220–35*]. Finally, the fear of inflation persisted; the Treasury's main priority was the 'transitional period' from a mobilized to a civilian economy. In this phase, all agreed that *in*flation not *de*flation would be the problem, and it was in this period that most of the Treasury's attention was concentrated [223, *289*].

The Beveridge Report brought these official-level disputes to the attention of ministers because the Treasury's ability to pay for Beveridge's proposals was dependent upon levels of postwar employment and unemployment. Disagreements over what would happen to postwar employment prevented the Cabinet from concluding its deliberations on postwar social insurance, to the great annoyance of Labour Party Ministers [1, *222–3*]. To resolve these differences, the Cabinet established an official steering committee on postwar employment, under Sir Richard Hopkins of the Treasury. The debates of the steering committee and the role of Hopkins have come under very close scrutiny in recent years [see 223; 24]. In brief, the committee considered what policies might be deployed against (1) insufficient domestic demand resulting from a fall in consumption or investment and (2) a collapse of exports or a severe structural problem. The report was a masterful compromise, opting for cheap money, counter-cyclical public works and Meade's social security contributions scheme, though there were considerable reservations about the last item. This mix represented both the Economic

Section's programme and the broad approach innovated by th
Treasury in the 1930s. The highly divisive issues which remained
like budgetary policy, were fudged. They may have been a slight bia
to the Keynesian position of the Economic Section, as Keyne
described the report as 'an outstanding State Paper which, if on
casts one's eyes back ten years or so, represents a revolution ii
official opinion' [165, *364*]. A compromise 'Keynesian' postwa
policy seemed near to hand. However, as the steering committe
report was being completed and discussed, a critical stage wa
reached in the talks on the postwar external settlement. As we sha
see below, ministers were asked to take decisions which the Treasur
believed would reduce its freedom to defend the postwar balance (
payments. Against this background, Treasury officials began
campaign to try to regain the ground lost to the Economic Sectior
they suddenly became much more concerned about the effects (
postwar employment policy on inflation, the budget and on foreig
confidence in British public finance.

Before we can appreciate why the Treasury was so alarmed in earl
1944, it is essential to examine Britain's war and postwar balance (
payments problems. By 1943, Britain's export volumes were le;
than 30 per cent of the 1938 figure [244, *495*]. Import volumes wer
also down but by a lesser amount, giving a substantial deficit o
visible trade which was covered in large part by Lend-Lease aid fro:
the USA. However, there was no indication of what would happen 1
Lend-Lease after the war; Britain's external position was certain 1
be dire. It would take some time to restart the civilian expo
industries, but imports would be higher than in 1938 to feed a large
better nourished population and to provide raw materials f(
factories which would be booming in the immediate postwar perio(
Britain would have a massive deficit on visible trade for some tin
after the war. Invisibles would also be much reduced from the loss (
shipping and the sale or destruction of British overseas investmen
during the war. Moreover, the obvious major postwar source (
supply was certain to be the USA, but British reserves of gold ar
dollars had been depleted during the war, partly by the way Len(
Lease had been administered. The low reserves were also inadequa
in relation to the debts Britain had incurred to a wide range (
countries during the war. If this were not enough, there were certa
to be problems in production and distribution immediately after tl
war. Most of Britain's manufacturing base had been disrupte
capital equipment had been badly run down and many workers h;
not practised their skills for years. The main domestic energy sourc
coal, had experienced enormous problems in meeting wartin
demand; new investment and further recruitment would be postw

priorities. The ports and railways had been severely bombed and had enjoyed minimal maintenance and repair. To put it bluntly, Britain's postwar balance of payments was certain to be excessively weak and beyond the ability of the market economy to handle. It was already clear that the government would have to retain much of the mechanism of wartime control (though the future of manpower controls was uncertain) to protect the balance of payments.

Reinforcing these worries about Britain's immediate postwar balance of payments position was the enormous controversy in the government and administration in early 1944 unleashed by developments in the talks on the postwar international settlement. Talks with the Americans on the postwar international economic and financial system had begun early in the war and had been dominated on the British side by Keynes. His original thoughts had turned to a restrictive, protective scheme to allow Britain to defend her very difficult postwar external position [277, 25–6]. However, he saw very quickly that a more liberal tide was running in the USA, and turned his attention to the creation of a more liberal, multilateral framework in which Britain's likely postwar problems could be accommodated. The basic requirement was a postwar settlement which enabled trade to expand but which did not jeopardize the freedom of countries to pursue domestic economic goals (such as full employment). Expansion presupposed fixed exchange rates and the creation of additional reserve assets. Keynes's plan involved the establishment of an International Clearing Union, the members of which would have to fix par values for their currencies and to give up certain restrictive trade and payments measures. The new reserve asset, Bancor, would expand international liquidity substantially (and also increase enormously potential US liability) and provide a dynamic centre to the world economy. In this environment, Britain's exports might prosper. The Keynes plan envisaged fairly frequent adjustment of the fixed exchange rates if the level of 'efficiency wages' in any one country grew out of line with prevailing world levels. This provision was especially necessary for a country like Britain which hoped to pursue an active full employment policy and might suffer from inflationary pressures [164, 274–5].

US opinion, led by Harry White, also favoured freer multilateral trade and payments but could not support the degree of financial commitment proposed by Keynes. White's Stabilization Fund was, in effect, a gold exchange standard with fixed but adjustable exchange rates tied to the gold value of the dollar. Member countries of the Fund would have to keep some of their national reserves with the Fund, but loans could be made available to meet immediate balance of payments difficulties. White hoped that the Fund would be able to impose conditions (especially changes in domestic policy) on those countries receiving assistance [244, 93]. The White plan demanded that member countries obtain permission from the Fund before altering their exchange rates.

Although both schemes shared common principles, it was clear that the experts in the two countries had drawn up plans to protect their own national self-interest. Where there were differences of view, it was almost inevitably the US view which prevailed. However, Keynes accepted the rejection of most of his ideas with very good grace and fought vigorously to persuade London to accept White's proposals [288, 100]. Despite the loss of most of his specific suggestions, Keynes seems to have been encouraged by the fact that the US wartime view was similar to that which he himself had proposed in the 1930s, especially in The Means to Prosperity. He may also have been very relieved that the USA was finally accepting its international responsibilities [288, 100–1]. Finally, there is no doubt that the case of the optimists was becoming increasingly centred upon the long-term benefits to employment of an expanding, liberal international framework. The two leaders of the Economic Section, Robbins and Meade, were heavily involved with Keynes in the very difficult and protracted Anglo-American negotiations on postwar trade and payments.

In February 1944, the Cabinet was considering an American plan, backed by Keynes, to establish an International Monetary Fund. Because the plan implied some limits on Britain's freedom to vary its exchange rate, it was highly controversial [233, 290]. The liberal tone antagonized both the Labour left (who saw the terms of the international settlement as a barrier to socialist planning) and the Conservative right (because Imperial links were threatened). All these elements intensified worries about Britain's postwar balance of payments and gave the Treasury a lever with which to influence those who were turning the steering committee report into a white paper.

The White Paper

There was another problem for officials in early 1944; Beveridge was again in the background. He was known to be close to publishing a report on his own employment policy enquiry. The fear of being embarrassed a second time by Beveridge probably did more than anything to ensure that the Employment Policy white paper was produced quickly, but it made for an unsatisfactory document. The foreword committed the goverment to accept 'as one of [its] primary aims and responsibilities, the maintenance of a high and stable level of employment after the war' [117, *3*]. This was stirring stuff, but 'high and stable' had been deliberately chosen instead of 'full' [146, *43*] and even this attenuated commitment was made conditional on a favourable outcome of the Anglo-American external policy talks. The conditional elements were detailed in the first chapters of the paper, an ordering demanded by the Treasury [223, *291*]. Chapter 1 emphasized that Britain's domestic prosperity was dependent upon international factors. Britain was highly committed to trade. Thus, full employment depended upon a progressive expansion of world trade and the recovery and continuing efficiency of Britain's export industries. The need for efficiency was a recurrent theme in the white paper, again at the insistence of the Treasury [223, *291*]. Controls would be needed to give priority to export industries in the transition, but in the longer term governments would need to find fiscal and other devices to promote technological advance in British industry. Chapter 2 argued that the potential chaos of the transition was also a serious threat to long-term employment policy. Controls rather than the market should be used to allocate resources to avoid another exaggerated postwar cycle. The destructive power of inflation was underlined and the public was warned that, if industry was to recover from the war and be able to provide long-run prosperity, consumption must continue to be restrained to allow for heavy investment in the export industries. Both these chapters contained important material and sound argument, but their unremitting caution and appearance so early in the paper gave the impression that the authors were already looking for excuses should the policy fail.

Only in the third chapter, 'The Balanced Distribution of Industry and Labour', did a more positive tone emerge. This chapter bore the impress of politicians, Bevin and Dalton, rather than administrators. To overcome localized unemployment, this chapter suggested that, in the period of transition to a 'normal' peacetime economy, the release to the private sector of government factories and new factory building should be concentrated in the 'development areas' and, in the longer term, government should acquire a range of measures to influence the location of industry. There would also need to be measures to retrain and improve the mobility of labour.

The rest of the paper was concerned with ways of preserving high and stable employment after the transition. Three general propositions had to be followed: total expenditure on goods and services had to be maintained; prices and wages had to be stabilized; and labour mobility be encouraged. The first element may appear to be an endorsement of the Keynesian view, but the Treasury insisted upon a very cautious approach. The white paper noted that aggregate expenditure consisted of five components: private consumption, public expenditure on current services, public investment, private investment and the foreign balance. The most unstable were private investment and the foreign balance. These two were also the most difficult to control. The only possible solution to these problems was to insist upon making industrial efficiency a priority for all. Having completed their list of the threats to the policy, the authors now turned to positive steps to maintain total expenditure. Cheap money could help encourage private investment and the government could encourage firms to programme their investment expenditures according to the needs of the employment situation. However, little was expected under this heading. Public investment offered rather more and local authorities would be asked to submit a five-year investment programme to central government which would accelerate or postpone work by changing grant conditions. However, there was a considerable amount of scepticism about this proposal in the Treasury [223, 292]. The white paper noted that government current expenditure could be phased counter-cyclically to some extent. Finally, measures to influence private consumption were mentioned in the white paper (among them Meade's plan to vary social security contributions). It was pointed out, however, that no scheme had been approved by ministers. Predictably, the Treasury was hostile to Meade's plan [223, 292].

The sections of the white paper dealing with the budgetary implications of employment policy were confused. The fudges of the steering committee report remained, and the Treasury view again came first. It was argued that none of the proposals implied the deliberate planning of budget deficits [117, para 74]. There followed the Keynesian assumption that the burden of public indebtedness could increase if mass unemployment returned [para 75]. Finally, there was a compromise in a pledge to balance the budget over a period of years [para 77]. The Treasury was signalling its willingness to tolerate budget deficits in crisis years, such as 1931, as long as there was no pressure to see budget deficits as an everyday feature of British public finance. The Treasury rounded off this section by warning that the acid test of economic policy would be seen in foreign and domestic confidence, and that the major threat to confidence lay in the growth of public indebtedness [para 79].

It is difficult to avoid the view that the white paper was a pusillanimous document aimed primarily, though probably subconsciously, at reducing the pressure on politicians to make extravagant postwar promises. It is also certain that the Treasury was very wary of disturbing foreign opinion, given Britain's very weak external position [223, *295–6*]. Treasury officials, who rightly suspected that Meade's social security contributions scheme would run into insuperable problems [223, *292*], regarded the white paper as having given approval to a return to Treasury policies of the 1930s. The white paper did promise more immediate and concerted action than hitherto and proposed to retain specialist economists and statisticians in government to ensure that informed advice was available, but there was no indication that these specialists would be any more successful than the Economic Advisory Council had been in the 1930s. The pessimism over the balance of payments cast a cloud over Whitehall's expectations in early 1944.

Ministers, on the other hand, could not be as pessimistic. Public opinion on postwar reconstruction was now in a very delicate state. There was a strong determination not to allow conditions after the war to be as bad as they had been in the 1930s, but at the same time there was a sinking feeling, sometimes approaching a dread, that the depression would return [187, *179*]. Some ministers were afraid that this despondency about domestic prospects would react with the tremendous public admiration for the achievements of the Soviet economy and people during the war to produce a demand for very radical solutions to postwar problems [187, *184, 207*]. Once again, the British political establishment appears to have concluded that social stability was fragile and required careful nurturing. This fear communicated itself even to ministers without well-developed political antennae; Lord Woolton, the chairman of the Cabinet committee dealing with the white paper was certainly aware of the mood [297, *268–9*]. Accordingly, when Bevin presented the white paper to Parliament, he portrayed it (as did the Conservative industry spokesman, Henry Brooke) as a pledge to *prevent* unemployment. Bevin made much of the way that the experience of unemployment had burnt itself into working class consciousness and how bitterly servicemen would resent returning to the dole [38, *319–20*]. The force of public opinion, thus, compelled ministers to treat the very equivocal pledges of the white paper's draftsmen as unambiguous promises of full employment. The force of this emotional commitment helped create the myth that the white paper was the cornerstone of a new postwar order. There was nothing in the very timid text to justify this interpretation; it could be read equally justifiably as a statement that the government would do its best to reduce unemployment, but really there was very little which could be done.

The text was not only timid, it was no guide to subsequent policy. The white paper was built upon two propositions: that the government's macroeconomic role should be exercised with extreme caution; and that enormous vigilance was needed to maintain microeconomic efficiency. However, after 1947–8, postwar employment policy consisted almost entirely of a macroeconomic role with comparatively little direct effort to maintain microeconomic efficiency, at least until the 'modernization drive' of the early 1960s. On taking office, the Attlee government followed the white paper plan of maintaining controls to favour the export industries, a policy which coincided with Labour's long-standing belief that economic planning would be necessary to create a prosperous economy. In its first years of office, the government took decisive steps to forestall rising unemployment in the former depressed areas by a vigorous development of its regional policy. K. O. Morgan claims that Labour had a powerful claim to be the party of full employment which exorcised the ghosts of Jarrow, Wigan and Merthyr Tydfil [210, *183–4*]. However, Labour's production drive to promote exports and full employment soon ran into an inflationary crisis which was exacerbated by the imposition, as one of the conditions of the 1946 US loan, of free convertibility for sterling. To curb inflation, Treasury officials advocated a return to the Keynesian budgetary arithmetic which had been so successfully deployed between 1941 and 1945 but which had gone into abeyance at the end of the war [24, *121*]. Although Labour also briefly strengthened its planning machinery in 1947–8, from 1947 both it and subsequent governments (until 1979) relied heavily upon macroeconomic management to achieve employment targets, albeit in a context of excess rather than deficient demand for much of the period.

The reasons for the failure to pursue microeconomic efficiency more strongly are more complex. One very difficult part of the discussions of the steering committee on employment had been concerned with industrial policy [see 25]. Whitehall considered in detail two choices. On the one hand, the Economic Section pushed strongly for the reopening of as much of the British economy to the forces of free competition as was possible. The economists argued that the government should take firm steps to enforce market disciplines by actively prohibiting restrictive agreements and by helping to create a liberal international economic order. On the other hand, Board of Trade officials wanted to resume the *ad hoc* cartelization schemes which they had implemented in the 1930s for the staple industries and which Kirby had discussed very fully in Chapter 10. The option of retaining and developing 'planning' as the normal peacetime system was not considered. This might appear to be an unusual omission at a time when the success of British wartime planning was very evident but Whitehall clearly saw the planned economy as an expedient to be used only in the emergency of war.

The Civil Service was, thus, a barrier to planning as a means of maintaining microeconomic efficiency in industry, but it was not the only one. Both sides of industry were opposed equally to full planning and to the free market. British industry knew that it would not be able to recover fully from the war without the rebuilding of the infrastructure which had been devastated or run down since 1939. Reconstruction could be undertaken without fierce competition for scarce resources only if the government were to direct the economy. But industry's longer-term ideal, beyond the immediate reconstruction phase, seems to have been to have a government which was both obedient to industry's wishes and remained at arm's length, leaving private industrialists to regulate their own affairs [20, 38].

In the same way, the TUC insisted in its reconstruction policy statement of 1944 that the unions should be free to function without state interference and to represent their members through free collective bargaining. The white paper took a sympathetic line, especially on incomes policy by merely noting that the government would try to continue its policy of stabilizing the cost of living and leaving both sides of industry to act responsibly over wages. The Treasury had, of course, been very concerned about the effects of rising wages at full employment in the early stages of the war, and the Economic Section had argued in each of its employment policy papers that an incomes policy was essential if a full employment regime was to be adopted. Once the government had failed in wartime to impose a planned wages policy there was little likelihood of that measure appearing in reconstruction plans.

Thus, there were few obvious indications of how the draftsmen of the white paper hoped to achieve increasing microeconomic efficiency. Planning was rejected; the foreword proclaimed very loudly that governments could only create favourable conditions, the achievement of full employment and efficiency was a matter for both sides of industry to work out. Given the size of Britain's postwar economic problems, both sides of industry were obliged to co-operate and work with the Labour government, but this system was as much concerned with short-term crisis avoidance as with long-term planning [see, 210, 120]. Nor was there any attempt to turn British industry to face the full blasts of market competition, especially from the USA, even when Labour's limited concept of planning faded in 1948. It scarcely needs adding that free competition with US industry would have been disastrous at this time. Thus, despite the vital importance of industrial efficiency to all sides of the employment policy debate, the only real policy weapon which the draftsmen of the white paper gave to policy-makers was strident exhortation.

191

We might conclude by attempting to measure the effect of the war on the white paper. Clearly, the impact on the actual policies set out in the paper was marginal. Apart from the very special conditions and problems of the transitional period, the white paper looked back to the policy programme of the 1930s rather than to the innovations of the war. The new expansionist, Keynesian aspects were blunted by the Treasury's unwillingness to shift on budgetary policy and its increasingly successful attempts to curtail any initiative which might have jeopardized foreign confidence. There is also ample internal evidence to suggest that the 1944 white paper intended a policy regime after the transition which would make only minor inroads into the liberal attitudes and assumptions so deeply entrenched in British society. The traditional lines of demarcation between public and private sectors and between economic and political affairs were scarcely blurred by the white paper. The most obvious example was the failure to consider planning as a long-term solution to Britain's economic problems. There was, however, a more positive tone to parts of the white paper and especially to the way politicians chose to interpret the document as a whole. There is absolutely no doubt that the sceptics and critics of employment policy in the Coalition government were forced into this more generous mood by the power of wartime opinion. The main ingredient in public opinion in 1943–4 was fear of the return of unemployment and its associated degradations. Whiteside and Deacon have demonstrated very clearly, in Chapters 2 and 3, that similar strong emotions were evident also in the 1930s. The war merely induced changes which gave particular social and political resonance to working class insecurities; there is no evidence to support the view that a new deal for labour was being forged in the wartime administration [see also 225, *142–3*].

Postscript

In the event, full employment policies *appeared* to be remarkably successful in practice. Whitehall estimated that 5 per cent would be a reasonable target rate of unemployment, and that figure has been exceeded only since the mid-1970s. Britain, in common with much of the Western capitalist world, enjoyed thirty years of full employment between 1945 and 1975.

One of the foundations of the boom in Western economies was the creation in the 1940s and full implementation in the 1950s of a liberal trade and financial framework. In all the discussions of international economic and financial arrangements, the industrial powers were most concerned about future employment levels and this was the main reason for seeking to free trade and payments. The inter-connections between trade, growth and employment were a major theme in the debates on Bretton Woods [277] and in the discussions on an International Trade Organization [58, 76]. Although the ITO did not come into being, its successor, the General Agreement of Tariffs and Trade, did help to bring down levels of protection and so contribute to the establishment of a virtuous circle of increased trade and employment. Between the late 1940s and the mid-1970s, when the international economy was once more racked by very fierce discord, growth in the world economy created an expansionary environment which should have made the tasks of domestic policy-makers comparatively easy.

Between 1947 and 1951, government developed most of its techniques of macromanagement, and came to rely much more heavily upon fiscal rather than monetary instruments, a marked change from both the 1930s and the Treasury's interpretation of the 1944 white paper. Fiscal changes were concentrated on a very narrow range of indirect taxes and duties and on changes in the public capital programme. In monetary policy, governments up to 1975 tended to rely mainly on alterations in hire purchase terms and on the manipulation of interest rates, though for much of this period real interest rates were low or negative. Thus, new policy instruments have been added to the list discussed in 1943–4. Before the 1970s, governments tended to expand demand whenever a politically sensitive level of unemployment was reached (but that level tended to rise over time) and to cut demand whenever there was a balance of payments crisis [211]. However, these changes of demand rarely accounted for more than one per cent on the unemployment rate [44, 371]. British governments were 'fine-tuning' the economy in an inflationary context and not giving major boosts to demand in a deflationary environment as the wartime planners had anticipated. Inflation, which was at relatively low levels in the 1950s and 1960s, gathered momentum in the 1970s and accelerated after the enormous shift in the terms of trade in the middle of that decade. Macroeconomic policy has tended to be restrictive for much of the postwar period, with a current budgetary surplus which until 1973 met most of the borrowing requirements of the nationalized industries. This restrictive stance suggests that the impressive employment record of 1945–75 was not directly caused by postwar macroeconomic policy. The most careful study of the causes of postwar full employment has argued that the principal factor has been the postwar investment boom [192]. The backlog of investment resulting from the depressed 1930s and the war produced an initial surge which was carried forward by accelerated technical progress and the expansion of world trade [192,

124–5; 44, *373*]. This explanation appears to be independent of macroeconomic management, but low real rates of interest and the widely held belief that governments would not tolerate a slump aided business confidence [192, *125*; 44, *373–4*] and policy-makers should be given credit for fostering trade expansion.

Despite the surge in investment, Britain's relative industrial efficiency, the problem which so engaged wartime policy-makers, has declined. Freer trade and the discipline of the market have not promoted improvements in manufacturing productivity at a pace comparable to that in most other industrial nations. Britain's 'efficiency wages' have risen faster than in competitor countries, but devaluations in 1949 and 1968 and depreciations in 1972, 1976, and the more gradual, prolonged fall since 1982 appear not to have solved the problem. Britain's share of world trade fell consistently from the early 1950s to the mid–1970s, and in the mid–1980s Britain has become a net importer of manufactures for the first time since the Industrial Revolution. Once the dynamic expansionary force evaporated from the international economy in the mid–1970s, the British economy was in a weak position simply because too little attention had been paid to microeconomic efficiency in the years of full employment. Failure to resolve this problem in the near future runs enormous risks. A recent authoritative report has argued that unless the international competitiveness of Britain's manufacturing industry is revived, living standards will *fall* with potentially devastating repercussions on domestic economic and political stability [119, *48*].

The failure of Britain's manufacturing industry to achieve competitiveness in world markets is not a new problem. It manifested itself persistently in the late Victorian and Edwardian periods, in many sectors of the interwar economy, and again, more generally, since the mid-1950s. There have been comparatively few occasions when the British establishment has had an opportunity to give detailed consideration to the problem untroubled by immediate economic and political pressures. The chance could have been taken in the wartime discussions of postwar policy. All realized at the time that if the liberalization of world trade was the dynamic upon which international and national economic expansion were to be founded, it was essential that British industry should regain and retain its international competitiveness. Unfortunately, wartime policy-makers did not consider all the alternatives. Postwar experience has demonstrated that to leave questions of industrial efficiency solely to industrialists and market forces is pure folly.

Notes

1 PRO T171/349, 'Problems of War Finance and the Decision to Subsidise the Cost of Living', Memorandum by Lord Stamp, 4 Mch. 1940; PRO T171/355, 'The Control of Inflation', Memorandum by the Survey of Economic and Financial Plans, 12 July 1940; ibid. 'The Control of Inflation: Second Memorandum by the Survey of Economic and Financial Plans', 5 Sept. 1940.
2 The official cost of living index was based on Edwardian working class consumption patterns and had a very high weighting (60 per cent) for food expenditure. The government attempted to hold the index steady by subsidizing food prices. Comparisons between the official index and other estimates of the course of retail prices in the war can be found in [233, *211*; 225, *130*].
3 This does not mean, of course, that British and American officials were always in agreement on questions either of detail or broad strategy in the talks on the postwar international settlement [see 277].

Notes on Contributors

Alan Booth is Lecturer in Economic and Social History at the University of Sheffield, co-author of *Employment, Capital and Economic Policy: Great Britain 1918–39* and author of articles on twentieth-century economic policy.

Forrest Capie is Reader in Economic History at the City University, the author of *Depression and Protectionism* and a number of articles on the tariff of the 1930s, a co-author of one of the contributions to the Bank of England's Panel of Expert Academic Consultants Report on the UK Economic Recovery in the 1930s and is nearing completion of his three-volume monetary history of the UK.

Alan Deacon is Lecturer in Social Policy at the University of Leeds, the author of *In Search of the Scrounger* and co-author of *Reserved for the Poor: The Means Test in British Social Policy* and has contributed articles on social security and the history of unemployment relief to a number of books and journals.

W. R. Garside is Senior Lecturer in Economic and Social History at the University of Birmingham, and is author of *The Measurement of Unemployment* and numerous articles on aspects of interwar unemployment. He is completing his own major survey of the interwar unemployment problem.

Sean Glynn is Senior Lecturer in Economic and Social History at the University of Kent at Canterbury, the co-author of *Interwar Britain: A Social and Economic History* and articles on the interwar unemployment problem.

Tim Hatton is Lecturer in Economics at the University of Essex and the author of a number of articles on the possibilities of Keynesian policies between the wars.

Maurice Kirby is Lecturer in Economic History at the University of Lancaster, and the author of *The British Coalmining Industry 1870–1944*, and *The Decline of British Economic Power*, and of numerous articles on British industrial policy in twentieth century.

Rodney Lowe is Lecturer in Economic and Social History at the University of Bristol, author of numerous articles on interwar economic policy and has just completed a major study of the Ministry of Labour between the wars, *Adapting to Democracy*, which will shortly be published by Oxford University Press.

Roger Middleton is Lecturer in Economic History at the University of Durham. He is the author of *Towards the Managed Economy: Keynes, the Treasury and the Fiscal Policy Debate of the 1930s* and has produced a number of articles on interwar monetary and fiscal policies.

G. C. Peden is Lecturer in Economic and Social History at the University of Bristol, author of *British Rearmament and the Treasury*, of *British Economic and Social Policy*; *Lloyd George to Margaret Thatcher*, and of numerous articles on British interwar economic and social economic policy. He is currently working on a book on the influence of Keynes.

Noel Whiteside is Lecturer in Social Administration at the University of Bristol, the author of a number of articles on social welfare legislation during the First World War and the interwar years and is currently writing a book on the social consequences of interwar unemployment.

Bibliography

The works listed below are the ones to which reference has been made in this volume. The place of publication is London, unless otherwise stated.

[1] Paul Addison, *The Road to 1945; British Politics and the Second World War*, (Quartet edition), 1977.

[2] D. H. Aldcroft, 'The Impact of British Monetary Policy, 1919–1939', *Revue Internationale d'Histoire de la Banque*, 3, 1970.

[3] D. H. Aldcroft, *The Inter-War Economy: Britain 1919–1939*, 1970.

[4] D. H. Aldcroft, *The British Economy Between the Wars*, Oxford, 1983.

[5] D. H. Aldcroft, *Full Employment: The Elusive Goal*, Brighton, 1984.

[6] S. M. H. Armitage, *The Politics of the Decontrol of Industry: Great Britain and the United States*, 1969.

[7] William Ashworth, *An Economic History of England, 1870–1939*, 1960.

[8] M. N. Baily, 'Stabilization Policy and Private Economic Behaviour', *Brookings Papers on Economic Activity*, 1, 1978.

[9] E. W. Bakke, *Insurance or Dole?*, New York, 1935.

[10] Dennis Barnes and Eileen Reid, 'A New Relationship: Trade Unions in the Second World War' in Ben Pimlott and Chris Cook, eds. *Trade Unions in British Politics*, 1982.

[11] R. J. Barro, *Macroeconomics*, Chichester, 1984.

[12] M. Beenstock, 'Real Wages and Unemployment in the 1930s: A Reply to Critics', *National Institute Economic Review*, forthcoming, 1986.

[13] M. Beenstock and P. Warburton, 'An Aggregate Model of the UK Labour Market', *Oxford Economic Papers*, 34, 1982.

[14] M. Beenstock, F. Capie, B. Griffiths, 'Economic Recovery in the UK in the 1930s', *Bank of England Panel of Academic Consultants, Panel Paper 23*, 1984.

[15] M. Beenstock and P. Warburton, 'The Market for Labour in Interwar Britain', *Explorations in Economic History*, 23, 1986.

[16] S. H. Beer, *Modern British Politics*, 2nd edn. 1969.

[17] D. K. Benjamin and L. A. Kochin, 'Searching for an Explanation of Unemployment in Inter-War Britain', *Journal of Political Economy*, 87, 1979.

[18] W. H. Beveridge, *Unemployment: A Problem of Industry*, 1931.

[19] W. H. Beveridge, *Full Employment in a Free Society*, 1944.

[20] Stephen Blank, *Industry and Government in Britain: The Federation of British Industries in Politics, 1945–65*, Farnborough, 1973.

[21] Michael Bleaney, *The Rise and Fall of Keynesian Economics: An Investigation of its Contribution to Capitalist Development*, 1985.

[22] Alan Booth, 'An Administrative Experiment in Unemployment Policy in the Thirties', *Public Administration*, 56, 1978.

[23] Alan Booth, 'Corporatism, Capitalism and Depression in Twentieth Century Britain', *British Journal of Sociology*, 33, 1982.

[24] Alan Booth, 'The "Keynesian Revolution" in Economic Policy-Making', *Economic History Review*, 2nd ser. 36, 1983.

[25] Alan Booth, 'Simple Keynesianism and Whitehall, 1936–47', *Economy and Society*, 15, 1986.

[26 Alan Booth and Sean Glynn, 'Unemployment in the Interwar Period: A Multiple Problem', *Journal of Contemporary History*, 10, 1975.

[27] Alan Booth and A. W. Coats, 'Some Wartime Observations on the Role of the Economist in Government', *Oxford Economic Papers*, 32, 1980.

[28] Alan Booth and Melvyn Pack, 'Baldwin, Thatcher and the Aftermath of Industrial Disputes', *Political Quarterly*, 56, 1985.

[29] Alan Booth and Melvyn Pack, *Employment, Capital and Economic Policy: Great Britain 1918–1939*, Oxford, 1985.

[30] Robert Boothby, *et al.*, *Industry and the State: A Conservative View*, 1927.

[31] J. S. Boswell, *Business Policies in the Making: Three Steel Companies Compared*, 1983.

[32] J. Boyd Orr, *Food, Health and Income*, 1936.

[33] R. F. Bretherton, F. A. Burchardt and R. S. G. Rutherford, *Public Investment and the Trade Cycle in Britain*, Oxford, 1941.

[34] E. Briggs and A. Deacon, 'The Creation of the Unemployment Assistance Board', *Policy and Politics*, 2, 1973.

[35] S. N. Broadberry, 'Unemployment in Inter-War Britain: A Disequilibrium Approach', *Oxford Economic Papers*, 35, 1983.

[36] K. D. Brown, *Labour and Unemployment, 1900–1914*, Newton Abbot, 1971.

[37] J. M. Buchanan, J. Burton and R. E. Wagner, *The Consequences of Mr Keynes: An Analysis of the Misuse of Economic Theory for Political Profiteering, with Proposals for Constitutional Disciplines*, 1978.

[38] Alan Bullock, *The Life and Times of Ernest Bevin: Volume II: Minister of Labour, 1940–1945*, 1967.

[39] Kathleen Burk, ed. *War and the State: The Transformation of British Government, 1914–1919*, 1982.

[40] Kathleen Burk, 'The Treasury: From Importance to Power' in [39].

[41] E. M. Burns, *British Unemployment Programs, 1920–38*, Washington, DC, 1941.

[42] N. K. Buxton, 'The Role of the "New" Industries in Britain during the 1930s: A Reinterpretation', *Business History Review*, 49, 1975.

[43] Neville Cain and Sean Glynn, 'Imperial Relations under Strain: The Australian Foreign Debt Contretemps of 1933', *Australian Economic History Review*, XXV, 1985.

[44] Sir Alec Cairncross, 'The Postwar Years, 1945–77' in [90].

[45] Sir Alec Cairncross, 'An Early Think-Tank: The Origins of the Economic Section', *Three Banks Review*, 144, 1984.

[46] John Campbell, *Lloyd George: The Goat in the Wilderness*, 1977.

[47] E. Cannan, 'The Problem of Unemployment', *Economic Journal*, 40, 1930.

[48] Forrest Capie, 'Tariffs, Elasticities and Prices in Britain in the 1930s', *Economic History Review*, 2nd ser. 34, 1981.

[49] Forrest Capie, *Depression and Protectionism: Britain Between the Wars*, 1983.

[50] Forrest Capie and Michael Collins, *The Inter-War Economy: A Statistical Abstract*, Manchester, 1983.

[51] L. P. Carpenter, 'Corporatism in Britain, 1930–45', *Journal of Contemporary History*, 11, 1976.

[52] Mark Casson, *The Economics of Unemployment: A Historical Perspective*, Oxford, 1983.

[53] D. G. Champernowne, 'The Uneven Distribution of Unemployment in the UK, 1929–36', *Review of Economic Studies*, 5, 1937–8.

[54] Agatha L. Chapman and Rose Knight, *Wages and Salaries in the UK, 1920–38*, Cambridge, 1953.

[55] D. N. Chester, ed., *Lessons of the British War Economy*, 1951.

[56] Colin Clark, *National Income and Outlay*, 1937.

[57] Colin Clark, 'Determination of the Multiplier from National Income Statistics', *Economic Journal*, 48, 1938.

[58] Sir Richard Clarke (ed. Sir Alec Cairncross), *Anglo-American Economic Collaboration in War and Peace, 1942–1949*, Oxford, 1982.

[59] H. Clay, 'Unemployment and Wage Rates', *Economic Journal*, 38, 1928.

[60] H. Clay, *The Post-War Unemployment Problem*, 1929.

[61] Sir Henry Clay, *Lord Norman*, 1957

[62] Peter Cline, 'Winding Down the War Economy' in [39].

[63] D. C. Coleman, 'War Demand and Industrial Supply: The "Dope Scandal", 1915–19' in J. M. Winter, ed., *War and Economic Development*, Cambridge, 1975.

[64] M. Collins, 'Unemployment in Inter-War Britain: Still Searching for an Explanation', *Journal of Political Economy*, 90, 1982.

[65] Conference on Industrial Reorganisation and Industrial Relations, *Interim Joint Report on Unemployment* (Mond–Turner Conference), 1929.

[66] S. Constantine, *Unemployment in Britain Between the Wars*, 1980.

[67] Chris Cook, 'Liberals, Labour and Local Elections' in Gillian Peele and Chris Cooke, eds., *The Politics of Reappraisal, 1918–1939*, 1975.

[68] N. F. R. Crafts, *British Economic Growth During the Industrial Revolution*, Oxford, 1985.

[69] R. Cross, 'How Much Voluntary Unemployment in Inter-War Britain?', *Journal of Political Economy*, 90, 1982.

[70] M. A. Crowther, 'Family Responsibility and State Welfare in Britain Before the Welfare State', *Historical Journal*, 25, 1982.

[71] R. Davidson, *Whitehall and the Labour Problem in Late-Victorian and Edwardian Britain: A Study in Official Statistics and Social Control*, 1985.

[72] Ernest Davies, 'National' Capitalism: The Government's Record as Protector of Private Monopoly, 1939.

[73] Alan Deacon, In Search of the Scrounger, 1976.

[74] Alan Deacon, 'Concession and Coercion: The Politics of Unemployment Insurance in the Twenties' in Asa Briggs and John Saville, eds., Essays in Labour History, 1918–1939, 1977.

[75] A. Deacon, 'Unemployment and Politics in Britain since 1945' in A. Sinfield and B. Showler, eds., The Workless State, Oxford, 1980.

[76] A. Deacon and E. Briggs, 'Local Democracy and Central Control: The Issue of Pauper Votes', Policy and Politics, 2, 1974.

[77] A. Deacon and J. Bradshaw, Reserved for the Poor: The Means Test in British Social Policy, 1983.

[78] N. H. Dimsdale, 'British Monetary Policy and the Exchange Rate, 1920–1938', Oxford Economic Papers, Supplement, 33, 1981.

[79] N. H. Dimsdale, 'Employment and Real Wages in the Inter-War Period', National Institute Economic Review, 110, 1984.

[80] Bernard Donoghue and G. W. Jones, Herbert Morrison: Portrait of a Politician, 1973.

[81] J. A. Dowie, 'Growth in the Interwar Period: Some More Arithmetic', Economic History Review, 2nd ser. 21, 1968.

[82] J. A. Dowie, '1919–20 is in Need of Attention', Economic History Review, 2nd ser. 28, 1975.

[83] Elizabeth Durbin, New Jerusalems: The Labour Party and the Economics of Democratic Socialism, 1985.

[84] Barry Eichengreen, 'Keynes and Protection', Journal of Economic History, 44, 1984.

[85] D. Eisenberg and P. Lazarsfeld, 'The Psychological Effects of Unemployment', Psychological Bulletin, 35, 1933.

[86] E. W. Evans and N. C. Wiseman, 'Education, Training and Economic Performance: British Economists' Views, 1869–1939', Journal of European Economic History, 13, 1984.

[87] M. Falkus, 'United States Economic Policy and the "Dollar Gap" of the 1920s', Economic History Review, 2nd ser. 24, 1971.

[88] C. H. Feinstein, National Income, Expenditure and Output of the United Kingdom, 1855–1965, Cambridge, 1972.

[89] C. H. Feinstein, ed., The Managed Economy: Essays in British Economic Policy and Performance since 1929, Oxford, 1983.

[90] Roderick Floud and Donald McCloskey, eds., The Economic History of Britain since 1700: Volume II: 1860 to the 1970s, Cambridge, 1981.

[91] J. S. Foreman-Peck, 'The British Tariff and Industrial Protection in the 1930s: An Alternative Model', Economic History Review, 2nd ser. 34, 1981.

[92] J. S. Foreman-Peck, 'Seed-Corn or Chaff? New Firm Formation and the Performance of the Interwar Economy', Economic History Review, 2nd ser. 38, 1985.

[93] Milton Friedman, 'The Role of Monetary Policy', American Economic Review, 58, 1968.

[94] W. R. Garside, 'Management and Men: Aspects of British Industrial Relations' in [262].

[95] W. R. Garside, *The Measurement of Unemployment: Methods and Sources in Great Britain, 1850–1979*, Oxford, 1980.

[96] W. R. Garside, 'The Failure of the Radical Alternative: Public Works, Deficit Finance and British Interwar Unemployment', *Journal of European Economic History*, 14, 1985.

[97] W. R. Garside, *The British Unemployment Crisis: A Study in Public Policy*, forthcoming.

[98] B. B. Gilbert, *The Evolution of National Insurance in Britain*, 1966.

[99] B. B. Gilbert, *British Social Policy, 1914–1939*, 1970.

[100] Sean Glynn, 'Irish Immigration to Britain, 1911–1951: Patterns and Policy', *Irish Economic and Social History*, 8, 1981.

[101] Sean Glynn and A. Lougheed, 'A Comment on United States Economic Policy and the "Dollar Gap" of the 1920s', *Economic History Review*, 2nd ser. 26, 1973.

[102] Sean Glynn and John Oxborrow, *Interwar Britain: A Social and Economic History*, 1976.

[103] Sean Glynn and P. G. A. Howells, 'Unemployment in the 1930s: The "Keynesian Solution" Reconsidered', *Australian Economic History Review*, 20, 1980.

[104] Sean Glynn and Stephen Shaw, 'Wage Bargaining and Unemployment', *Political Quarterly*, 52, 1981.

[105] Sean Glynn and Alan Booth, 'Unemployment in the Interwar Period: A Case for Relearning the Lessons of the 1930s?', *Economic History Review*, 2nd ser, 36, 1983.

[106] M. M. Gowing, 'The Organisation of Manpower during the Second World War', *Journal of Contemporary History*, 7, 1972.

[107] HMSO *Memoranda on Certain Proposals Relating to Unemployment*, Cmd 3331, 1929.

[108] HMSO *Committee on Finance and Industry, Minutes of Evidence*, (Macmillan Committee) 1931; Evidence of Sir Richard Hopkins, 22 May 1930.

[109] HMSO *Royal Commission on Unemployment Insurance, First Report*, Cmd 3872, 1931; (Appendix 1).

[110] HMSO *Committee on Finance and Industry, Report* (Macmillan Report), Cmd 3897, 1931.

[111] HMSO *Committee on National Expenditure, Report* (May Report), Cmd 3920, 1931.

[112] HMSO *Unemployment Assistance Board, Report for 1935*, Cmd 5177, 1936.

[113] HMSO *Annual Returns for Expenditure on the Public Social Services*, Cmd 5609, 1937–8.

[114] HMSO *Royal Commission on the Distribution of the Industrial Population, Minutes of Evidence*, (Barlow Commission) 1938; 10th and 11th days.

[115] HMSO *Royal Commission on the Distribution of the Industrial Population, Report* (Barlow Report), Cmd 6153, 1939–40.

[116] HMSO *Social Insurance and Allied Services* (Beveridge Report), Cmd 6404, 1942.

[117] HMSO *Employment Policy*, Cmd 6527, 1944.

[118] HMSO *British Labour Statistics: Historical Abstract, 1886–1968*, 1971.

[119] HMSO *House of Lords Select Committee on Overseas Trade*, Report (Aldington Report), 1985.

[120] W. K. Hancock and M. M. Gowing, *British War Economy*, 1949.

[121] Leslie Hannah, 'A Pioneer Public Enterprise: The Central Electricity Board and the National Grid, 1927–1940' in [262].

[122] Leslie Hannah, *Electricity Before Nationalisation*, 1979.

[123] Leslie Hannah, *The Rise of the Corporate Economy*, 2nd edn. 1983.

[124] Wal Hannington, *Unemployed Struggles, 1919–1936*, 1936.

[125] Wal Hannington, *The Problem of the Distressed Areas*, 1937.

[126] C. K. Harley, 'Skilled Labour and the Choice of Technique in Edwardian Industry', *Explorations in Economic History*, 2, 1974.

[127] Jose Harris, *Unemployment and Politics*, Oxford, 1972.

[128] Jose Harris, *William Beveridge: A Biography*, Oxford, 1977.

[129] T. J. Hatton, 'Unemployment Benefits and the Macro-Economics of the Inter-War Labour Market: A Further Analysis', *Oxford Economic Papers*, 35, 1983.

[130] T. J. Hatton, 'Unemployment in the 1930s and the "Keynesian Solution": Some Notes of Dissent', *Australian Economic History Review*, 25, 1985.

[131] T. J. Hatton, 'Structural Aspects of Unemployment in Britain Between the Wars', *Research in Economic History*, 10, 1985.

[132] R. G. Hawtrey, 'Public Expenditure and the Trade Depression', *Journal of the Royal Statistical Society*, Series A, 96, 1933.

[133] J. R. Hay, *The Origins of the Liberal Welfare Reforms*, 1975.

[134] Ralph Hayburn, 'The National Unemployed Workers' Movement, 1921–36', *International Review of Social History*, 28, 1983.

[135] H. D. Henderson (ed. Henry Clay), *The Inter-War Years and Other Papers: A Selection of the Writings of Hubert Douglas Henderson*, Oxford, 1955.

[136] Susan Howson, *Domestic Monetary Management in Britain, 1919–38*, Cambridge, 1975.

[137] Susan Howson, 'The Management of Sterling, 1932–1939', *Journal of Economic History*, 40, 1975.

[138] Susan Howson, *Sterling's Managed Float: The Operations of the Exchange Equalisation Account, 1932–39*, Princeton Studies in International Finance, 46, 1980.

[139] Susan Howson, 'Slump and Unemployment' in [90].

[140] Susan Howson and Donald Winch, *The Economic Advisory Council, 1930–9: A Study of Economic Advice during Depression and Recovery*, Cambridge, 1977.

[141] J. J. Hughes and R. Perlman, *The Economics of Unemployment*, Brighton, 1984.

[142] J. Hurstfield, *The Control of Raw Materials*, 1953.

[143] T. W. Hutchison, Review of Howson and Winch, *Economic History Review*, 2nd ser. 31, 1978.

[144] A. Hutt, *The Condition of the Working Class in Britain*, 1933.

[145] M. Jahoda, *Employment and Unemployment: A Social Psychological Analysis*, 1982.

[146] John Jewkes, *A Return to Free Market Economics? Critical Essays on Government Intervention*, 1978.

[147] John Jewkes and A. Winterbottom, *Juvenile Unemployment*, 1933.

[148] G. Jones, *The State and the Emergence of the British Oil Industry*, 1980.

[149] M. E. F. Jones, 'The Regional Impact of an Overvalued Pound' *Economic History Review*, 2nd ser. 38, 1985.

[150] Russell Jones, 'The Wages Problem in Employment Policy, 1936–48', University of Bristol, MSc. 1983.

[151] R. F. Kahn, 'The Relation of Home Investment to Unemployment', *Economic Journal*, 41, 1931.

[152] R. F. Kahn, 'Unemployment as seen by the Keynesians' in G. D. N. Worswick, ed., *The Concept and Measurement of Involuntary Unemployment*, 1976.

[153] J. M. Keynes, 'Relative Movements in Real Wages and Output', *Economic Journal*, 49, 1939.

[154] J. M. Keynes, *The Collected Writings of John Maynard Keynes: Volume IV: A Tract on Monetary Reform*, 1971.

[155] J. M. Keynes, *The Collected Writings of John Maynard Keynes: Volume V: A Treatise on Money: The Pure Theory of Money*, 1971.

[156] J. M. Keynes, *The Collected Writings of John Maynard Keynes: Volume VI: A Treatise on Money: The Applied Theory of Money*, 1971.

[157] J. M. Keynes, *The Collected Writings of John Maynard Keynes: Volume VII: The General Theory of Employment, Interest and Money*, 1973.

[158] J. M. Keynes, *The Collected Writings of John Maynard Keynes: Volume IX: Essays in Persuasion*, 1972.

[159] J. M. Keynes, *The Collected Writings of John Maynard Keynes: Volume XIII: The General Theory and After: Part I, Preparation*, 1973.

[160] J. M. Keynes, *The Collected Writings of John Maynard Keynes: Volume XIX: Activities, 1922–1929: The Return to Gold and Industrial Policy*, 1981.

[161] J. M. Keynes, *The Collected Writings of John Maynard Keynes: Volume XX: Activities, 1929–1931: Rethinking Employment and Unemployment Policies*, 1981.

[162] J. M. Keynes, *The Collected Writings of John Maynard Keynes: Volume XXI: Activities, 1931–1939: World Crises and Policies in Britain and America*, 1982.

[163] J. M. Keynes, *The Collected Writings of John Maynard Keynes: Volume XXII: Activities, 1939–1945: Internal War Finance*, 1978.

[164] J. M. Keynes, *The Collected Writings of John Maynard Keynes: Volume XXV: Activities, 1940–1944: Shaping the Post-War World: The Clearing Union*, 1980.

[165] J. M. Keynes, *The Collected Writings of John Maynard Keynes: Volume*

XXVII: *Activities, 1940·1946: Shaping the Post-War World: Employment and Commodities*, 1980.

[166] Milo Keynes, ed., *Essays on John Maynard Keynes*, Cambridge, 1975.

[167] Charles P. Kindleberger, *The World in Depression, 1929–1939*, 1973.

[168] M. W. Kirby, 'The Lancashire Cotton Industry in the Inter-War Years: A Study in Organizational Change', *Business History*, 16, 1974.

[169] M. W. Kirby, *The British Coalmining Industry, 1870–1946: A Political and Economic History*, 1977.

[170] M. W. Kirby, 'The Politics of Coercion in Inter-War Britain: The Mines Department of the Board of Trade, 1920–42', *Historical Journal*, 22, 1979.

[171] Max Krafchik, 'Unemployment and Vagrancy in the 1930s', *Journal of Social Policy*, 12, 1983.

[172] Jurgen Kuczynski, *Hunger and Work*, 1938.

[173] Simon Kuznets, *Modern Economic Growth*, New Haven, Conn. 1966.

[174] R. Layard and J. Symons, 'Neo-Classical Demand for Labour Functions for Six Major Economies', *LSE Centre for Labour Economics, Discussion Paper 166*, 1983.

[175] C. H. Lee, *British Regional Employment Statistics, 1841–1971*, Cambridge, 1979.

[176] Liberal Industrial Inquiry, *Britain's Industrial Future*, 1928.

[177] Liberal Party, *We Can Conquer Unemployment: Mr Lloyd George's Pledge*, 1929.

[178] H. Llewellyn Smith, *New Survey of London Life and Labour*, Volume III, 1932.

[179] London and Cambridge Economic Service, *The British Economy: Key Statistics, 1900–1966*, 1968.

[180] Rodney Lowe, 'The Erosion of State Intervention in Britain, 1917–1924', *Economic History Review*, 2nd ser. 31, 1978.

[181] Rodney Lowe, 'Welfare Legislation and the Unions during and after the First World War', *Historical Journal*, 25, 1982.

[182] Rodney Lowe, *Adjusting to Democracy: The Role of the Ministry of Labour in British Politics, 1916–39*, Oxford, 1986.

[183] A. F. Lucas, *Industrial Reconstruction and the Control of Competition: The British Experiments*, 1937.

[184] R. E. Lucas, 'Econometric Policy Evaluation: A Critique' in K. Brunner and A. H. Melzer, eds., *The Phillips Curve and Labor Markets*, Amsterdam, 1976.

[185] R. E. Lucas, *Studies in Business Cycle Theory*, Cambridge, Mass. 1981.

[186] Stuart MacIntyre, *Little Moscows: Communism and Working Class Militancy in Interwar Britain*, 1980.

[187] Ian McLaine, *Ministry of Morale: Home Front Morale and the Ministry of Information in the Second World War*, 1979.

[188] J. Macnicol, *The Movement for Family Allowances, 1918–1945*, 1980.

[189] David Marquand, *Ramsay MacDonald*, 1977.

[190] Arthur Marwick, 'Middle Opinion in the Thirties: Planning, Progress and Political "Agreement"', *English Historical Review*, 79, 1964.

[191] Kent Matthews, 'High Wages Cause Unemployment', *Economic Affairs*, 5, 1985.

[192] R. C. O. Matthews, 'Why has Britain had Full Employment since the War' in [89].

[193] R. C. O. Matthews, C. H. Feinstein and J. C. Oddling-Smee, *British Economic Growth, 1856–1973*, Oxford, 1982.

[194] D. Metcalf, S. J. Nickell and N. Floros, 'Still Searching for an Explanation of Unemployment in Inter-War Britain', *Journal of Political Economy*, 90, 1982.

[195] Keith Middlemas, *Politics in Industrial Society: The British Experience of the System since 1911*, 1979.

[196] Keith Middlemas, 'Unemployment: The Past and Future of a Political Problem' in Bernard Crick, ed., *Unemployment*, 1981.

[197] Keith Middlemas and John Barnes, *Baldwin: A Biography*, 1969.

[198] Roger Middleton, 'The Constant Employment Budget Balance and British Budgetary Policy, 1929–1939', *Economic History Review*, 2nd ser. 34, 1981.

[199] Roger Middleton, 'The Treasury in the 1930s: Political and Administrative Constraints to the Acceptance of the "New" Economics', *Oxford Economic Papers*, 34, 1982.

[200] Roger Middleton, 'The Treasury and Public Investment: A Perspective on Interwar Economic Management', *Public Administration*, 61, 1983.

[201] Roger Middleton, *Towards the Managed Economy: Keynes, The Treasury and the Fiscal Policy Debate of the 1930s*, 1985.

[202] Frederic Miller, 'National Assistance or Unemployment Assistance: the British Cabinet and Relief Policy', *Journal of Contemporary History*, 9, 1974.

[203] Frederic Miller, 'The Unemployment Policy of the National Government, 1931–36', *Historical Journal*, 19, 1976.

[204] Frederic Miller, 'The British Unemployment Assistance Crisis of 1935', *Journal of Contemporary History*, 14, 1979.

[205] J. D. Millet, *The Unemployment Assistance Board*, 1940.

[206] Alan Milward, *War, Economy and Society, 1939–1945*, 1977.

[207] M. Mitchell, 'The Effects of Unemployment on the Social Conditions of Women and Children', *History Workshop Journal*, 19, 1985.

[208] D. E. Moggridge, *British Monetary Policy, 1924–1931: The Norman Conquest of $4.86*, Cambridge, 1972.

[209] D. E. Moggridge, 'The Influence of Keynes on the Economics of his Time' in [166].

[210] K. O. Morgan, *Labour in Power, 1945–1951*, Oxford, 1984.

[211] Paul Mosley, *The Making of Economic Policy: Theory and Evidence from Britain and the United States since 1945*, Brighton, 1984.

[212] C. L. Mowat, *Britain Between the Wars*, 1956.

[213] *The Next Five Years: An Essay in Political Agreement*, 1935.

[214] Euan O'Halpin, 'British Government and Society in the Twentieth Century', *Historical Journal*, 28, 1985.

[215] P. A. Ormerod and G. D. N. Worswick, 'Unemployment in Inter-War Britain', *Journal of Political Economy*, 90, 1982.

[216] George Orwell, *The Road to Wigan Pier*, 1937.
[217] George Orwell, *Inside the Whale*, 1940.
[218] A. D. K. Owen, 'The Social Consequences of Industrial Transference', *Sociological Review*, 29, 1937.
[219] PEP, *Report on the British Social Services*, 1937.
[220] PEP, *Report on the British Health Services*, 1937.
[221] Peter Payne, *Colvilles and the Scottish Steel Industry*, Oxford, 1979.
[222] G. C. Peden, 'Keynes, the Treasury and Unemployment in the Later Nineteen Thirties', *Oxford Economic Papers*, 32, 1980.
[223] G. C. Peden, 'Sir Richard Hopkins and the "Keynesian Revolution" in Employment Policy, 1929–1945', *Economic History Review*, 2nd ser. 36, 1983.
[224] G. C. Peden, 'The "Treasury View" on Public Works and Employment in the Interwar Period', *Economic History Review*, 2nd ser. 37, 1984.
[225] G. C. Peden, *British Economic and Social Policy: Lloyd George to Margaret Thatcher*, Deddington, 1985.
[226] G. A. Phillips, *The General Strike: The Politics of Industrial Conflict*, 1976.
[227] A. C. Pigou, 'Wage Policy and Unemployment', *Economic Journal*, 37, 1927.
[228] A. C. Pigou, *The Theory of Unemployment*, 1933.
[229] Pilgrim Trust, *Men Without Work*, Cambridge, 1938.
[230] Ben Pimlott, *Labour and the Left in the 1930s*, Cambridge, 1977.
[231] Ben Pimlott, *Hugh Dalton*, 1985.
[232] D. E. Pittfield, 'Labour Migration and the Regional Problem in Britain, 1920–1939', University of Stirling, PhD, 1974.
[233] Sidney Pollard, *The Development of the British Economy, 1914–1980*, 3rd edn. 1983.
[234] L. S. Pressnell, '1925: The Burden of Sterling', *Economic History Review*, 2nd ser. 31, 1978.
[235] T. Prosser, 'The Politics of Discretion' in M. Adler and S. Asquith, eds., *Discretion and Welfare*, 1981.
[236] W. J. Reader, 'Imperial Chemical Industries and the State, 1926–1945' in [262].
[237] J. Redmond, 'The Sterling Overvaluation in 1925: A Multilateral Approach', *Economic History Review*, 2nd ser. 37, 1984.
[238] Richard Roberts, 'The Administrative Origins of Industrial Diplomacy: An Aspect of Government-Industry Relations' in [274].
[239] Joan Robinson, *Economic Philosophy*, Harmondsworth, 1976.
[240] E. A. G. Robinson, 'The Overall Allocation of Resources' in [55].
[241] B. S. Rowntree, *Poverty and Progress*, York, 1941.
[242] W. G. Runciman, *Relative Deprivation and Social Justice*, 1966.
[243] P. Ryan, 'Poplarism, 1894–1930' in Pat Thane, ed., *The Origins of Social Policy*, 1978.
[244] R. S. Sayers, *Financial Policy*, 1956.
[245] R. S. Sayers, 'The Return to Gold, 1925', in Sidney Pollard, ed., *The Gold Standard and Employment Policies Between the Wars*, 1970.

[246] R. S. Sayers, *The Bank of England, 1891–1944*, 3 vols, Cambridge, 1976.
[247] R. S. Sayers, 'The First Keynesian Budget' in [89].
[248] E. F. Schumacher, 'Public Finance: Its Relation to Full Employment' in Oxford University Institute of Statistics, *The Economics of Full Employment*, Oxford, 1944.
[249] Stephen Shaw, 'The Attitude of the TUC towards Unemployment in the Inter-War Period', University of Kent, PhD, 1979.
[250] Robert Skidelsky, *Politicians and the Slump: The Labour Government of 1929–31*, Harmondsworth, 1970.
[251] Robert Skidelsky, *Oswald Mosley*, 1975.
[252] Robert Skidelsky, 'The Reception of the Keynesian Revolution' in [166].
[253] Robert Skidelsky, 'Keynes and the Treasury View: The Case for and against an Active Unemployment Policy, 1920–1939' in W. J. Mommsen, ed., *The Emergence of the Welfare State in Britain and Germany*, 1981.
[254] Gareth Stedman Jones, *Outcast London: A Study in the Relationship between the Classes in Victorian Society*, Oxford, 1971.
[255] John Stevenson, *British Society, 1914–1945*, Harmondsworth, 1984.
[256] John Stevenson and Chris Cook, *The Slump: Society and Politics during the Depression*, 1977.
[257] Michael Stewart, *Keynes and After*, 2nd edn, Harmondsworth, 1972.
[258] J. R. N. Stone and W. M. Stone, 'The Marginal Propensity to Consume and the Multiplier', *Review of Economic Studies*, 1, 1938.
[259] J. R. N. Stone, 'The Use and Development of National Income and Expenditure Estimates' in [55].
[260] Susan Strange, *Sterling and British Policy: A Political Study of an International Currency in Decline*, 1971.
[261] I. Svennilson, *Growth and Stagnation in the European Economy*, Geneva, 1954.
[262] Barry Supple, ed., *Essays in British Business History*, Oxford, 1977.
[263] R. H. Tawney, 'The Abolition of Economic Controls, 1918–21', *Economic History Review*, 1st ser. 13, 1943.
[264] Pat Thane, 'The Working Class and the Welfare State in Britain, 1880–1914', *Historical Journal*, 27, 1984.
[265] A. P. Thirlwall, 'Keynesian Employment Theory is not Defunct', *Three Banks Review*, 131, 1981.
[266] R. L. Thomas and P. J. M. Storey, 'Unemployment Dispersion as a Determinant of Wage Inflation in the UK' in M. Parkin and M. T. Sumner, eds., *Incomes Policy and Inflation*, Manchester, 1972.
[267] T. J. Thomas, 'Aggregate Demand in the United Kingdom, 1918–1945', in [90].
[268] R. M. Titmuss, *Problems of Social Policy*, 1950.
[269] S. Tolliday, 'Tariffs and Steel, 1916–1934: The Politics of Industrial Decline' in [274].
[270] S. Tolliday, 'Steel and Rationalization Policies, 1918–1950' in B.

Elbaum and W. Lazonick, eds., *The Decline of the British Economy*, 1985.

[271] Jim Tomlinson, 'Why was there never a "Keynesian Revolution" in Economic Policy?', *Economy and Society*, 10, 1981.

[272] Jim Tomlinson, *Problems of British Economic Policy, 1870–1945*, 1981.

[273] J. D. Tomlinson, 'Women as Anomalies: The Anomalies Regulations of 1931', *Public Administration*, 62, 1984.

[274] J. Turner, ed., *Businessmen and Politics: Studies of Business Activity in British Politics, 1900–1945*, 1984.

[275] H. Tyszynski, 'World Trade in Manufactured Commodities, 1899–1950', *Manchester School*, 19, 1951.

[276] Unemployment Unit, Bulletin, Nov. 1985.

[277] Armand van Dormael, *Bretton Woods: Birth of a Monetary System*, 1978.

[278] B. A. Waites, 'The Effect of the First World War on Class and Status in England, 1910–1920', *Journal of Contemporary History*, 11, 1976.

[279] W. B. Walker, 'Britain's Industrial Performance, 1850–1950: A Failure to Adjust' in K. Pavitt, ed., *Industrial Innovation and British Economic Performance*, 1980.

[280] E. Warburton and C. Butler, *Disallowed: The Tragedy of the Means Test*, 1935.

[281] G. C. Webber, 'Patterns of Membership and Support for the British Union of Fascists', *Journal of Contemporary History*, 19, 1984.

[282] Charles Webster, 'Healthy or Hungry Thirties?', *History Workshop Journal*, 13, 1982.

[283] Charles Webster, 'Health, Welfare and Unemployment during the Depression', *Past and Present*, 109, 1985.

[284] Hugh Weeks, 'Anglo-American Supply Relationships' in [55].

[285] Noel Whiteside, 'Welfare Legislation and the Unions during the First World War', *Historical Journal*, 23, 1980.

[286] Noel Whiteside, 'Private Agencies for Public Purposes', *Journal of Social Policy*, 12, 1983.

[287] Noel Whiteside, 'Counting the Cost: Sickness and Disability among Working People in an Era of Industrial Depression', forthcoming.

[288] John Williamson, 'Keynes and the International Economic Order' in G. D. N. Worswick and J. Trevithick, eds., *Keynes and the Modern World*, Cambridge, 1983.

[289] Philip Williamson, 'Safety First: Baldwin, the Conservative Party and the 1929 General Election', *Historical Journal*, 25, 1982.

[290] Philip Williamson, 'Financier, the Gold Standard and British Politics, 1925–1931', in [274].

[291] Elizabeth Wilson, 'Unemployment Insurance and the Stability of Wages in Great Britain', *International Labour Review*, 30, 1934.

[292] P. H. St. J. Wilson, 'The Ministry of Labour', *Crucible*, 1966.

[293] Donald Winch, *Economics and Policy: A Historical Study*, 1969.

[294] Donald Winch, 'Britain in the Thirties: A Managed Economy?' in [89].

[295] J. M. Winter, 'Infant Mortality, Maternal Mortality and Public Health in Britain in the 1930s', *Journal of European Economic History*, 8, 1979.

[296] J. M. Winter, 'Unemployment, Nutrition and Infant Mortality in Britain, 1920–1950' in J. M. Winter, ed., *The Working Class in Modern British History*, Cambridge, 1983.

[297] Lord Woolton, *The Memoirs of the Rt. Hon. Earl of Woolton*, 1959.

[298] J. F. Wright, 'Britain's Inter-War Experience', *Oxford Economic Papers*, Supplement, 33, 1981.

[299] J. F. Wright, 'Real Wage Resistance: Eighty Years of British Cost of Living', *Oxford Economic Papers*, 36, 1984.

[300] Chris Wrigley, 'The Ministry of Munitions: An Innovatory Department' in [39].

Index

211